Teaching the Works of
EUDORA WELTY

Teaching the Works of

EUDORA WELTY

Twenty-First-Century Approaches

Edited by **Mae Miller Claxton** and **Julia Eichelberger**

University Press of Mississippi / *Jackson*

www.upress.state.ms.us

The University Press of Mississippi is a member
of the Association of American University Presses.

Copyright © 2018 by University Press of Mississippi
All rights reserved
Manufactured in the United States of America

First printing 2018
∞

Photographs by Eudora Welty reprinted by the permission of Mississippi
Department of Archives and History and Russell & Volkening as agents
for the author. Copyright © by Eudora Welty, renewed by Eudora Welty, LLC.

Introduction to Welty (1980) by Toni Morrison.
Used by Permission. All rights reserved.

Library of Congress Cataloging-in-Publication Data

Names: Claxton, Mae Miller, editor. | Eichelberger, Julia, 1959– editor.
Title: Teaching the works of Eudora Welty : twenty-first-century approaches /
edited by Mae Miller Claxton and Julia Eichelberger.
Description: Jackson : University Press of Mississippi, [2018] | Includes
bibliographical references and index. |
Identifiers: LCCN 2017033435 (print) | LCCN 2017033551 (ebook) | ISBN
9781496814548 (epub single) | ISBN 9781496814555 (epub institutional) |
ISBN 9781496814562 (pdf single) | ISBN 9781496814579 (pdf institutional)
| ISBN 9781496814531 (hardback) | ISBN 9781496814630 (paperback)
Subjects: LCSH: Welty, Eudora, 1909–2001—Study and teaching. | Welty,
Eudora, 1909–2001—Criticism and interpretation. | BISAC: EDUCATION /
Teaching Methods & Materials / Arts & Humanities. | LANGUAGE ARTS &
DISCIPLINES / Study & Teaching. | LITERARY CRITICISM / Women Authors.
Classification: LCC PS3545.E6 (ebook) | LCC PS3545.E6 Z876 2018 (print) | DDC
813/.52—dc23
LC record available at https://lccn.loc.gov/2017033435

British Library Cataloging-in-Publication Data available

*To the Eudora Welty Society
and all of our students
and to absent friends*

CONTENTS

xi	Acknowledgments
xiii	Introduction —Mae Miller Claxton and Julia Eichelberger

I. Invitations to Welty's "Mountain of Meaning"

3	Some Notes on Teaching Welty —Suzanne Marrs
13	Introductions to Welty —Carolyn J. Brown and Lee Anne Bryan
17	Teaching the Art of Welty's Letters —Julia Eichelberger
24	How She Wrote and How We Read: Teaching the Pleasure and Play of Welty's Modernist Techniques —Harriet Pollack
32	Teaching Welty's Narrative Strategies in *Delta Wedding* —Sarah Gilbreath Ford

II. New Perspectives on Welty and the US South

41	Teaching Welty's *A Curtain of Green* in an American Studies Freshman Seminar —Susan V. Donaldson

48 Matters of Life and Death: Teaching Welty in a Course on Death, Dying, and Funerals in Southern Literature
—David A. Davis

55 Indigenizing Welty
—Mae Miller Claxton

62 Taking *The Wide Net* to the Waters of *La Frontera* along Eudora Welty's Natchez Trace
—Dolores Flores-Silva

III. "Lifting the Veil": Teaching Welty and African American Identity

71 Teaching "A Curtain" in the Thick of Things: Welty and Race in Diverse Classrooms
—Christin Marie Taylor

78 The Matter of Black Lives in American Literature: Welty's Nonfiction and Photography
—Ebony Lumumba

84 "Powerhouse" and the Challenge of African American Representation: Teaching Eudora Welty and Race in an American Literature Survey
—Jacob Agner

90 "We Must Have Your History, You Know": African/Soul Survivals, Swallowed Lye, and the Medicine-Journey of "A Worn Path"
—Keith Cartwright

IV. "Learning to See": Bodies in Welty's Texts

101 Picturing Difference and Disability in Our Classrooms
—Keri Watson

109 Queering Welty's Male Bodies in the Undergraduate Classroom
—Gary Richards

115	Loch of the Rape: Welty Stories and Sexual Violence —**Michael Kreyling**
122	Welty's Place in the Undergraduate Theory Classroom —**Annette Trefzer**

V. Worldly Welty: International and Transcultural Contexts

133	Teaching Welty and/in Modernism —**David McWhirter**
141	Post Southern and International: Teaching Welty's Cosmopolitanism in "Going to Naples" —**Stephen M. Fuller**
147	Umbrellas and Bottles: Teaching Welty's Mythology in the Hong Kong Classroom —**Stuart Christie**
158	Transcontinental Welty: Teaching Welty with South African Writers Nadine Gordimer and Sindiwe Magona —**Pearl Amelia McHaney**

VI. Teaching Welty in Our Writing Classrooms

167	Finding the Freshman Voice: Using *One Writer's Beginnings* in the Classroom —**Virginia Ottley Craighill**
172	"He Going to Last": Why Phoenix Jackson's Grandson Still Matters **Dawn Gilchrist**
177	How I Teach "Livvie" in Welty's Home County —**Alec Valentine**
181	"Something Beautiful, Something Frightening": Using Welty's Stories to Teach Critical Thinking in Undergraduate Writing Courses —**Laura Sloan Patterson**

188	"A Worn Path" in the Creative Writing Classroom: Writing, Attention, and the Ecological Thought —**Amy Weldon**

VII. Casting Wider Nets: New Interdisciplinary Contexts for Teaching Welty

195	Teaching Welty in Dialogue with Other Artists in a Social Justice Course —**Adrienne Akins Warfield**
202	Using "A Worn Path" to Explore Contemporary Health Disparities in a Service-Learning Course —**Casey Kayser**
208	Folk and Fairy Tales, Opera, and YouTube: Teaching Welty's Fiction in a Folklore and American Literature Course —**Kevin Eyster**
215	Teaching Welty to Future Teachers: *The Wide Net*, *The Golden Apples*, and Inquiry-Based Learning —**Rebecca L. Harrison**
224	Finding Hope: Listening to Welty's Words in "Lily Daw and the Three Ladies" —**Sharon Deykin Baris**
231	Resources for Teachers and Students
241	About the Contributors
249	Index

ACKNOWLEDGMENTS

This book would not have been possible without the generosity of many colleagues.

We've always believed that teaching, which extends and deepens our understanding of Welty's oeuvre, is vital to our scholarly work, and the contributors to this book have proved us right. We're most grateful to these colleagues, who often had bigger fish to fry, for producing essays that are useful to busy instructors as well as to researchers. We salute their expertise in drafting essays, in revising them promptly and repeatedly upon request, and in waiting patiently as we searched for the right home for this book.

Numerous colleagues offered welcome advice and encouragement as we drafted proposals for this project and recruited contributors: we especially want to thank Susan Donaldson (William and Mary), David McWhirter (Texas A&M), Harriet Pollack (Bucknell University), Barbara Ladd (Emory University), Sarah Gilbreath Ford (Baylor University) Annette Trefzer (University of Mississippi), Tim Carens and Scott Peeples (College of Charleston), and Annette Debo, Laura Wright, and Brian Gastle (Western Carolina University). Over forty colleagues took the time to respond to a survey on how instructors are now teaching Welty.

The Eudora Welty Society's expertise, encouragement, and collaborative spirit have proved indispensable to this book—indeed, we would not have undertaken the project without knowing that society members would be pitching in and cheering us on. Many thanks, y'all.

Thanks are due to College of Charleston students who assisted with the final stages of manuscript preparation, Matt Woodward, Blake Taylor, and Cara Scott, and to the College for funding graduate assistantships for Blake and Cara. We thank the College of Charleston's Department of English and School of Humanities and Social Sciences and the Department of English at Western Carolina University for supporting our travel to half a dozen academic conferences where we discussed this project with colleagues. Special thanks go to Jonathan Wade, Michele Hawes, and the WCU Coulter Faculty Commons for help in developing and maintaining a companion website for this volume.

We are very grateful to Mary Alice Welty White and Eudora Welty, LLC for their encouragement of our work and for permission to use Welty's works in this volume. Thanks to Jeanne Luckett and the Eudora Welty Foundation for supplying us with teaching materials we hadn't seen before, and to Forrest Galey and other staff members at the Mississippi Department of Archives and History who assisted us with locating and reproducing images. We're also grateful to the editorial and production staff at the University Press of Mississippi, first for supporting our vision for this book, and for their editorial guidance, production and design, and marketing skills. Their efforts are a crucial part of reaching all the readers who may benefit from this book.

Through the years as we have worked on this project, family members have been loyal supporters of efforts that seemed as if they might never bear fruit. To David Claxton, who has been hearing about Welty projects for over twenty years now, and to Roy Hutchinson, who never stopped asking kindly about our most recent two-hour phone conference, we will always be grateful. We also thank our children and extended families. You continue to inspire us.

INTRODUCTION

> As you have seen, I am a writer who came of a sheltered life. A sheltered life can be a daring life as well. For all serious daring starts from within.
> —**Eudora Welty,** *One Writer's Beginnings*

> Volcanoes be in Sicily
> And South America
> I judge from my Geography
> Volcanoes nearer here
> A Lava step at any time
> Am I inclined to climb
> A Crater I may contemplate
> Vesuvius at Home
> —**Emily Dickinson,** Poem #1705

The essays in this volume attest to Eudora Welty's "daring writing life." Recent scholarship has amply demonstrated that Welty was a writer with cosmopolitan sensibilities and progressive politics, a woman whose love of travel enabled her to maintain close friendships with artists and intellectuals throughout the world. Throughout her writing career, however, this innovative artist was known to much of the general public as "Miss Welty," the genteel spinster who wrote her sharply tuned fiction in the upstairs bedroom of her parents' comfortable Tudor home in Jackson, Mississippi (see, for example, Claudia Roth Pierpont's 1998 article "A Perfect Lady" in the *New Yorker*). She continues to be categorized—narrowly and sometimes dismissively—as a "regionalist" writer, a white southern "lady" too polite to criticize the society she emerged from. Many have assumed that Welty's lyricism was a ladylike celebration of her region, and that her works valorize the white privilege from which she benefited. To assume this is Welty's intention is to misread much of her work, as more attentive readers of Welty have always known.

To those of us who know her work well, Welty's texts are acts of "serious daring," expressing not only affection and humor, but also biting sarcasm, anger, and a radical form of empathy for her characters. However, too few instructors are aware of Welty's depth and range, most often assigning one or two of the handful of stories most often anthologized ("A Worn Path," "Why I Live at the P.O.," "Petrified Man," "Livvie," "Powerhouse"). Without familiarity with Welty's entire body of work and without the aid of the powerful scholarly readings of these works produced in the past thirty years, readers may assume that these well-known stories are only what they seem on a first reading: straightforward, affectionate, and humorous portrayals of rural southerners. Although Welty is lauded for her documentary detail, her fiction is not always a transparent record of her time and place; any Welty text contains much more than can be absorbed on a first reading. Readers often need guidance to become accustomed to the complexity of Welty's tone, which can encompass humor and tragedy, reverence and whimsy, within the same sentence or paragraph. This volume offers ways to navigate Welty's prose and enriches readers' understanding of Welty's era and region. It offers teachers less simplistic approaches to the stories most frequently taught, and it steers them to less familiar texts, helping them to navigate these rich works. In addition, this book seeks to move Welty beyond a discussion of region to reflect new scholarship that remaps her work onto a larger canvas.

Despite the many accolades Welty received and the profusion of scholarly books and articles assuring her academic reputation, no collection as yet has focused solely on information designed to aid instructors of Welty's works. Now more than ever, teachers need guidance in navigating the critical landscape and in preparing to introduce her texts to students in varied teaching settings and diverse classrooms. As the essays in this book demonstrate, Welty's works are being read and taught across the globe: Mississippi, Israel, Florida, Hong Kong, Texas, among many other locations. Welty's works enrich courses taught at many levels, from high school to community college to the university level. One essay discusses teaching Welty's fiction to students in advanced placement high school classes in Appalachia. Other essayists teach Welty's works in large university settings, at the Eudora Welty House in Jackson, at a historically black college in Mississippi, at liberal arts institutions in Iowa and Pennsylvania as well as in the South. Each essayist has successfully translated his or her expertise into useful pedagogical strategies. This book gives readers a window into the teaching practices of distinguished and veteran scholars and also those at the beginning of their careers. Their work can guide instructors new to Welty as well as seasoned Welty scholars who are eager for fresh classroom approaches and new material to offer a new generation of students.

The pedagogical approaches presented in these essays succeed in part because they are informed by decades of scholarly work on Welty. Academic work on Welty has been active since the 1940s, but new directions in southern and American studies make this a particularly opportune time to revisit Welty's works and encourage their use in the classroom, using many of the scholarly lenses that are now available to study her work. Earlier generations of scholars began the crucial work of unraveling some threads of Welty's prose: her allusions to classical literature and myth, her mastery of free indirect discourse, her skill at capturing the speech of a wide range of characters, her documentation of everyday details found in her home region. While Welty's rich use of language and her interest in myth and folklore lend credence to this kind of close reading, scholars of the 1970s and 1980s expanded our understanding of Welty using other theoretical and historical contexts. Welty's photography, and especially its documentation of the lives of African Americans in the 1930s, has received increased critical attention since the publication of Welty's *One Time, One Place* in 1971 and *Photographs* in 1989. Feminist readings of Welty significantly altered the landscape of Welty studies beginning in the 1980s, but exciting developments in the twenty-first century have given us new eyes to see even more of Welty's continuing relevance as a writer and thinker. Other developments in Welty scholarship include the posthumous release of archival material from the Eudora Welty Collection at the Mississippi Department of Archives and History, including letters, manuscript drafts, photographs, and other materials now available to researchers and in book form.

Recent Welty scholarship reflects these developments in the academy. Scholars who study the US South are more likely now to look beyond the region to understand it. Critical studies that challenge traditional ideas of "regionalism," that redefine the US South in terms of a "global south," and that investigate it alongside South Africa, the Caribbean, and Latin America, are all aspects of what was called "new southern studies" in 2001, though by now this approach is more standard practice among all critics who work on the region, including leading Welty scholars. Welty scholarship is also increasingly informed by interdisciplinary perspectives and new investigations of place and space, globalization and border crossings. New dimensions in Welty's work are continually being revealed via these theoretical developments—in narratology, queer theory, trauma theory, critical race studies, disability studies, modernist studies, memory studies, ecocriticism, the ethics of reading. Concurrent with these critical and theoretical advances, pedagogical developments of the past thirty years have given us new understandings of how our students learn; many of the essays in this book demonstrate that Welty's works are excellent vehicles for teaching critical thinking, writing, and visual thinking strategies, and for fostering deeper understandings of diversity and difference.

This volume provides answers to questions many teachers will have: why should I study a writer who documents white privilege? Why should I give this "regional" writer space on an already crowded syllabus? Why should I teach Welty if I don't study the South? How can I help my students make sense of her innovative modernist narratives? How can Welty's texts help me teach my students about literary theory, about gender and disability, about cultures and societies with which my students are unfamiliar? Our essayists assist instructors in grappling with Welty's rich and challenging texts, where we find ample evidence of Welty's engagement with gender identity, racism, class, and an unbalanced power structure, issues that continue to appear in contemporary newspaper headlines, social media, and videos captured on cell phones. Welty's works belong in our classrooms, not because they were written by a "perfect lady," but because they contain the surprising, even dangerous, eruptions of a volcanic talent, "Vesuvius at home."

Readers need not proceed through our collection according to our sequence, but may prefer to browse the table of contents to find essays that interest them. As instructors ourselves, we know that prep time before a scheduled class can be scarce. Instructors may productively read a single essay while preparing for a class on a specific Welty work, or they may spend more time with groups of essays when planning new courses or looking for ways to fit texts that they have not tried before into their existing courses. For readers interested in studying our entire volume, our grouping of essays is designed to lead readers through an increasing number of contexts in which instructors can teach Welty successfully.

The first group of essays in this volume should be useful to any instructor preparing to teach Welty. We've titled this section "Invitations to Welty's 'Mountain of Meaning,'" a phrase we borrowed from Welty's memoir to suggest the wealth of insight and artistic innovation her work contains. Our research for this volume confirmed that many instructors never teach Welty, or teach only one or two stories. Even those who teach a wider range of her work acknowledge the challenge of leading students to engage deeply with texts that are often difficult and sometimes disturbing. Accordingly, we begin the volume with essays focused on motivating readers to immerse themselves in Welty's work. Leading Welty scholar and biographer Suzanne Marrs shares insights gleaned from teaching Welty's work throughout her career, including guidance from Welty herself. As Marrs reminds us, quoting Welty, fiction "contains everything but a clear answer," and this is especially helpful to remember when teaching Welty's work. Other essayists detail how they use biographical materials to attract new audiences for Welty (Brown and Bryant) and how personal letters, another genre at which Welty excelled, can enhance a wide range of teaching situations (Eichelberger). With so much correspondence and other archival material now available for study, instructors may use Welty's letters as an entrée to the distinctive voice of the author, whose works often take unexpected turns. The last two essays in this section provide expert guidance on how to help our students enjoy those aspects of Welty's work that may initially frustrate and baffle them—Welty's modernist artistry, her narratives that thwart readerly expectations (Pollack), and her complex arrays of characters and relationships (Ford). These essays demonstrate that the very things that may have prevented readers from enjoying Welty can become sources of immense pleasure and insight.

Each section of the volume that follows offers a new thematic or pedagogical context for teaching Welty's work. In our second section, instructors share their expertise in southern studies and their approaches to teaching Welty in the context of her home region. Each essay is built on the assumption that the US South is culturally and ideologically diverse and that Welty's texts attest to this diversity. Welty's narratives provide an opportunity to explore southerners' rituals and beliefs (Davis); detailed knowledge of the South's history reveals that Welty's texts interrogate her region's constructions of racial identity and of southern womanhood (Donaldson). Welty's work can also enrich courses designed to highlight the experiences and perspectives of Native southerners (Claxton), and can even serve as a bridge between Anglo-American cultures and the South's Latin American communities and cultural retentions (Flores-Silva).

In the third section of the book are essays that help instructors and students discover how deeply Welty's work engages with African American identity and agency, once we "lift the veil" that assumes that Welty was quietist or complacent in her position of white privilege. Offering innovative new readings as well as pedagogies, these essayists explore the way an early Welty story facilitates classroom discussions of race (Taylor) and how Welty's portrayals of African American experiences contribute to American literature courses (Lumumba, Agner). One essayist teaches at a historically black college where students analyze which American experiences are included and which are discounted in the literary canon. In another American literature classroom, an essayist situates the main character in "Powerhouse" within the New Negro

Renaissance. Finally, Keith Cartwright's teaching of "A Worn Path" explores the way the heroine's "medicine-journey" reflects "initiatory tales and rituals of the black Atlantic world."

Bodies abound in Welty's works, including many that no "perfect lady" would acknowledge but that our students should recognize and contemplate. In the fourth section, which takes its title from a chapter in Welty's memoir, essayists offer ways of "learning to see" how Welty's works engage with issues related to the body—disability (Watson), queerness (Richards), the representation of sexual trauma (Kreyling), and pleasure; the last essay by Annette Trefzer argues that these concerns make Welty's texts particularly useful in teaching literary theory. Our fifth section on "Worldly Welty" remaps Welty in several interesting ways, demonstrating numerous rewards available when we teach Welty as an international rather than regional writer. One essayist finds that Welty's works illuminate and are illuminated by South African writers (McHaney), while students in a course taught in Hong Kong have found Welty's texts relevant to a twenty-first-century political context far from Mississippi (Christie). One scholar teaches Welty as an international modernist whose texts respond to southern and American modernities, putting them in conversation with Joyce, Conrad, and Woolf (McWhirter), and another scholar focuses on Welty's cosmopolitanism in her narratives set outside the South (Fuller). Clearly, Welty's texts can work well in classes—and scholarly work—whose focus extends beyond her home region.

Essayists in our sixth section, "Welty in the Writing Classroom," discuss Welty as an exemplar and as a productive subject of analysis for writing students. Before this book, relatively few publications connected Welty's work to what we know about the teaching of writing, even though her work is widely admired by many writers (Nadine Gordimer, Alice Munro, Toni Morrison, Ann Patchett, Richard Ford, William Maxwell, to name a few), and is regularly assigned by writing teachers. Since most English and literature teachers often teach writing and introductory-level classes, the sixth section will benefit a very large number of readers, whether they are teaching Advanced Placement English (Gilchrist), community college students (Valentine), a first-year writing class focused on literature (Craighill), analysis and critical thinking (Patterson), or a creative writing class (Weldon).

In our seventh section, we provide five essays offering interdisciplinary contexts for teaching Welty, demonstrating the relevance of her work to disciplines besides literary studies—folklore (Eyster), teacher education (Harrison), anthropology (Baris), and medical humanities (Kayser). These essayists open up new windows onto Welty's works, and several describe innovative courses built around exciting new themes such as social justice (Warfield) and new pedagogies such as inquiry-based learning (Harrison) and service learning (Keyser). One of the essays in this section may prove perfectly suited to a course that a particular reader plans to teach, but the variety of these essayists' approaches is instructive to any reader, showing how adaptable Welty's work is to new and unexpected contexts. These essays may inspire readers to develop their own courses and approaches—contexts and confluences that we have not yet imagined, but that will surely be discovered in the future.

Following our contributors' essays, our short essay, "Resources for Teachers and Students," offers further information on Welty's publications, points instructors to helpful teaching aids available online and elsewhere, and discusses scholarship on Welty that will be particularly useful for teachers and students. As we note in that essay, the Library of America editions of Welty's works, which contain most of her published fiction as well as some nonfiction, are the standard editions for all of these texts. Our essayists use these volumes unless quoting from other works by Welty.

The teacher-scholars whose essays appear in this volume do more than illuminate Welty's work, as important as that endeavor is. They also demonstrate that our work as teachers advances our scholarly understanding of Welty's oeuvre—and that we often have our students to thank for our discoveries. Our contributors have learned new things about Welty by seeing her through the eyes of students who identify with the kinds of communities Welty depicts, who delight in Welty's humor or lyrical descriptions, who enjoy her subtle critiques of characters' restricting circumstances, and who connect her work to present-day contexts Welty could not have anticipated. Even students who do not share their instructor's enthusiasm for this writer have shown us ways to teach her more effectively, leading us to discoveries that advance our scholarly work. We are better readers of Welty because of our time in the classroom. We hope that readers will learn as much from our contributors' essays as we have learned by preparing this book.

I

Invitations to Welty's "Mountain of Meaning"

Like distant landmarks you are approaching, ... suddenly a light is thrown back, as when your train makes a curve, showing you that there has been a mountain of meaning rising behind you on the way you've come, is rising there still.
—***One Writer's Beginnings*** (933)

Some Notes on Teaching Welty

—**Suzanne Marrs**, Millsaps College

During the course of my forty-plus-year academic career, I have had the great good fortune to teach Eudora Welty's fiction on a regular basis. At first I often taught a story or two or perhaps even a novel as part of an American or southern literature class. But eventually I taught entire courses devoted to Welty. Here are some notes about my years in the classroom, recollections offered in the hope that they may prove useful to others.

Notes on Helping Students Prepare for Class

I rely on Welty's statements about the nature of fiction, the art of writing it, and the art of reading it to help students read Welty's stories and novels. Other instructors might like to distribute the following list of quotations at the beginning of a Welty unit or class, or you might prefer to bring individual quotations to bear at opportune moments as you discuss a particular work.

1. "Great fiction . . . abounds in what makes for confusion; it generates it, being on a scale which copies life, which it confronts. It is very seldom neat, is given to sprawling and escaping from bounds, is capable of contradicting itself, and is not impervious to humor. There is absolutely everything in great fiction but a clear answer" (*Stories* 806). Students often expect stories to end in a conclusive fashion, but they will not typically find resolution in a Welty story; they will eventually come to appreciate that lack and Welty's explanation for it.

2. "A narrative line is in its deeper sense . . . the tracing out of a meaning, and the real continuity of a story lies in this probing forward" (817). Though Welty's stories are not plot driven, their plots are vehicles carrying meaning. The journeys in stories like "Death of a Traveling Salesman," "A Worn Path," and "No Place for You, My Love" are cases in point—these journeys prove to be both external and internal, literal and metaphoric.

3. "The writer must accurately choose, combine, superimpose upon, blot out, shake up, alter the outside world for one absolute purpose, the good of his story. To do this, he is always seeing double, two pictures at once in his frame, his and the world's, a fact that he constantly comprehends; and he works best in a state of constant and subtle and unfooled reference between the two. It is his clear intention—his passion, I should say—to make the reader see only one of the pictures—the author's—under the pleasing illusion that it is the world's; this enormity is the accomplishment of a good story" (789). Students often view stories as literal transcriptions of actual people or places. I like to encourage them to look for differences between an actual locale—say the house called Waverly, which lies near West Point, Mississippi—and a fictional setting based upon it—Marmion in *Delta Wedding*, in this instance. The differences, it seems to me, can illustrate the power of the writer's imagination and serve as a guide for interpretation.

4. "Fictional time may be more congenial to us than clock time, precisely for human reasons. An awareness of time goes with us all our lives. Watch or no watch, we carry the awareness with us. It lies so deep, in the very grain of our characters, that who knows if it isn't as singular to each of us as our thumbprints. In the sense of our own transience may lie the one irreducible urgency, telling us to do, to understand, to love.

"We are mortal: this is time's deepest meaning in the novel as it is to us alive" (*Eye* 168).

A focus on mortality and the urgency this brings to human lives is a crucial issue in most of Welty's fiction. *The Golden Apples*, in particular, depicts a small-town community seeking to block out this disturbing knowledge and a circle of wanderers who are driven by it. This double response is particularly evident during the funerals in "June Recital" and "The Wanderers," two key stories in *The Golden Apples*.

5. In 1981, discussing her use of allusion in *The Golden Apples*, Welty told an interviewer: "Well, you know, now I think I'd think twice before I threw around myths and everything so freely. I'm glad I did then [late 1940s]

because I just used them as freely as I would the salt and pepper. They were part of my life, like poetry, and I would take something from Yeats here and something from a myth there. I had no system about it" (*Conversations* 330). I think it is a good idea to discourage students from viewing Welty's allusions to myth, fairy tales, or poetry in too rigid a fashion. The allusions are significant and suggestive, but as Welty indicates, she was not writing allegory or simply retelling other texts.

6. "We start from scratch, and words don't; which is the thing that matters—matters over and over again" (*Eye* 134). Welty asks readers to look carefully at words, at their derivations and connotations, and we must ask the same of our students. The periodical versions of Welty's stories are to varying degrees different from the book publications. Students might find it valuable to examine shifts in phrasing and to speculate about the import of these shifts.

7. In 1965, in the midst of the civil rights movement, Welty wrote: "*A Passage to India* is an old novel now. It is an intensely moral novel. It deals with race prejudice. Mr. Forster, not by preaching at us, while being passionately concerned, makes us know his points unforgettably as often as we read it.... The points are good forty years after their day because *of the splendor of the novel*. What a lesser novelist's harangues would have buried by now, his imagination still reveals" (*Stories* 810). Welty here distinguishes between the novel that crusades, that seeks to bring about social change, and the novel that reflects or conveys social realities as its characters develop. But she nevertheless believes the novelist takes and must take a moral stand: her own fiction does just that. The essays in *Eudora Welty and Politics: Did the Writer Crusade?* address this issue.

8. "I never doubted that . . . imagining yourself into other people's lives is exactly what writing fiction is" ("Looking Back" 755). In her stories, Welty imagines herself into the lives of young and old, white and black, affluent and poverty stricken, and she adopts voices from this diverse array of characters, sometimes creating dialogue for them, at other times subtly shifting into free indirect discourse. A keen awareness of voice and of shifts in voice is crucial to any reading of Welty.

9. "The home tie is the blood tie. And had it meant nothing to us, any other place thereafter would have meant less, and we would carry no compass inside ourselves to find home ever, anywhere at all" (*Stories* 794). Reading about Mississippi and especially Welty's hometown of Jackson provides an

invaluable context for her fiction even though that fiction transcends state and city boundaries. Students can also visit, either literally or virtually, the Eudora Welty House, the house Welty called home for seventy-six years. In what is now a literary house museum, they can look at the 5,000-volume library she compiled, at the artwork she hung throughout the house, at the room in which she wrote, at the music she collected, at the snapshots she took of family and friends. Interpreting the relationship between her home and her writing life can serve as a compass for students as they explore Welty's fiction.

Notes on Selecting Individual Stories to Teach

1. If teaching a class on the short story, instructors might like to use a CD/DVD combination that is available for free at eudorawelty.org. It is titled *Welty and the Craft of Writing* and focuses on three stories: "Why I Live at the P.O.," "Petrified Man," and "A Worn Path." The CD teachers will receive includes drafts of the stories, letters concerning their composition, and Welty photographs related to the stories. Those who include "A Worn Path" on their syllabi might also like to look at Welty's essay "Is Phoenix Jackson's Grandson Really Dead?"

2. If you are teaching a class about translations of fiction into film, there are film versions of a number of Welty stories: *The Hitch-Hikers*, directed by Alan Bergmann; *The Key*, directed by Francis James; *The Ponder Heart*, directed by Martha Coolidge; *The Purple Hat*, directed by Gregory Doucette; *A Visit of Charity*, directed by Tom Ptasinski; *The Frost Whistle*, a version of "The Whistle," directed by Catherine Owens; *Why I Live at the P.O.*, directed by Jodie Markell; *The Wide Net*, directed by Anthony Herrera; and *A Worn Path*, directed by Bruce Schwartz.

3. When teaching an American literature survey, I recommend including some of these stories.

"Powerhouse" is a story Welty wrote after hearing Fats Waller in concert. The narrative point of view in parts 1 and 3 of the story lies in the white audience but shifts to an authorial perspective in part 2. In the course of the story, a portrait of race relations in the 1930s South emerges as does a portrait of the artist as itinerant musician. Biographical accounts of Welty's work on the story and recordings of Fats Waller's music are useful teaching aids. Students can also listen to a recording of Welty herself reading the story.

"The Whistle" recounts the events of one night in the life of a tenant farming couple, vividly describing the poverty and desperation such individuals faced during the Great Depression. The story might well be taught alongside "Bright and Morning Star" by Richard Wright. And students might like to read about the biracial Southern Tenant Farmers Union for historical perspective. There is a teaching unit on "The Whistle" available at eudorawelty.org.

"First Love" and "A Still Moment" are Welty's ventures into historical fiction. "First Love" is set in 1807 during Aaron Burr's trial in the Mississippi territory. "A Still Moment" arranges for an early nineteenth-century meeting of three historical figures: John James Audubon, Lorenzo Dow, and James (actually John) Murrell. Both stories, though set in the past and drawing upon American history, also comment obliquely on issues of the second World War, the time in which Welty wrote the stories.

"June Recital" and "The Wanderers" are both included in Welty's story cycle, *The Golden Apples*. Set primarily in the post–World War I through post–World War II fictional town of Morgana, Mississippi, they are richly allusive and profoundly metaphysical in import, but they are also grounded in the authentic details of small-town American life.

"No Place for You, My Love" might be called a postmodern story; at least your students might like to discuss that possibility. It is most certainly a story in which place carries the story's import to an impressive degree. Welty wrote of this story in the essay "Writing and Analyzing a Story" (*Stories* 773–80).

"Where Is the Voice Coming From?" is the story Welty wrote in the wake of Medgar Evers's assassination. It is a monologue delivered by the assassin, who undermines himself with every word. The story went through intensive revision, and students can study those revisions. Early versions are available in John Kuehl's book *Write and Rewrite* and in the *Jackson Clarion-Ledger* archive ("From the Unknown"). There is a teaching unit on this story available at eudorawelty.org. Instructors who are able to bring students to Jackson can arrange a tour of the Medgar Evers House.

Notes on Designing Welty Courses

Here are brief descriptions of courses I have taught with success in the last few years.

1. Eudora Welty's Short Fiction. I taught this course as my swan song, and a joy it was. My students read all of the stories in *A Curtain of Green*, *The*

Wide Net, The Golden Apples, and *The Bride of the Innisfallen,* in addition to reading *The Robber Bridegroom,* "Where Is the Voice Coming From?" and "The Demonstrators." We were not able to discuss every story, but we were able to consider the continuities and shifts in Welty's artistic strategies and in her thematic concerns. We paid particular attention to the biographical, social, cultural, and historical contexts from which her fiction emerged and on which it comments. By semester's end all of the class embraced Ann Patchett's assessment of Welty as "the greatest short story writer of our time" (209).

2. Eudora Welty: The Writer as Reader. In this course, I first taught works by Jane Austen, Anton Chekhov, and Virginia Woolf along with Welty's essays about each of these writers.[1] Then I taught books by Welty that I thought paired well with these texts. Other instructors might prefer to alternate texts: *Pride and Prejudice,* then *Delta Wedding*; Chekhov's stories (I used "The Privy Councilor," "About Love," "The Kiss," "Gooseberries," "The Darling," and "The Lady with the Dog"), then *The Golden Apples*; *To the Lighthouse,* then *The Optimist's Daughter.* Suzan Harrison's book *Eudora Welty and Virginia Woolf: Gender, Genre, and Influence* was particularly helpful. There is a teaching unit on *The Optimist's Daughter* available at eudorawelty.org. At this website you may also request a pamphlet describing the ways Welty's home served as a source for setting in that novel.

3. Welty and Politics. Though critics for many years assumed Welty's fiction to be essentially apolitical, she herself operated under a different assumption. As Welty once noted, "I assumed that my whole life I had been writing about injustice." In this course I asked students to look at the political implications of Welty stories from the Great Depression, the World War II era, and the postwar decades of the fifties and sixties. We studied seven stories from *A Curtain of Green* ("Powerhouse," "The Whistle," "Death of a Traveling Salesman," "The Hitch-Hikers," "Flowers for Marjorie," "Keela, the Outcast Indian Maiden," "A Worn Path"); moved to *The Robber Bridegroom* and *Delta Wedding*; looked at five stories from the fifties ("Circe," "The Bride of the Innisfallen," "Kin," "Going to Naples," "The Burning"); and then finished the semester with "Where Is the Voice Coming From?" "The Demonstrators," and *Losing Battles*. A collection of essays titled *Eudora Welty and Politics: Did the Writer Crusade?* would be a useful one to consult as would another titled *Eudora Welty, Whiteness, and Race.*[2]

4. Welty and Friends: In this class I paired texts by Welty with works by Elizabeth Bowen, Reynolds Price, and Ross Macdonald. Bowen's novels *The*

House in Paris and *A World of Love* I taught in conjunction with *A Curtain of Green* and *The Golden Apples*. Welty's *The Bride of the Innisfallen* I paired with Price's *The Names and Faces of Heroes*. And Macdonald's *The Underground Man* and *Sleeping Beauty* I taught in conjunction with *The Optimist's Daughter*. If there is time in your course, I suggest adding William Maxwell's *So Long, See You Tomorrow*. I think a biography of Welty (I recommend my own), the collection of letters between Welty and Macdonald, and another letter collection, one between Welty and Maxwell, would prove useful to anyone teaching or taking this course. An actual or virtual visit to the Eudora Welty House, where Welty entertained all of these friends and where their works and their photographs are among the many artifacts on display, would also complement course content.[3]

I have compiled these notes with a sense of melancholy—I won't be teaching any more on a regular basis—but also with a sense of exhilaration: I may in these pages encourage younger teachers to bring Welty more centrally into their classrooms and to devise new and more exciting approaches than my own. That is a happy thought. Teach on!

Notes

1. Welty's essays about Austen and Chekhov appear in *The Eye of the Story*. Her discussion of Woolf's *To the Lighthouse* is the foreword to an edition of this book published by Harcourt, Brace, Jovanovich in 1981.

2. Here is the course description I included on my syllabus:

In her essay "Must the Novelist Crusade?" Eudora Welty distinguishes between the editorial writer and the writer of fiction, contending that the editorial writer must deal in generalities whereas generalities in works of fiction "make too much noise for us to hear what people might be trying to say." And she adds, "there is everything in great fiction but a clear answer." Nevertheless, she asserts that fiction can "show us how to face our feelings and face our actions and to have new inklings about what they mean." She offers E. M. Forster's depiction of race prejudice in *A Passage to India* as a case in point, writing that "The points are good forty years after their day because of the splendor of the novel. What a lesser novelist's harangues would have buried by now, his imagination still reveals." In short, Welty contends that fiction must not crusade, but that it is inherently and powerfully political.

In English 3350, we will discuss the political beliefs and acts that typified Eudora Welty's life, and we'll investigate the political import of her fiction. Throughout the course, we'll ask ourselves what Welty's fiction reveals about the crucial political issues of the twentieth century.

3. Here is the course description I gave to students:

Eudora Welty had a genius for friendship, and a magical use of language often was both the spark for and the result of her friendships. In this class, we will discuss three of the most powerful friendships that marked Welty's life between 1950 and her death in 2001. These three friendships were each with fellow writers, whom Welty first met in the pages of their stories. Was her own fiction influenced by her love for the work of novelists and story writers who became her friends? Was their work influenced by hers? Do the novels and stories of these friends ever seem to be in dialogue with each other? Such are questions we will attempt to answer as we discuss the artistry and thematic complexity of fiction by Welty, Elizabeth Bowen, Reynolds Price, and Ross Macdonald.

Some years before she met Elizabeth Bowen, Welty had read her stories and novels. She admired them and felt Bowen was especially astute in her characterization of women. For her part, Bowen had read and reviewed Welty's work before the two met. In a review of *Delta Wedding*, Bowen wrote, "I don't imagine that anyone who is on the lookout for anything new and great in writing can by now have overlooked the work of this young American, or that anybody susceptible to the magic of writing can have forgotten hers, once met." And after reading *The Golden Apples*, Bowen praised Welty for "having found a means of communications which spans oceans." The two writers seemed destined to become friends, and friends they did become when Welty first visited Ireland and Bowen's Court in 1950.

Reynolds Price entered Eudora Welty's life five years later. In 1955, invited by Duke University to speak and to meet with its writing students, Welty was scheduled to arrive at the Durham train station in the wee hours, but wary of cloying student attention, she had asked not to be met. Price chose to disregard her request—he knew that finding a cab after midnight in Durham would prove difficult. So there he was, in his ice cream suit (according to Welty's memory), to meet her and to promise immediately that he would not trap her in conversation. That, as Humphrey Bogart said to Claude Rains in *Casablanca*, was the beginning of a beautiful friendship. At Duke, Welty read the stories of this young writer and was impressed. She volunteered to put him in touch with her agent and recommend him for a Guggenheim Fellowship. Subsequently, during more than four decades that followed before Welty's death, the two would correspond and would frequently meet. In writing or in person, they discussed the work of writers they admired, commented on each other's fiction, and offered support in seasons of difficulty.

It was not until 1971 that Welty met Kenneth Millar (aka Ross Macdonald), a mystery writer whom she revered. She had reviewed his novel *The Underground Man*, and the two had established a correspondence both literary and personal in nature. Their first meeting, however, was an unexpected one (for Welty, at least) in the lobby of New York's Algonquin Hotel. Common friends had told Millar that Welty was staying there, and he waited in the lobby hoping to catch sight of her. Welty recalled that "As I came into the lobby and got my key and went for the elevator . . . a man came across the lobby and said, 'Miss Welty? Kenneth Millar.' I just couldn't believe it! . . . Isn't this just like a Ken story? You know how he used to say, there's no such thing as coincidence? So I just saddown [*sic*] in the lobby and threw my coat down and we started talking, and we just didn't stop for I don't know how long" (Tom Nolan, *Ross Macdonald: A Biography* [New York: Scribners, 1999], 310). The next day Ken took Eudora to a cocktail party given by Alfred and Helen Knopf and then out to dinner. Afterward they walked about Manhattan and into the theater district. They each had discovered a soul mate. They each would have a tremendous impact upon the future work of the other, and their connection would even transcend the barrier that arose when Ken encountered Alzheimer's disease.

Late in life, Welty mused upon the importance of friendship to her life and fiction. In her introduction to the *Norton Book of Friendship*, she asked, "Did friendship between human beings come about in the first place along with—or through—the inspiration of language?" And then she attempted to answer her own question: "It can be safe to say that when we learned to speak to, and listen to, rather than to strike or be struck by, our fellow human beings, we found something worth keeping alive, worth possessing, for the rest of time. Might it possibly have been the other way round—that the promptings of friendship guided us into learning to express ourselves, teaching ourselves, between us, a language to keep it by? Friendship might have been the first, as well as the best teacher of communication. Which came first, friendship or the spoken word? They could rise from the same prompting."

During our semester study of works by four friends, we will examine the promptings of friendship and language as they manifest themselves in a series of magnificent texts (*The Golden Apples*, *The Bride of the Innisfallen*, *The Optimist's Daughter*, *A House in Paris*, *A World of Love*, *The Names and Faces of Heroes*, *The Underground Man*, and *Sleeping Beauty*), and we will examine the extent to which these texts take friendship, in both its triumphs and its failures, as their subject.

Works Cited

Harrison, Suzan. *Eudora Welty and Virginia Woolf: Gender, Genre, and Influence*. Baton Rouge: LSU P, 1997.
Kuehl, John. *Write and Rewrite: A Study of the Creative Process*. New York: Meredith, 1967.
Patchett, Ann. *This Is the Story of a Happy Marriage*. New York: Harper, 2013.
Pollack, Harriet. *Eudora Welty, Whiteness, and Race*. Athens: U of Georgia P, 2013.
Pollack, Harriet, and Suzanne Marrs, eds. *Eudora Welty and Politics: Did the Writer Crusade?* Baton Rouge: Louisiana State UP, 2002.

Welty, Eudora. *Conversations with Eudora Welty*. Ed. Peggy Whitman Prenshaw. Jackson: UP of Mississippi, 1984.

———. *The Eye of the Story: Selected Essays and Reviews*. New York: Random House, 1978.

———. "From the Unknown." *Clarion-Ledger* [Jackson, MS], June 2, 2013: C4. Newspapers.com. Web. May 18, 2017.

———. "Looking Back at the First Story." *Georgia Review* 33.4 (Winter 1979): 755.

———. *Stories, Essays, and Memoir*. Ed. Richard Ford and Michael Kreyling. New York: Library of America, 1998.

Introductions to Welty

—**Carolyn J. Brown and Lee Anne Bryan,** independent scholars

In our roles as a biographer of Eudora Welty and as the education and outreach coordinator at the Eudora Welty House and Garden, we often find ourselves in front of a variety of audiences where we have a limited amount of time—sometimes only an hour—to introduce Eudora Welty and her work with the goal of leaving the audience more knowledgeable about the author and with a desire to read further. We have engaged in conversation with people of all kinds, from grade school students to senior citizens, to find where their interests lie. Sometimes they come to tour the Eudora Welty House knowing that Welty wrote about her fellow Mississippians; sometimes they know very little about her at all. Sometimes they are students who are clueless about the Pulitzer Prize–winning author; sometimes they are excellent readers but want some guidance in understanding her fiction. We have both found that one effective way to engage learners of all ages is through Welty's life story. There are family pictures, archival materials, and Welty's photographs and artwork that give a full portrait of her creative life. Depending on the age of the audience, we recommend emphasizing different aspects of Welty's biography and selecting a variety of texts that will appeal to each age group individually.

To engage a younger audience who today expect multimedia presentations, we recommend using a PowerPoint or a Prezi to give students an image of Eudora Welty as a child and a visual framework for her words. Pictures of her riding a bicycle to check books out of the library, her first pen-and-ink drawings, and attempts at writing poetry and stories captivate students. Even a century later, they can relate to Welty and find similarities in their own lives. Engaging middle and high school students also requires visual images. Photographs, drawings, and doodles show that Welty's artistic vision grew from multiple sources and that she was not committed to becoming a writer at a very young age. She was creative and as a high school and college student contributed artwork and cartoons to yearbooks and humor magazines. These images are amusing and entertaining, and can now be viewed firsthand in Carolyn J. Brown's *A Daring Life: A Biography of Eudora Welty* and in Patti Carr Black's book *Early Escapades*. Students enjoy knowing that she was talented in many creative arts and had her first photography exhibit the same year that she published her first short story! Her life story also demonstrates the hard work and effort required to publish one's work, unlike in today's society where self-publishing has become a common phenomenon.

Selecting works of Welty's that are grade-level appropriate is essential, and one that is especially effective with elementary students is the autobiographical essay "The Little Store." It serves as both a reading lesson and as a writing exercise because it illustrates the importance of detail and imagery to tell a story. The "little store" of the work is a neighborhood grocery, whose location was the corner of Congress Street and George Street, blocks away from Welty's birth home at 741 North Congress Street. Both structures—the Congress Street house and the grocery (although repurposed)—are visible today. "The Little Store" is a "looking back" essay, meaning that the author is recounting events from her childhood. It allows teachers to ask: "In what ways is this information useful to a writer? How is her view of the 'little store' different as an adult than it was as a child?" The essay can also serve as an effective springboard, encouraging students to write their own autobiographical essays.

Most often, we work with middle and high school students as they tour Welty's home at 1119 Pinehurst Street in Jackson. They can see examples of Welty's art and photographs in the Education and Visitors Center, and the orientation film offers the opportunity to hear Welty reading from her own works. The focus of the tour for students is Welty's writing process: the dining room table is laid with draft pages of *One Writer's Beginnings*, showing Welty's "cut-and-pin" method of revision; the writing desk in her bedroom is covered with notes taken on scraps of paper and checkbook registers, which she then used to type the pages of her fiction. Staff and docents also reveal the sources of Welty's work as part of the tour. Students are excited to learn that Welty's short stories sprang from her life, often from visual or auditory images, which she then transformed into the characters or scenarios of her fiction.

Two examples that are often selected as reading for the middle or high school classroom are "The Whistle" and "A Worn Path." "The Whistle" is based on an experience that Welty had while visiting a friend in Utica, Mississippi. A whistle sounded in the night to warn the farmers of a freeze, and Welty woke to see crops covered in quilts, clothing, and anything else the farmers owned in an attempt to save the plants. Welty converts the experience into the story of a married farming couple and the extreme poverty in which they live. A unit on teaching "The Whistle" is available on the Eudora Welty Foundation website at www.eudorawelty.org. It offers several methods to teach the story by providing the historical background of tenant farming in Mississippi, information on Welty's writing process from scholar Suzanne Marrs, questions about the text, and a creative portion that challenges students to produce their own original work.

Likewise, Welty's story "A Worn Path" was inspired by a single visual image. Welty was accompanying an artist friend on a sketching trip, and she saw a woman walking in the distance. This simple image was reimagined as Phoenix Jackson's journey in the story set on the Natchez Trace. An excellent resource to teach "A Worn Path" is available from the Welty Foundation, with no cost to educators, and can be ordered from the foundation website. Titled "Welty and the Craft of Writing," the kit includes a DVD of Welty herself reading the story, Welty's photographs, and manuscripts. We find that the footage of Welty reading is particularly valuable, because the rhythm and cadence of her voice helps students process the dialogue in the story. A teacher's guide is also on the website, with a list of questions to generate discussion. Again, this story can be an inspiration for a creative assignment. Learning what sparked Welty's imagination prompts students to choose an image or a moment from their own lives and draw from their own experiences to write a short story.

Perhaps the most receptive audience for learning about Welty's life and work is adults. When we have only an hour to introduce the writer on a tour of the Welty House, at a library program, or to a reading group, adult readers enjoy hearing about a childhood not so distant from their own. The tour of the home for adults differs slightly from the one given to students in that more emphasis is given to the furnishings, the artwork, the correspondence, and personal photographs. Adults see firsthand Welty's love of books and how they were her most faithful companions as they are scattered throughout every room, covering sofas and chairs. The furniture and paintings that are tributes to her parents reveal her love for her family. Adult readers also may relate to the themes in Welty's mature works—grief, love, loss, memory, and the passage of time—which are all made more poignant when visitors learn that Welty's father died when she was only twenty-two years old; that she was a caregiver to her mother and brothers for much of her life; and that she overcame great tragedy (the death of her mother followed by the death of her brother Edward four days later in January 1966) to write the Pulitzer Prize–winning novella *The Optimist's Daughter*. The tour also includes references to her large circle of friends, and her connection to famous authors and celebrities such as Elizabeth Bowen, E. M. Forster, and Roger Mudd corrects the frequent misconception that she rarely left Jackson. Hearing stories about her life from the docents, watching the video that begins the tour (and can only be viewed at the house), and walking through the garden that is dotted with quote-markers showcasing her expert knowledge of flowers and nature—all introduce adult readers to the author and prepare them to read her fiction.

Adults also enjoy hearing about Welty's reading life and what authors she especially liked. Suzanne Marrs's biography of Eudora Welty sheds light on Welty's friendships and relationships with other important twentieth-century writers, and *Occasions* and *Eye of the Story* are useful texts to learn more about Welty through writers that she considered important to the canon, such as Jane Austen, Anton Chekhov, Ross Macdonald, and Elizabeth Bowen. We have led a monthly book club named "Cereus Readers" (pun intended) for four years now, where during an hour-long meeting we have connected Welty with some of her favorite writers. The short stories of Chekhov have particularly resonated with our group, in large part because Welty's essay "Reality in Chekhov's Stories" was used as our guide and as a way into his fiction. Studying Chekhov, Elizabeth Bowen, and Isak Dinesen has made us better readers of the short story in general, including Welty's own work.

To schedule a tour of the Welty house, a museum of the Mississippi Department of Archives and History, call (601) 353-7762. For those not in the Jackson area, a virtual tour of the home is featured at the Eudora Welty House website. Our experiences have shown that when you have only an hour, it is critical to find a connection to Welty quickly, a way in to her life and work that encourages further study. Welty herself was, first and foremost, a reader; the greatest tribute would be to ensure new generations of readers for her body of work.

Further Reading and Resources

Black, Patti Carr. *Early Escapades*. Jackson: UP of Mississippi, 2005.

Brown, Carolyn J. *A Daring Life: A Biography of Eudora Welty*. Jackson: UP of Mississippi, 2012.

Marrs, Suzanne. *Eudora Welty: A Biography*. New York: Houghton, 2005.

Welty, Eudora. *The Eye of the Story: Selected Essays and Reviews*. New York: Random, 1978.

———. *Occasions: Selected Writings*. Ed. Pearl Amelia McHaney. Jackson: UP of Mississippi, 2009.

———. *Stories, Essays, and Memoir*. Ed. Richard Ford and Michael Kreyling. New York: Library of America, 1998.

For teaching units and *Welty and the Craft of Writing*: www.eudorawelty.org.

Teaching the Art of Welty's Letters

—Julia Eichelberger, College of Charleston

Anyone who teaches or conducts research on Welty's works should become acquainted with her remarkable correspondence. Whether studied on their own or as aids for interpreting other Welty texts, these letters are impressive linguistic and literary achievements that deserve a place in our classrooms. In addition to providing biographical and historical information about an acclaimed author, they also capture Welty's private voice in intimate conversation with friends who cherished her wit, compassion, and creativity.

Some letters display Welty's sharp-edged humor, as in one where she complains about another writer at Yaddo:

> Thank God I am not in the same house with her again. I won't be glad when she is dead, particularly, but I don't stop in my tracks and send up thanks ever that she is alive. I know you wouldn't like her if you only knew her! (she said eagerly). [...] Just to think of her here at my kitchen table makes me furious and I will start banging pots and pans in a minute. (*Tell* 29)

Whether satirical or sincere, Welty's letters document a supremely attentive mind observing impressions as they enter it. She often imagined her correspondent sharing the moment with her:

> There is a blue sky, small silver clouds. A thrush is singing by himself. I must go now. When I got your letter I played the Mozart and some of the other things to think how they would sound in Sicily with maybe ocean sounds behind them. Don't forget how the Mozart symphony is, ever. I must go. It is so good to hear from you and it changes everything sometimes when things have happened in

the world that make a fresh mystery of how you are. Please take care of yourself. (*Tell* 101)

In particularly memorable letters, new meanings coalesce as the letter concludes:

> Every evening between 8 and 9 you can watch the Calypso daylily opening—it is a night daylily—palest pure yellow, long slender curved petals, the color of the new moon. To see it actually open, the petals letting go, is wonderful, and its night fragrance comes to you all at once like a breath. What makes it open at night—what does it open to? in the same progression as others close, moment by moment. Tell about night flowers. Love, Eudora. (*Tell* 63)

Welty did not revise or revisit these letters; her insights seem to have appeared on the page as she wrote. Deploying powers of observation that matched her stylistic gifts, whenever Welty the correspondent records what she is doing, thinking, or feeling, she captures transitory moments and creates a powerful connection with a faraway reader.

Now that so much correspondence is available for study, Welty's letters can enhance our teaching in numerous ways.[1] First, instructors can encourage students' exploration by directing them to four volumes of letters that have now been published. A brief description of each book can steer students toward eras and subjects that interest them. Michael Kreyling's *Author and Agent* quotes extensively from Welty's thirty-year correspondence with her friend and literary agent Diarmuid Russell. Suzanne Marrs's collection *What There Is to Say We Have Said: The Correspondence of Eudora Welty and William Maxwell* presents almost all extant correspondence between Welty and her *New Yorker* editor Maxwell and his wife, Emily. My project, *Tell about Night Flowers: Eudora Welty's Gardening Letters, 1940–1949*, includes Welty's letters to Russell and John Robinson (Welty's 1940s love interest). *Meanwhile There Are Letters: The Correspondence of Eudora Welty and Ross Macdonald*, coedited by Marrs, contains 1970–1982 correspondence between Welty and another man she loved, the mystery writer Ross Macdonald (Kenneth Millar).[2] Students will be interested to know that recent collections include photographs and examples of Welty's handwritten or typed letters.[3] We can also remind students that a book's index will help them find references to a particular story or topic, and that three of these volumes include helpful endnotes that can bring letters to life by identifying the people and events mentioned in them.[4]

For more focused classroom learning, instructors may present particular letters for study. For an upper-level course with three weeks allotted to Welty's works, I had students explore selected letters as a homework assignment. Groups of students were assigned letters relevant to the day's reading.[5] I scanned these letters and their editorial annotations (unfortunately positioned at the end of the volume), then posted the scans inside my institution's learning management system. Students completed a worksheet responding to four prompts: describe important information found in these letters; discuss possible connections between letters and fiction we are studying; identify memorable, interesting, or disturbing parts of these letters; offer advice for reading and enjoying these letters and Welty's fiction. Students made photocopies or took photos of their worksheets before submitting them at the beginning of class, so both student and teacher could refer to them during discussion. This low-stakes assignment was equivalent to a quiz grade; students were free to submit carefully argued paragraphs or informal notes. I used a similar exercise in an American Literature survey course in which the only Welty text was "Petrified Man."[6] In survey courses, reading these letters could be an optional extra credit activity. Welty could also be one of several authors from different eras whose letters are available for study throughout the semester. For teachers who prefer not to assign more homework, a mini-lesson using letters can facilitate richer discussion of a work of fiction. After presenting a letter or two in class, instructors can invite students to identify Welty's shifts in tone or subject, and then to speculate on what makes each letter enjoyable or meaningful.

More ambitious learning opportunities exist for advanced students; teachers could ask them to comment on or supplement the annotations provided by the letters' editors, or have students use letters to document Welty's political views, her favorite artists, her social class, or some aspect of daily life in Jackson, where many letters were written. With hundreds of letters available for research in the Eudora Welty Collection in the Mississippi Department of Archives and History, instructors can travel there with student researchers, an enjoyable experience I have found genuinely useful to my own work. Unlike writing literary criticism, where it can be more difficult to collaborate with students, archival research and textual editing can be significantly advanced by carefully trained graduate or undergraduate students. My students have proved quite helpful in researching factual information for footnotes and conducting the multiple rounds of proofreading necessary to eliminate errors in transcription. Students accompanying me to the archive have helped me locate letters and transcribed photocopies after we return. Some institutions, like mine, may offer undergraduate research grants for such travel, covering students' expenses and honoring them with a competitive award. Students enjoy the chance to work in an archive, to tour Welty's house and hometown, and to contribute to a future publication.[7]

For all my students, reading these letters has proved an enjoyable way to get to know Welty. They become intrigued by her relationships with her correspondents and by her interest in politics, art, and the unspoken rules of Jackson society. Letters help students become more accustomed to encountering whimsy and poignance, sincerity and mockery, within a few sentences. Students find that some letters' rapid twists and turns that are confusing at first are pleasing by the end of the letter, as in the Easter 1942 letter that, in three paragraphs, goes from Welty's plans for a seed box to a description of zoot suits worn in Jackson on Easter to an evocative dream about an iris (*Tell* 56–57). Whereas students are reluctant to admit being confused or put off by a story their teacher clearly considers important, one that (they assume) should be admired from a respectful distance, they are usually willing to explore the meandering in a Welty letter.[8] Once students have noticed and even been puzzled by gaps in a letter, they may be better prepared for the poetic shifts and gaps within Welty's fiction.

Students' homework suggests that the letters deepen their engagement with Welty's work. Several students have praised Welty's lyrical accounts of nature and gardening. "She can make something as simple as smelling a flower a spiritual experience," one student wrote. Aspiring fiction writers were intrigued by Welty's comments on her work in progress.[9] Another student "laughed aloud" over Welty's snide remarks about Carson McCullers, delighted that a revered American author could write letters that were as entertaining as "gossip about your own town ... They are meant to be enjoyed not to be intimidating." One student wrote that, after reading Welty's epistolary skewering of some of her acquaintances, he'd decided the tone of "Petrified Man" and "Lily Daw and the Three Ladies" was more humorous than moralizing. He wrote of being equally intrigued by a 1941 letter describing "the emotions of a wanderer" and the "journey through or towards something" that Welty hoped her stories would express. These letters, he said, helped him stop searching for a Welty story's "meaning"; he could relax and enjoy it as an exploratory experience, with no definite message or denouement.

Welty's letters, rewarding in their own right, can equip instructors and students to take greater pleasure in her stories and novels. Compared with her published fiction, Welty's private letters are more accessible and less intimidating—briefer, more straightforward accounts of daily life and the people and ideas she found funny, admirable, or infuriating. These accounts are like her fictional texts in that they do not always advance in a clear direction, but linger within an individual's subjectivity. While updating her correspondent on her recent activities—reminiscing, complaining, gossiping, meditating, free-associating, and delighting in the transaction between reader and writer—Welty performs the same complicated sensibility that informs her fiction. As one of my students wrote, when asked for advice on how to read and enjoy the letters, "I'm not sure how to tell people to enjoy them because I enjoy them inherently—but I guess I'd say just to feel, remember to feel the language she uses and watch how she takes some little moment—some tiny scene in nature—and transforms it into this vast far-reaching idea, and you're not really sure how she does it, but it's wonderful."

I understand why readers are initially puzzled by some of Welty's narratives, wondering what their "message" may be. As the narrator of "A Curtain of Green" puts it, "Just to what end Mrs Larkin worked so strenuously in her garden, her neighbors could not see" (*Stories* 131). Welty does not explain why the rain at the end of that story is described as "the sound of the end of waiting" for Mrs. Larkin (134) or why, after she collapses and the rain strikes her face, "her lips began to part" (134). Similarly, in Welty's "Powerhouse," the "marvelous, frightening" artist (158) never tells the crowd at the World Café what has happened between himself and his wife: "Truth is something worse, I ain't said what, yet" is all he discloses (168). No resolution has appeared at the end of "The Winds," either. The storm has passed, leaving Josie with only a fragment of a letter, addressed to someone else, asking, "when are you coming for me? . . . When?" (267).

If Welty's texts—her fiction and her letters—do not solve a riddle, reach a clear destination, or attain a denouement, what *are* they doing? Both kinds of texts allow readers to experience something intensely, as Welty herself experienced her world. An encounter with mystery, a re-creation of someone else's wonder and awe, may be, for Welty, the most important "message" of any letter or any story. The letter-writing artist is a little like Powerhouse, "giving all [he's] got, for an audience of one" (160). Thanks to these letters, readers now have new ways "to enter into the mind, heart and skin of a human being who is not myself." According to Welty, this is no small achievement: "It is the act of a writer's imagination that I set most high" (829).

Notes

1. In addition to Kreyling's groundbreaking monograph *Author and Agent*, three volumes dedicated to Welty's correspondence appeared between 2011 and 2015. Additional letters are quoted in Suzanne Marrs's *One Writer's Imagination*, her 2005 biography, Fuller's *Welty and Surrealism*, and McHaney's *A Tyrannous Eye*. Welty's forty-year correspondence with Frank Lyell, a friend from Jackson who became an English professor, is mostly unpublished, but

Marrs and Stephen Fuller both quote from these letters. As of 2016, publications of Welty's correspondence with Lyell and with literary women, especially Welty's friend and editor Mary Louise Aswell, were in the planning stages. Welty's family correspondence will open for study after 2021.

2. Welty's personal relationship with Millar was not widely known before Marrs's 2005 biography. It was mostly long distance and apparently platonic, continuing even after Millar's Alzheimer's disease ended the correspondence.

3. Fuller also includes drawings and photographs Welty sent Lyell. *Early Escapades* includes drawings Welty sent Lyell in the 1930s.

4. While Kreyling's book is not an edition per se, his monograph often furnishes explanations for references in the letters he quotes. Although his book does not include an index, one has been published; see Shimkus.

5. These letters appear, in chronological order, in *Tell* and *What There Is to Say*. A sample worksheet is posted on our Teaching Welty website.

Group one: "The Wide Net," "The Winds," "Livvie": (1) Welty to Russell, May 1941 ["Hotel Bristol"], June 17, 1941, August 28, 1941; (2) Welty to Russell, December 23, 1941, April 5, 1942.

Group two: "Shower of Gold," "June Recital," "Moon Lake," "The Wanderers": (3) Welty to Robinson, September 1, 1943, April 14, 1945, May 1, 1945; (4) Welty to Robinson, February 17, 1948, March 19, 1948.

Group three: "No Place for You, My Love," "Where Is the Voice Coming From?": (5) August 7, 1952, August 11, 1952, Welty to Maxwell; (6) August 23, 1952, August 30, 1952, to Maxwell; September 2, 1952, from Maxwell.

Students analyzed these groups of letters after two earlier class periods discussing "Lily Daw and the Three Ladies," "Petrified Man," "Why I Live at the P.O.," "A Curtain of Green," "Powerhouse," and "A Worn Path."

Thanks to Ainsley Davis, Bailey Burns, and J. D. Brookbank for permission to quote from their Spring 2016 homework.

6. For "Petrified Man" (composed 1939, published in book form 1941) I transcribed excerpts from three unpublished letters to Frank Lyell documenting Welty's irreverent exuberance and cosmopolitan sensibility, from 1933 and 1942. For a published letter indicating Welty's view of traditional womanhood, see June 23, 1941, to Diarmuid Russell (*Tell* 31).

7. To learn about Welty materials at MDAH, begin with Marrs's *The Welty Collection* (1988). Following Welty's death, seventy-two cubic feet of material were added, and Marrs wrote several online finding aids describing new material in the reorganized collection. More information about letters in MDAH can be found in published books of letters; the appendix to *Tell about Night Flowers* gives details on each letter cited, many of which were not quoted in full. Before planning a trip to MDAH, contact Eudora Welty Collection's archivists to learn of current procedures in the reading room, collections scheduled to close or open, and more detailed information about a particular correspondent. Forrest Galey has published an updated overview of the collection annually in the *Eudora Welty Review*.

8. For other activities that facilitate students' discussion by acknowledging their initial confusion, unease, or boredom with Welty's challenging texts, see Taylor, Patterson, and Trefzer in this volume.

9. *Tell about Night Flowers* charts Welty's artistic development and creative process in the 1940s. The introduction discusses links between Welty's references to gardening and work in progress, subjects which often appeared in the same sentence or paragraph and even shared similar terminology. Some letters' descriptions resemble scenes Welty would later use in her fiction.

Works Cited

Fuller, Stephen. *Eudora Welty and Surrealism*. Jackson: UP of Mississippi, 2013.

Galey, Forrest. "Practical Matters: Eudora Welty Collection, Mississippi Department of Archives and History." *Eudora Welty Review* 8 (2016): 149–56.

Kreyling, Michael. *Author and Agent: Eudora Welty and Diarmuid Russell*. New York: Farrar, 1991.

Marrs, Suzanne. *Eudora Welty: A Biography*. New York: Harcourt, 2005.

———. *One Writer's Imagination: The Fiction of Eudora Welty*. Baton Rouge: Louisiana State UP, 2002.

———. "Series 29b: Correspondence by Eudora Welty." *Z/0301.000: Welty (Eudora) Collection*. Mississippi Department of Archives and History. Web. July 18, 2016.

———. *The Welty Collection*. Jackson: UP of Mississippi, 1988.

McHaney, Pearl. *A Tyrannous Eye: Eudora Welty's Nonfiction and Photographs*. Jackson: UP of Mississippi, 2014.

Shimkus, James H. "Index to Author and Agent: Eudora Welty and Diarmuid Russell." *Eudora Welty Newsletter* 31.2 (Summer 2007): 15–20.

Welty, Eudora. *Early Escapades*. Ed. Patti Carr Black. Jackson: UP of Mississippi, 2005.

———. *Meanwhile There Are Letters: The Correspondence of Eudora Welty and Ross Macdonald*. Ed. and intro. Suzanne Marrs and Tom Nolan. New York: Arcade, 2015.

———. *Stories, Essays, and Memoir*. Ed. Richard Ford and Michael Kreyling. New York: Library of America, 1998.

———. *Tell about Night Flowers: Eudora Welty's Gardening Letters, 1940–1949*. Ed. Julia Eichelberger. Jackson: UP of Mississippi, 2013.

———. *What There Is to Say We Have Said: The Correspondence of Eudora Welty and William Maxwell*. Ed. Suzanne Marrs. New York: Houghton, 2011.

How She Wrote and How We Read

Teaching the Pleasure and Play of Welty's Modernist Techniques

—Harriet Pollack, Bucknell University

My teaching of Welty stresses the pleasure created by her nonfulfillment of readers' expectations. Thus, this essay models how to steer students to enjoy the swerves in four stories—"Lily Daw and the Three Ladies," "A Memory," "Powerhouse," and "The Wide Net"—as a lesson to take forward to other of her fictions. The topic is one I have written about elsewhere, but not yet from the classroom perspective.

    I teach Welty's fiction and sometimes her photography in a wide variety of courses, but whatever the course, I ask students to share their initial reading questions before class, disclosing this part of their process, as we ask about interpretation: who makes meaning when we read, and how is meaning made?[1] In the responses of new Welty readers, I often see perplexed pleasure. One articulate student reaction makes clear what instructors need to anticipate and what I mean to address: "I leave my first reading of Welty's stories feeling delight. I also leave not quite sure I've mastered her stories, at least in terms of being sure how to discuss the fiction analytically, or even in terms of being entirely certain of what's happened in all of them. Stories like 'Lily Daw and the Three Ladies,' 'A Memory,' and 'Powerhouse,' seem to have changed up on me from what I initially expected. But maybe that's the source of my pleasure."

    Getting students set to enjoy reading her, I share Welty's commentary on surprised expectation as "the source of the deepest pleasure we receive from a writer" ("The Reading and Writing of Short Stories" 49). Her observation then becomes the on-ramp to discussions identifying Welty's signature modernist techniques, artistic maneuvers that make use of a reader's literary memory and competence while creating delight by veering from literary convention. My aim is to make our way toward understanding Eudora Welty's characteristic play with point of view and focalization, with plot and detail, with allusion and genre, as well as with humor, parody, and with "the female swerve," a woman's dissident revoicing of literary history's familiar narratives, elements, and patterns—repetitions with a mischievous difference. I want to demystify certain characteristic Welty techniques, to suggest how surprised expectation often directs her readers to the heart of a story. Welty—perhaps wryly impersonating the self-serious language of criticism—called this the pleasure of a writer's "quondam obstruction" (49), or more simply, obstruction that once was.

My first classes unfold Welty's early stories, particularly "Lily Daw," "A Piece of News," "Petrified Man,"[2] "A Memory," and "Powerhouse." In ninety minutes, we typically discuss four stories, and touch on a few others. In my second class on *A Curtain of Green*, I take additional time for "Powerhouse" because the complex and quite remarkable story is so helpful to making my point and thematically relevant to my interest in reading the representation of race as well.

To be specific, "Lily Daw and the Three Ladies" leads us to consider Welty's sly and comic play with the conventional literary endings to a woman's story—marriage, madness, or death—and the clear but restricted choice open to heroines in nineteenth- and early twentieth-century fiction of marrying suitably or being certifiable.[3] In Welty's play with the traditional literary ending to the story of a woman, the choice—according to the comic ladies—is unexpectedly unvarnished. The first option is for Lily to be confined at the state institution for the "Feeble-Minded," a euphemistic resolution for potentially "Wayward Girls" capturing Welty's satire of 1930s eugenic attitudes toward women of the lower classes.[4] Or, then again, she might be secured in a respectable marriage. And hilariously the ladies and the story present these alternatives as absolutely equal and interchangeable choices! The comic surprise is that, unlike the familiar endings that Welty parodies, her ending can barely distinguish between these two limited literary outcomes for a woman's maturity, and in its final line, we see Lily as caught one way or another: "Some of the people thought Lily was on the train, and some swore she wasn't. Everybody cheered, though, and a straw hat was thrown into the telephone wires" (*Stories* 15).

Another case in point is "A Memory." At first centered on an adolescent's unexpressed first love for a schoolroom classmate, the plot unpredictably culminates in the gesture of a large woman on a beach as she turns her bathing suit down to shake sand away from her breasts. Thus the girl's conventional love story is unexpectedly displaced by this display of a woman's body, leading us to ask about the linkage between the central conscious character's associated memories of the boy and the woman on the beach, memories that each concern the girl's anxieties about female self-exposure. Escaping parental protection and preoccupied with her discovery of secret life around her, the remembered girl makes "small frames with [her] fingers to look out at everything," and we question if her gesture is primarily artistic, defensive, or both (92). Setting up to consider the woman on the beach, we discuss the narrator's recollection that "such people were called 'common'" (94), and explore the issue of social class not only as it applies to the girl's fears about the boy who attracts her, but critically, to her own timidity, as she lives in a time and place where white women of a certain class are protected with vehemence, a practice having much to do with culturally prevalent notions of class and racial purity.[5] Relatedly, we discuss the size of the beach woman and her fleshiness that disturbs the girl; Patricia Yaeger calls this other woman "gargantuan" (117), marking her large break with the conventional female miniature and its restrictions. Then in the unexpected climax of the now adult narrator's memory, the girl reacts to this woman who pulls "down the front of her bathing suit, turning it outward, so that the lumps of mashed and folded sand came emptying out. [The girl] felt a peak of horror" (97). Unpacking this climax, I introduce the idea of Welty's play with the literary double—a technique useful in signifying internal conflict and self-division, capable of expressing both anxiety and desire for the transformation of the self. For the girl, the vulgar bather's gesture is a disturbing difference based on class, physicality, and sexual maturity, but above all, on the woman's comfort with exposure that the exceedingly protected daughter fears and yet both tentatively and demonstrably seeks. Finally, we assess how the adult narrator has changed from the reticent child she once was, since she now obliquely but willingly risks unconditionally exposing herself to the reader, making no effort to tell her audience how to judge her. "A Memory" bewilders when read with conventional expectations that it does not fulfill. A novitiate lady dreams about a first romantic love, but the expected boy of the story—the representative of the conventional script for the girl's future—appears only briefly. He slips from our attention when female exposure, rather than romantic love or the traditional lady, takes center stage.[6]

The third story I'll model here as illustrating Welty's play with surprised expectation is "Powerhouse," the story I give most time to in class. The story begins: "Powerhouse is playing!" Importantly, he is, and so is Welty in this story puzzle where musical and narrative performances are one. Initial readings need to relinquish expectations following the too literal question of how Gypsy "come . . . to die?" and so to acknowledge that Powerhouse is not mourning a wife, but improvising a song (161). The performance articulates his racial blues as he plays for a segregated 1930s white dance. To start I share two of Welty's comments: first, she describes the plot as about "the life of the traveling artist . . . in the alien world" (Prenshaw, *Conversations* 85), and second, she tells of composing it immediately after seeing Fats Waller perform at a dance: "Of course what I was trying to do was express . . . what I thought of as improvisation . . . by making [Powerhouse] improvise this crazy story" (*Conversations* 328). Then, before opening the topic of Welty on racial interactions in 1930s Mississippi, I introduce today's students to Waller with bits of YouTube clips: "Your Feets Too Big" and "Hold Tight, I Want Some Seafood, Mama." (Welty had originally ended "Powerhouse" with "Hold Tight" before the *Atlantic* rejected it as lewd.) In these clips, students see Waller's penchant for comic, bawdy, and transgressive performance. Like Louis Armstrong, his strategy as a performer was to wear the mask foisted onto him as black jazzman and then, to be creative with it, by combining humor and transgression in his lyrics, his routine, and his artistic manner. Waller owed his fame to this burlesque lampooning tinged with aggression. Like "Powerhouse," even when Waller played a tune "very delicately" there remained an impression of "mockery," a daring undercurrent, something underground (Bearden 68). Examining what might be masked in a black jazzman's performance in the 1930s, we talk about life in the Jim Crow world: by illustration, I return to my YouTube search for "Hold Tight" to show that the Andrews Sisters' reissue of Waller's song even now tops his version—and a quick, amusing sample of their rendering adequately demonstrates the cooptation of black music by white performers earning greater recognition and reward. Asking my students about evidence from within Welty's story of what would frustrate a black performer delivering to a white dance audience, students call up details: the gawking first narrator; the need to rely for support on a pit orchestra full of musicians who usually don't do jazz improvisation; the problem of performing for white audiences calling for another kind of music. When intermission arrives, segregation compels Powerhouse and his group to go across the tracks to the "World Café" for refreshment. Linking these racial, artistic blues to Waller and Powerhouse's performances, I ask students to call up the initial white narrator's descriptions of the "obscene" and "monstrous" jazzman attempting to give his art to an audience, transgressing as he displays "such a leer for everybody" (159). Then I connect my students' collected evidence, along with what we saw in film clips of Waller's strategic comic mugging, with Welty herself, identifying her as another "traveling artist . . . in the alien world" attempting to give this complex, comic, and rule-breaking story to readers who may or may not follow her.

Having established this as a complicated story about race, art, and performance, I ask students to name Powerhouse's several audiences to assess their receptivity (the white dancer, the far section of band musicians that "don't count," the customers at World Café, and Powerhouse's coterie of musician collaborators). Further considering the complexity and playfulness of the text, we close-read the tricky language of Powerhouse's blues song, calling it his response to feeling "like a man lost, down in a whirlpool" as he delivers his art to the white dance crowd (159). Discussing the musical rhythms of the story, we note the ambiguity of whether Powerhouse's first invention of Gypsy's death is told in lyrics or stage whispers, or if the story isn't the music itself, told with "wandering fingers?" (161–62). Finally, we discuss Welty's play throughout the invention of Uranus Knockwood. The name starts in a rude joke—Powerhouse's response to Scoot the drummer, who challenges him (as a drum might be the beat against which an improvisation develops) with "what name has it got signed if you got a telegram?" (161). Powerhouse's brazen banter back to the contesting drum is a roguish flare of "signifying" insult: "Uranus Knockwood." Then at World Café, in a narrative rather than musical riff, the performer elaborates on this blues boogie man: "Listen how it is" (165). His Negrotown audience "moans with pleasure" (167) and recognizes the man who brings the blues: "'Middle size man,' 'Wears a hat'" (167). Powerhouse's creation of Knockwood—the man who brings the blues—becomes a means of chasing them away. Artistic transformation in progress, Powerhouse, recharged, back in the dance hall, moves from his theme "I got a telegram my wife is dead" to the requested number "Somebody Loves Me." As a "vast, impersonal and yet furious grimace transfigures his wet face," he challenges, "Maybe it's you!" (170). In this last line Welty, in direct confrontation, asks, do we love her in her story? Did we follow her beyond our initial expectations to appreciate her masterful play?[7]

Here I'm modeling discussion of three stories from *A Curtain of Green*, but of course the technical pattern I'm highlighting applies to most others. For example, "The Wide Net"—another story in which the theoretical death of a wife oddly becomes genuinely celebratory—demonstrates Welty's uses of allusion (another form of literary memory) to please the reader with nonfulfillment.[8] A reader doesn't need to recognize its specific allusions (Virgil, Carthage) to the *Aeneid* to experience barely conscious awareness of Welty's comic parody and transformation of the heroic quest genre: a band of men eager to seek, stomp, and paw each other while their leaders apply to a wise oracle (Old Doc) who could foretell the day's outcome. We expect the questing hero to survive his ordeals, but when he dances with a catfish hanging from his belt in genuine celebration, his quest has *failed* and yet he's strutting anyway, leaving us to ask, why? In a triple play on reader's expectations, Welty has set up initial anticipation for a realistic narrative about a backwoods couple's marital squabble, switched readers into expectations based on a comic male quest, and then, in one more sleight of hand, switched the story to a female pastoral. William Wallace's wife, Hazel, by sending him to drag the river as the seasons change, has sent him toward some insight that will help him understand her in her pregnancy and the "changing time" that has caused trouble between them. What he brings home from his male quest is unexpectedly the secret of the natural world and its physical changes: as he dives within the river, the text suggests that he had perhaps "suspected down there . . . the real, true trouble Hazel had fallen into . . . , how . . . she had been filled to the brim with that elation . . . that comes of great hopes and changes, sometimes simply of the harvest time" (217).

If I'm teaching a course with only a short class period for Welty, we can develop my point with one story. But if the class will return to Welty to treat different periods in her story-writing career (recommended since students in this way develop the skill to read her), the point previously made becomes a useful touchstone for *The Golden Apples*, *The Bride of the Innisfallen*, or some topical grouping of Welty stories (I often bring together "A Worn Path," "Keela," "The Burning," "Where Is the Voice Coming From?" "The Demonstrators," "Must the Novelist Crusade," and selections from Welty's *Photographs* in a class exploring her representation of race). In courses where I include Welty's photography, I follow a related notion: we can understand Welty's displacement of conventional expectation for plot with attention to a detail (as I above suggest happens in "A Memory") by considering how photographs often frame an arresting detail to move a viewer to reverie—a photographic convention influencing her sometimes surprising use of detail in, or as, plot.[9]

Treating Welty's playful obstruction of reader expectations as a characteristic technique and as a source of a reader's pleasure, I nevertheless take care to avoid the impression that Welty values obscurity. In a 1977 interview, Welty explains that she abominates "deliberate obscurity," but that "mysterious is something else." Conveying the complex difference between being obscure—"a fault in the teller"—and being "mysterious"—a virtue in a writer—is essential to this approach.[10] My emphasis throughout is on the puzzle of fiction: the play in Welty's puzzle texts and the play invited by them. It is exactly Welty's innovative play with literary forms and conventions, with a reader's experience and competencies, producing surprised expectations, that makes her a paramount modernist, a woman writer with a most cunning swerve, a short-story writer of the first rank, and a remarkable literary innovator.

Notes

1. To name a few surveys: American Modernism, Southern Literature, Women Writers, The Short Story. And to name a few seminars: Faulkner, Welty, and The Reading Process, Mississippi Writers from Plantation Memory to the Social Disaster of Katrina, and Unsettling Memories: Body, Culture, and Trauma in Southern Literature, History, and Photography.
2. Chapter 4 in *Eudora Welty's Fiction and Photography* discusses my teaching of "Petrified Man."
3. See Rachel Blau DuPlessis, *Reading beyond the Ending: Narrative Strategies of Twentieth-Century Women Writers*, though she does not discuss Welty. Also see Prenshaw on Lily's choice.
4. For a fuller "Lily Daw" and eugenics discussion, see *Eudora Welty's Fiction and Photography*, 11–12.
5. For more on whiteness and female sheltering, see *Eudora Welty's Fiction and Photography*, 3–11, and its chapter on Welty's "girl stories," 23–70.
6. On "A Memory," see *Eudora Welty's Fiction and Photography*, 37–44.
7. For the fuller discussion, see my "Words between Strangers."
8. I'm referring to "On Welty's Use of Allusion."
9. See my essays "Photographic Convention and Story Composition" and its correction: "Too Far to Walk It?"
10. Prenshaw, *Conversations*, 190.

Works Cited

Bearden, Kenneth. "Monkeying Around: Welty's 'Powerhouse,' Blues-Jazz, and the Signifying Connection." *Southern Literary Journal* 31.2 (Spring 1999): 65–79.

Pollack, Harriet. *Eudora Welty's Fiction and Photography: The Body of the Other Woman*. Athens: U of Georgia P, 2016.

———. "On Welty's Use of Allusion: Expectations and Their Revision in Welty's 'The Wide Net,' *The Robber Bridegroom*, and 'At the Landing.'" *Southern Quarterly* 29.1 (Fall 1990): 5–33. Rpt. in *The Critical Response to Eudora Welty's Fiction*. Ed. Laurie Champion. Westport, CT: Greenwood Press, 1994. 312–34.

———. "Photographic Convention and Story Composition: Eudora Welty's Use of Detail, Plot, Genre, and Expectation from 'A Worn Path' through *The Bride of the Innisfallen*." *South Central Review* 14.2 (Summer 1997): 15–33.

———. "Words between Strangers: On Welty, Her Style, and Her Audience." *Mississippi Quarterly* (Fall 1986): 481–507. Rpt. in *Eudora Welty: A Life in Literature*. Ed. Albert Devlin. Jackson: UP of Mississippi, 1987. 54–82.

———. "Eudora Welty's 'Too Far to Walk It': Out Farther Still?" *South Central Review* (Fall-Winter 1997): 114–16.

Prenshaw, Peggy. "Welty's Transformations of the Public, the Private, and the Political." *Eudora Welty and Politics: Did the Writer Crusade?* Ed. Harriet Pollack and Suzanne Marrs. Baton Rouge: Louisiana State UP, 1996. 19–46.

———. *Conversations with Eudora Welty*. Jackson: UP of Mississippi, 1984.

Vande Kieft, Ruth M. *Eudora Welty*. Boston: Twayne, 1962.

Welty, Eudora. "The Reading and Writing of Short Stories." *Atlantic Monthly*, March 1949: 46–49.

———. *Stories, Essay, and Memoir*. Ed. Richard Ford and Michael Kreyling. New York: Library of America, 1998.

Yaeger, Patricia. *Dirt and Desire: Reconstructing Southern Women's Writing, 1930–1990*. Chicago: U of Chicago P, 2000.

Teaching Welty's Narrative Strategies in *Delta Wedding*

—**Sarah Gilbreath Ford,** Baylor University

Teaching Eudora Welty's work can be challenging. She relies on a well-read reader to grasp her allusions, she experiments with form, and she often de-emphasizes plot in favor of character or point of view. The very qualities that make her writing complex and appealing to critics can leave students bewildered or bored. *Delta Wedding* is certainly indicative of this challenge. It is a novel in which a white family revels in its wealth, in which the only rebellion is a spoiled bride's choice of the overseer for her groom, and in which in the end nothing much actually happens. Despite these difficulties, reading the novel can be very rewarding. Not only does *Delta Wedding* carefully document a particular place and time (Mississippi in the 1920s), its multiple perspectives can help students think through the intricacies of family dynamics as well as the perpetuation of racism through cultural blindness. The key is using the students' innate interest in character to help them perceive that the multiple perspectives replace plot as the active component of the narrative. Once my students were able to read for point of view, they were able to unpack the complexities of the novel and were excited about their discoveries.

Before this success, however, were a few failures. One approach that did not work was discussing the scholarship detailing the dense allusions to other texts that occur on every page of the novel. Although this intertextuality answers the seeming lack of plot progress in almost any given passage, without discovering these links for themselves, the students felt left out of the conversation. They could understand, for instance, how the depiction of Dabney marrying the overseer echoed the mythic story of Persephone and Hades, but this connection did not amplify their reading of Dabney's character or elucidate the family dynamics. Another unsuccessful approach I tried was helping students perceive the shifts in point of view by introducing them to the concept of free indirect discourse, defined by Dorrit Cohn as "the rendering of a character's thoughts in his own idiom, while maintaining the third-person form of narration" (100). Although a third-person narrator tells the story in *Delta Wedding*, this narrator takes on one character's opinions, thoughts, and language for a period of time and then shifts to another character, giving us the point of view of several different white female characters. Every detail of the text, then, is shaped by character, but free indirect discourse is not always easy to discern or track.[1] Students learned to identify which character the narrator was using as a focalizer in individual passages, but they were not engaged in the interplay between characters. What I realized about both these failed approaches is that I was not starting from my students' own interests or expertise.

My students have always been quite adept at reading for character. Susan Keen, in exploring the ability of novels to develop empathy in readers, discusses the habits of "middlebrow" readers, which may include students, and finds they "tend to value novels offering opportunities for strong character identification. They report feeling both empathy with and sympathy for fictional characters" (ix). To build from my students' interest in character, I assigned every student in a senior-level Literature of the South class one character to follow when reading the novel. Each student was to track their character's appearances, descriptions, and opinions and be ready to report each day to the class. Most students listed page numbers, but a few marked their books with sticky notes, which allowed them a concrete visual reference to the sections of the text that most involved their characters. I assured the students that as a class we would cover the larger issues of context, allusions, and form; their job was to read character.

In a sense I was asking the students to turn the narrative into a kind of first-person account, and each student became quite invested in his or her randomly selected character. The student who was following Maureen, for example, was devastated by the family's complete disregard for this disabled character. When Dabney finds out that the house she wants was inherited by Maureen, she first exclaims, "Marmion can't belong to Maureen!" and then asks her, "Look, honey—will you give your house to me?" (*Complete Novels* 119). The focus on a single character allowed students even in their first reading of this challenging text a kind of mastery in that each student was the expert on his or her character. One student followed Dabney and found that although Dabney appears as a spoiled bride to other characters, the descriptions and details Dabney focuses on when her point of view is given show her to be using her unconventional marriage to escape from the family, as when she rides out early in the morning on horseback to have time to herself and thinks, "I will never give up anything!" (210).

When we put the differing perspectives into conversation in the classroom, we then reenacted the novel's experiment in multiple points of view. When the student tracking the nine-year-old character India, for example, argued that India understands all of the other characters well because she is always observing and eavesdropping, the students tracking adults answered that they had read India as childish and obtrusive. With specific examples of multiple viewpoints reenacted in the classroom, we were then able to discuss how these points of view place *Delta Wedding* in the category of modernism.[2] The modernist splitting of point of view now became the students' focus and led them to perceive the complex family dynamics. In one class period each student argued that his or her character is the outsider in the family. One student explained that while Ellen as the mother of the Fairchild children should be an insider, she is from Virginia and has never been completely comfortable living at the Fairchild house on a farm. Another student remarked that Shelley shares her true feelings about her family only in her diary because she cannot talk about them. A third student added that even George, who is the center of the family's attention, lives away in Memphis, perhaps to escape that very attention. Discussing who made up the inside of the family that each character seemed to be rejecting was interesting because we saw the unsolvable contradictions in the family members' views of each other.

Beginning with character actually led the students to the intertextuality that I had wanted them to see. For example, the student tracing Troy was disturbed by the repeated references to his "darkness" and "red hair"; another student chimed in with the Persephone/Hades allusion, and the class discussed whether Troy, as both groom and overseer, was figured as an evil character stealing the daughter away from the family. Instead of feeling daunted by a mythic reference they did not catch, the students launched into a discussion of class issues in the novel, pondering how the family's pride leads them to imagine Dabney's marriage to a lower-class character as her descent into hell. I could now point interested students to the scholarship unpacking the novel's mythic allusions.[3]

The students also found on their own the complicated gender dynamics. Each student analyzed his or her character's feelings about the family's positioning of George as the hero figure. In earlier classes, my students had simply accepted the family's positive view, but considering George's character through the eyes of individual family members led to a more complex discussion. The student following Ellen perceived Ellen's need for George's attention but wanted input from the class on why George wounds Ellen by admitting he slept with the lost girl. The student following Dabney wondered if she was reading too much into Dabney's seemingly inappropriate feelings for her uncle, expressed through her memory of hugging his naked body after he breaks up a fight. The class decided that the incest was not literal but a means to convey the claustrophobic family relationships.

Most significantly, by focusing on individual characters, the students clearly saw how the white family members are blind to the African American workers in their midst. Students discussed how racism can be a lack of awareness or a cultural blindness and thus came to the same conclusion as recent Welty scholarship: that Welty's works do not skirt the problem of racism but instead depict white characters oblivious to their own racism.[4] The students following African American characters found that the details associated with these characters can show us their agency. The student following Vi'let discovered that she is always connected in the text with beautiful things such as flowers and dresses. Another student found the two brief passages that are presented from Roxie's point of view. Even scholars writing on the different perspectives in the novel often miss these. The second of these passages is when Ellen faints and Roxie expresses compassion: "Poor Miss Ellen just wasn't strong enough *any longer* for such a trial" (257). Roxie's guess at the cause of Ellen's weakness, however, comes when she asks, "Wasn't it pitiful to see her so white?" (257). My student took this passage as the starting point for a research paper arguing that while Vi'let's actions suggests that she supports the white family, Roxie's actions mask her disapproval.

When it came time to choose research topics for their major paper assignment (ten pages, open topic), almost half the students in the class chose to write about *Delta Wedding*, not only showing their enthusiasm for the text but teaching me new things about the novel as well. One paper compared the novel with Ellen Douglas's *Can't Quit You, Baby* and discussed the giving of gifts between white families and their African American domestic servants. This paper explored Partheny's gift of the patticake infused with the conjure-laden power to bring George's wife back to him. I had always read the patticake as a sign of African American agency that the family ignores, but the student argued the cake showed Partheny's care for the family. The family's disparaging remarks about Roxie's gift of nasturtiums for the wedding, the student argued, shows in return their lack of care for their servants. Another excellent paper analyzed the many mentions of Fairchild foreheads in the novel, a detail I had never seen. The student had traced the younger brothers throughout the novel and found that the similar physical traits referred to repeatedly are an indication of the family's insularity.

Although this technique of assigning each student a character is admittedly simple, the results for the reading of *Delta Wedding* were dramatic. I have since tried versions of this technique with other texts, most recently in a graduate class with *The Golden Apples*. My students have always found the structure of *The Golden Apples* challenging. The text is a short-story cycle, which means it is a collection of loosely connected short stories, similar to modern texts such as Ernest Hemingway's *In Our Time* or Sherwood Anderson's *Winesburg, Ohio*. Past students have tended to read the stories as isolated, struggling to find meaningful connections. This semester I assigned each graduate student a character. Not only were the students able to read the collection as a connected whole, each noticed his or her character appearing briefly in stories focusing on other characters. These appearances, though slight, elicited revelations that helped students read the characters better in the stories where they were actually spotlighted. Snowdie MacLain, for example, plays a key role in the first story, as Katie Rainey gossips about Snowdie and her husband, King. The student following Snowdie found that her small role in the last story, when she prepares Katie's body for burial, is a crucial answer to this first story, so that Snowdie and Katie provide the frame to the text. Another student tracing King convinced me that more characters are his children than I had realized. The connections the students found tracing characters made our discussion of the book as a whole richer.

Assigning students the task of focusing on individual characters allows them entrance into texts where Welty's experiments in form may prove challenging. Lower-level students can build from their interest in character to generate insightful readings while upper-level students or graduate students can more quickly latch onto a recurring pattern or interesting question. Giving each student this discrete task also allows him or her a domain of expertise. When students share their insights in class and even teach the teacher something, they can participate in the sheer fun of reading Eudora Welty's work. Before this class, I had always appreciated Welty's range in her depiction of different characters; as she explains, "what I do in writing of any character is to try to enter into the mind, heart, and skin of a human being who is not myself. Whether this happens to be a man or a woman, old or young, with skin black or white, the primary challenge lies in making the jump itself" (*Stories* 829). It was only, however, in following my students' exploration of the differing perspectives that I realized how much Welty's work allows for a sympathetic reading from many different viewpoints at once, giving students the chance to practice "making the jump" themselves.

Notes

1. For a good general discussion of free indirect discourse, see McHale. For discussion of free indirect discourse in *Delta Wedding*, see Ford.
2. For discussion about Welty's use of multiple points of view, see Gygax, Harrison, and Kreyling.
3. See, for example, Sprengnether.
4. See, for example, McMahand and McWhirter.

Works Cited

Cohn, Dorrit. *Transparent Minds: Narrative Modes for Presenting Consciousness in Fiction.* Princeton, NJ: Princeton UP, 1978.

Ford, Sarah. "Laughing in the Dark: Race and Humor in *Delta Wedding*." *Eudora Welty, Whiteness, and Race.* Ed. Harriet Pollack. Athens: U of Georgia P, 2013. 131–47.

Gygax, Franziska. *Serious Daring from Within: Female Narrative Strategies in Eudora Welty's Novels.* New York: Greenwood P, 1990.

Harrison, Suzan. "'The Other Way to Live': Gender and Selfhood in *Delta Wedding* and *The Golden Apples.*" *Mississippi Quarterly* 44.1 (1990–91): 49–67.

Keen, Suzanne. *Empathy and the Novel.* New York: Oxford UP, 2007.

Kreyling, Michael. *Eudora Welty's Achievement of Order.* Baton Rouge: Louisiana State UP, 1980.

McHale, Brian. "Free Indirect Discourse: A Survey of Recent Accounts" in *Narrative Theory: Critical Concepts in Literary and Cultural Studies.* vol. 1. Ed. Mieke Bal. New York: Routledge, 2004. 187–222.

McMahand, Donnie. "Bodies on the Brink: Vision, Violence, and Self-Destruction in *Delta Wedding.*" *Eudora Welty, Whiteness, and Race.* Ed. Harriet Pollack. Athens: U of Georgia P, 2013. 165–84.

McWhirter, David. "Secret Agents: Welty's African Americans." *Eudora Welty, Whiteness, and Race.* Ed. Harriet Pollack. Athens: U of Georgia P, 2013. 114–30.

Sprengnether, Madelon. "Delta Wedding and the Kore Complex." *Southern Quarterly* 25.2 (1987): 120–30.

Welty, Eudora. *Complete Novels.* New York: Library of America, 1998.

———. *Stories, Essays, and Memoir.* Ed. Richard Ford and Michael Kreyling. New York: Library of America, 1998.

II

New Perspectives on Welty and the US South

By reading her through such so-called "southern" filters as place, humor, race, history, and the grotesque, our critical vocabulary, our cultural assumptions, have protected us from the parts of Welty's work that might unsettle and threaten us since they are actually subversive of those so-called "values" of family and community—"place"—that are so much a part of what we have been taught to think of as central to "southern" literature.

But we can no longer ignore what is so manifestly there in Welty's work.

—**Noel Polk,** *Faulkner and Welty and the Southern Literary Tradition* (19)

Teaching Welty's *A Curtain of Green* in an American Studies Freshman Seminar

—**Susan V. Donaldson,** College of William and Mary

Thirty years ago my first efforts at teaching Eudora Welty's short stories—specifically the 1949 volume *The Golden Apples*—were singularly unsuccessful, partly, I suspect, because of the difficulty and elusiveness of those particular stories, but largely because I confined our discussions to close readings of modernist texts without paying sufficient attention to the critical conventions underlying those readings or the cultural context shaping southern women writers coming of age in the era of New Women and rapidly shifting gender and racial roles. What I needed to do was provide my students with a critical and cultural vocabulary for understanding the central concerns of Welty's fiction. In this respect, I received significant tutoring from the leading figures in Welty criticism I was beginning to read—particularly Suzan Harrison, Peggy Whitman Prenshaw, Peter Schmidt, Rebecca Mark, and Harriet Pollack—but also from my students, particularly young women who were new to Welty's fiction but who hailed from similar worlds in small Virginia towns and who immediately recognized that implicitly female world of piano recitals, claustrophobia, youthful yearnings, and secret rebellions portrayed in arguably the most famous story in *The Golden Apples*—"June Recital." My students' intuitive understanding of key motifs in Welty's stories—confinement, disruption, interrogation, and rebellion, motifs now bywords in feminist criticism in general and in critical approaches to Welty in particular—underscored for me the importance of re-creating for readers new to her work the peculiarly enclosed world of the twentieth-century American South and its special preoccupations with rigidly defined gender, class, and racial boundaries and roles.

That early experience teaching Welty also made it all too clear to me that novice readers needed to start not with her 1949 masterpiece but with her earliest stories—those in her first collection *A Curtain of Green* (1942), where she was learning her craft, building on her experience with photography, and encountering firsthand the complicated world of Jim Crow Mississippi. But to read those stories also meant to have some understanding of the world that produced them—in particular the rigid expectations of gender, race, and class facing character after character as well as the frustration, anger, and even comedy arising from conflicts between community rules and standards and individual aspirations. Hence, about a dozen years ago, when I first began teaching a freshman seminar on women writers of the US South—sometimes for the American Studies Program at my institution and sometimes for the English department—I turned to those early stories in *A Curtain of Green* and situated them halfway through the semester so that we could spend some time ascertaining why so many of those strangely lonely and outcast figures in Welty's early stories were quickly pronounced to be portraits of the "demented, the deformed, the queer," in the words of a contemporary *Time* magazine reviewer (qtd. in Peterman 106). Accordingly, I opened the semester with a broad cultural introduction to the region's cultural stereotypes of womanhood by showing the film *Gone with the Wind*, followed by a discussion of its lasting impact on American culture, from the stereotypes of black and white womanhood reified in American culture by Hollywood to revisions and parodies produced by writers ranging from Margaret Walker to Alice Randall and Eudora Welty herself, no fan of the film or the book. I've continued to show the film as an opening to the seminar over the years, but to help prod discussion and early informal writing assignments, I've paired the film with excerpts from three excellent secondary sources that explore the historical and cultural antecedents of southern female stereotypes: Betina Entzminger's *The Belle Gone Bad: White Southern Women Writers and the Dark Seductress*, Thavolia Glymph's *Out of the House of Bondage: The Transformation of the Plantation Household*, and Laura Edwards's *Scarlett Doesn't Live Here Anymore: Southern Women in the Civil War Era*. These three texts are particularly helpful in pointing out the interdependent nature of black and white womanhood as paired opposites and in emphasizing the tenacious power wielded by images of the white southern lady in cultural myths of the region and in scholarly writing about the region and its institutions.

From this broad introduction to the mythology of southern womanhood, the syllabus moves into exploring critiques of that mythology by some of Welty's predecessors and successors—Harriet Jacobs in *Incidents in the Life of a Slave Girl* (1861), Kate Chopin in the 1899 novel *The Awakening* and her short story "Desirée's Baby," and Zora Neale Hurston's *Their Eyes Were Watching God*, accompanied by Julie Dash's 1991 independent film *Daughters of the Dust*. These are all works that explore the constraints imposed by the constructions of black and white womanhood, the delimiting dichotomies arising from those constructions, and the possibility of new narratives rising in opposition as New Women entered the public sphere in the early twentieth century. But these are also works that frankly confront the barriers facing those new narratives and rebellions against the old. The tensions arising between those barriers of tradition and aspirations of the new help provide beginning students with an expanded critical vocabulary for approaching women's literature in general and Welty's earliest stories in particular.

Situating Welty within a tradition of southern women writers critical of their region's mythology of womanhood and the barriers presented for achieving one's individual identity is in fact one of the strongest sources of comedy in *A Curtain of Green*, particularly in some of the most famous stories in the collection—"Why I Live at the P.O," "Lily Daw and the Three Ladies," and "Petrified Man." These are the stories with which I begin our discussion of the book as a critique of the myth of the white southern lady and of the racial caste system erected in its defense. In laying out that critique I have relied heavily on Nina Baym's early essay "The Myth of the Myth of Southern Womanhood," included in *Feminism and American Literary History*, and Hazel Carby's pioneering chapter on the racial binary of southern femininity in *Reconstructing Womanhood*. For models of close readings of Welty's work, I have turned to criticism by Suzan Harrison, Harriet Pollack, and Peter Schmidt, all of which have proven to be particularly helpful in targeting some of Welty's central concerns—those recurring motifs of confinement, entrapment, and repression so apparent in the volume's stories, as well as the comical pretensions of self-designated guardians of order. So too, though, is Welty's own photography, which by her account led her to explore in fiction some of the questions raised by the photographs she began to take of her fellow Mississippians during the 1930s. These are photographs that highlight her sensitivity to the politics of public space implicit in the era's rigidly observed color line, in the brief glimpses of black interiority revealed to a white photographer, in the fleeting moments of exchange and communication captured in her pictures of black subjects, and in quiet meditations upon the dynamics of gazing and being gazed upon in a culture of hypervisual surveillance. Among the most helpful photographs as introductions to these three stories in particular are *A Woman of the 'thirties/Hinds County/1933*; *Delegate/Jackson/1938*; *Dolls/Jackson/1930s*; *Courthouse Steps/Fayette/1930s*; *Jackson/1930s*; and *Hello and Goodbye/Jackson/1930s*.[1]

From these photographs it is an easy transition to "Why I Live at the P.O.," which has benefited from numerous audio clips featuring Eudora Welty herself as well as dramatic representations, including Jodie Markell's witty 1998 film of the story. I begin our discussion of these three stories about white southern ladies frustrated and confined by the expectations of ladyhood with an examination of the first-person narrator as a figure who can consolidate her own credentials as a lady—and as a wronged one at that by an ungrateful family—only by talking herself into isolation and taking up residence in the second smallest post office in the state of Mississippi. From first to last she projects her own petty grievances into slights and injuries suffered at the hands of her family, until at last the only way she can maintain her own sense of being in the right is to withdraw altogether into the tiny post office where she serves as postmistress. That misplaced sense of self-righteousness is a trait she shares with the self-appointed guardians of the town charity case named Lily Daw in "Lily Daw and the Three Ladies," the story that opens the volume of *A Curtain of Green*. Positioning these two stories together underscores their parodic bent and humor in their respective portrayals of white southern ladies as enforcers of probity and respectability. The three ladies in this opening story share with the narrator of "Why I Live at the P.O." a garrulous and unswerving confidence in their own moral uprightness and their prerogative in taking charge of the impoverished and motherless Lily Daw to ensure that she maintain some semblance of white middle-class respectability. But the ladies of this story are even less successful than the narrator of "Why I Live at the P.O." in living up to their roles as models and guides of respectable white ladyhood. Just as they think they have succeeded in shipping Lily off on a train to the Ellisville Institute for the Feeble-Minded of Mississippi, they discover that Lily has made plans of her own by striking up a romance with an itinerant xylophone player. The story ends with the self-appointed guardians in disarray as they watch the train leave the station—apparently without Lily, who has thwarted their best-laid plans, disembarked from the train, and joined her suitor in the station waiting room, where she awaits her own story to unfold.

The story's ending offers a highly pointed commentary on the limits of self-designated ladies to live up to their own or anyone else's ideal, for that matter, and thereby underscores the irrelevance of their identities as ladies in charge as well as their ineffectiveness as models for the rest of the community to follow. Even more acerbic and broadly humorous is "Petrified Man," set wholly in the female sanctuary of a white beauty parlor, where beauticians and customers collaborate and compete in the elaborate rituals required to achieve the appearance of ladyhood. What's telling about this story is the way the characters scrutinize and measure each other's respectability and ladylike appearance. They criticize each other's failings while neglecting to acknowledge their own and inadvertently reveal their own limitations of observation while discussing a traveling sideshow attraction known as a "petrified man," who is supposedly turning into stone before the eyes of paying customers. When a turn of events suddenly reveals the "petrified man" to be far more than a mere sideshow attraction—an escaped rapist whose capture offers a sizable reward—all the women in the beauty shop are set on their heels, confronted with the unsettling revelation that their assumptions and expectations have been abruptly overturned and that nothing is really what it seems to be—at least not from the perspective of white women whose initial self-complacency is a large part of the story's comedy.

One of the most important lessons my students draw from these discussions is Welty's highly effective use of unreliable narrators/characters and her deft handling of limited third-person narration. By the time students in my seminar have finished discussing these initial stories, in fact, they have learned to be highly skeptical of those Welty characters most given to posturing and public moralizing, and it has been highly gratifying to see how these budding feminist critics learn to question those characters, like the first-person narrator of "Why I Live at the P.O.," who loudly try to occupy the higher moral ground of the domestic conflicts in which they engage. Not all of the students are bold enough to take on Welty in the short informal and formal writing assignments required in the seminar, but those who do have managed to demonstrate that much of the comedy in Welty's stories draws from the gap between her characters' limited self-knowledge and her readers' growing perceptions of those limitations.

Hence by the time my students turn to the last two stories of the volume, "Powerhouse" and "A Worn Path," they have acquired a special sensitivity to issues of reliable and unreliable characters and narrators, and they are often especially attuned to the delicate politics of racial encounters and the possibilities of white and black characters differing radically on the meanings of those encounters. In class discussions and in their writing assignments, questions begin arising about how Powerhouse's white audience sees and seeks to classify him and how the whites Phoenix Jackson encounters on the Natchez Trace and in Natchez interpret the meaning of her errand into town.

Those last two stories, after all, focus on African American figures whose complexity and interiority elude and baffle the whites who scrutinize them and seek to box them into small, tidy categories. Having discovered how so many of Welty's stories seem to scrutinize and question those who readily assume authority, especially if those tales appear to be about self-designated white southern ladies, my students learn to take on some of the metafictional issues brought up in two stories now read as powerful indictments of a highly racialized, segregated society. They learn to turn a skeptical eye on those characters who too easily profess certainty of judgment and who inadvertently reveal their own lapses in judgment and awareness, and they also learn to question the stories and the conclusions reached by those characters. Above all, what my students learn in this seminar is that so many of the portraits of white southern ladies in *A Curtain of Green*, especially those in "Why I Live at the P.O.," "Lily Daw and the Three Ladies," and "Petrified Man," are both comical and highly critical of those professed ideals of white southern womanhood, the protection of which was repeatedly cited during the whole era of Jim Crow to justify the maintenance of segregation as a racial caste system. The stories poke fun at the pretensions and posings of white southern ladies, but Welty's first volume of apprentice stories also points to the deeply flawed and even damaging nature of the ideal that confined generations of white and black southern women writers—and propelled them into rebellion against that ideal and the incarceration for which it came to stand. In this respect, Welty's *A Curtain of Green* serves my seminar very well as a turning point of sorts, one that underscores the long tradition of iconoclastic women writers working in the region and Welty's own pivotal place in that tradition.

Note

1. These photos are numbered in Welty's collection *Photographs*.

   1. A Woman of the 'thirties/Hinds County/1933
   2. Delegate/Jackson/1938
   51. Dolls/Jackson/1930s
   64. Courthouse Steps/Fayette/1930s
   63. Jackson/1930s
   84. Hello and Goodbye/Jackson/1930s

Works Cited and Consulted

Baym, Nina. *Feminism and American Literary History*. New Brunswick, NJ: Rutgers UP, 1992.
Carby, Hazel. *Reconstructing Womanhood: The Emergence of the Afro-American Woman Novelist*. New York: Oxford UP, 1987.
Chopin, Kate. *The Awakening and Selected Stories*. 1899. Intro. Sandra M. Gilbert. New York: Penguin, 1983.

Dash, Julie. *Daughters of the Dust: The Making of an African American Woman's Film*. New York: New Press, 1992.
Edwards, Laura F. *Scarlett Doesn't Live Here Anymore: Southern Women in the Civil War Era*. Urbana: U of Illinois P, 2000.
Entzminger, Betina. *The Belle Gone Bad: White Southern Women Writers and the Dark Seductress*. Baton Rouge: Louisiana State UP, 2002.
Glymph, Thavolia. *Out of the House of Bondage: The Transformation of the Plantation Household*. New York: Cambridge UP, 2008.
Harrison, Suzan. *Eudora Welty and Virginia Woolf: Gender, Genre, and Influence*. Baton Rouge: Louisiana State UP, 1997.
———. "'It's Still a Free Country': Constructing Race, Identity, and History in Eudora Welty's 'Where Is the Voice Coming From?'" *Mississippi Quarterly* 50 (Fall 1997): 631–46.
Hurston, Zora Neale. *Their Eyes Were Watching God*. 1937. Intro. Mary Helen Washington. New York: HarperPerennial, 2000.
Jacobs, Harriet. *Incidents in the Life of a Slave Girl, Written by Herself*. 1861. Ed. Jean Fagan Yellin. Enlarged Ed. Cambridge, MA: Harvard UP, 2000.
Mark, Rebecca. *The Dragon's Blood: Feminist Intertextuality in Eudora Welty's* The Golden Apples. Jackson: UP of Mississippi, 1994.
Peterman, Gina D. "*A Curtain of Green*: Eudora Welty's Auspicious Beginning." *Mississippi Quarterly* 46 (1992/1993): 91–114.
Pollack, Harriet, ed. *Eudora Welty, Whiteness, and Race*. Athens: U of Georgia P, 2013.
———. "Words between Strangers: On Welty, Her Style, and Her Audience." *Welty: A Life in Literature*. Ed. Albert J. Devlin. Jackson: UP of Mississippi, 1978. 54–81.
———, and Suzanne Marrs, eds. *Eudora Welty and Politics: Did the Writer Crusade?* Baton Rouge: Louisiana State UP, 2001.
Prenshaw, Peggy Whitman. *Composing Selves: Southern Women and Autobiography*. Baton Rouge: Louisiana State UP, 2011.
———. "Woman's World, Man's Place: The Fiction of Eudora Welty." *Eudora Welty: A Form of Thanks*. Ed. Louis Dollarhide and Ann J. Abadie. Jackson: UP of Mississippi, 1979.
Randall, Alice. *The Wind Done Gone*. New York: Houghton, 2001.
Schmidt, Peter. *The Heart of the Story: Eudora Welty's Short Fiction*. Jackson: UP of Mississippi, 1991.
Walker, Margaret. *Jubilee*. New York: Houghton, 1966.
Welty, Eudora. *Stories, Essays, and Memoir*. Ed. Richard Ford and Michael Kreyling. New York: Library of America, 1998. 3–179.
———. *Photographs*. Jackson: UP of Mississippi, 1989.
Weston, Ruth D. *Gothic Traditions and Narrative Techniques in the Fiction of Eudora Welty*. Baton Rouge: Louisiana State UP, 1994.

Matters of Life and Death

Teaching Welty in a Course on Death, Dying, and Funerals in Southern Literature

—**David A. Davis,** Mercer University

Death is both profoundly personal and extremely social. It is one of the most prominent literary themes, and through literary depictions of death, we can explore aesthetic issues of symbolism and narrative, emotional issues of grief and memory, cultural issues of burial practices and religious customs, and economic issues of estate succession and the funeral industry. As a critical lens, death reveals how people live. In 2013, I heard Victoria Bryan, then a graduate student at Ole Miss, give a fascinating paper about the funeral industry and cremation in *Absalom, Absalom!*, and by the time she was done with her talk, I had begun to imagine a course about death in the South. The potential discussion topics and reading list unfolded quickly, and since I was already scheduled to teach a course on southern literature since 1900 for the next semester, I proceeded to design a syllabus. Eudora Welty's novel *The Optimist's Daughter*, published in 1972, was one of the texts that came immediately to mind because it raises issues of family, memory, modernity, migration, and death in the South.

My students are traditional, capable students at a small liberal arts college, and most of the students who enroll in upper-level southern literature classes at Mercer are English, history, or southern studies majors. With this in mind, I developed a reading list and a set of assignments. Eudora Welty's novel *The Optimist's Daughter* was an obvious choice, and we read it after James Agee's *A Death in the Family* and before William Faulkner's *As I Lay Dying*, Lillian Smith's *Strange Fruit*, Ernest Gaines's *A Lesson before Dying*, Randall Kenan's *A Visitation of Spirits*, and Matthew Guinn's *The Resurrectionist*. Since the course was intended for majors, I put together a set of assignments that asked them to practice literary analysis and research. Each student was assigned a secondary text to read in the form of a book about death practices, literary criticism, or cultural history, and they then had to give a presentation to the class based on the text and to write a review of the book. Students were also assigned in small groups of four or five to write close readings of selected passages from the novels, and at the end of the semester, each student also wrote a ten-page research-based literary analysis that related to the texts and themes we discussed during the semester.

In an essay published, unfortunately for me, two years after I taught the course, Travis Rozier explains that "Eudora Welty's *The Optimist's Daughter*, a work centered on mourning, memorialization, and funerary ritual, depicts a South undergoing social change as a growing consumer culture offered new opportunities for self-creation and social climbing" (138). Beyond the facts that Welty is an important writer and that the novel is an excellent work of literature, I put the book on the syllabus because it represents an encounter with death in a middle-class white family in the twentieth century, which created useful points of contrast for our discussions of death in working-class, African American, or contemporary settings, and these conversations about differences allowed us to trace the values of different social groups and the evolution of death culture. The novel allowed us to talk about issues of social class, family dynamics, gender, domesticity, community construction, regional difference, symbolism, and the invention of tradition among other topics.

Our class discussions focused on the issues of death, memory, and family in *The Optimist's Daughter*. In the first class session, we discussed Laurel's errand of filial piety and her father's undignified death in an antiseptic New Orleans hospital room during Mardi Gras.[1] At the beginning of class, a student gave a presentation on *The Denial of Death* by Ernest Becker. His book argues that the development of symbolic culture is an attempt to establish the illusion of immortality, and he describes symbolic culture as all of the elements of civilization that humans have created to separate themselves from their own physicality, including architecture, art, language, music, clothing, and social relations. In other words, all of the processes that define our humanity are means to deny death, and he asserts that this drive to deny death motivates the vain human attempt to find a meaning to life. After the student presented this book to the class, we talked about the implications of this idea. They were reluctant to agree with his position as none of them felt the compulsion for immortality, but I asked them to imagine what about them would live on after they die. They soon listed their children, their creative works, their possessions, and their memory in their loved one's imagination. We used this conversation to frame a discussion of the opening of *The Optimist's Daughter*. We noted that Judge McKelva dies near the beginning of the book, so most of the novel concerns those elements that live on after him and how those vestiges of immortality complicate the lives of his surviving family.

We then discussed the way that Welty frames Judge McKelva's death with a juxtaposition between order and chaos. The antiseptic hospital in New Orleans represents the emergence of medical technology as a means of extending life spans, and the clinical setting of hospitals and doctors, we observed, has displaced the spiritual setting of churches and preachers. Judge McKelva enters the hospital for a routine procedure, but Welty foreshadows his death with references to his first wife's death, his failing eyesight, and the sensation of coldness and silence in the hospital room. Outside, meanwhile, New Orleans celebrates Mardi Gras, a frenzy of carnival affirming life in the face of death. We then discussed Fay's role in the scene as a chaos agent. Her obsession with Mardi Gras precipitates Judge McKelva's death when she attempts to drag him out of bed to celebrate her birthday. Later in our discussions, we pointed out that Welty consistently characterizes her as a disruptive force in the book who complicates the issues of mortality and immortality in the novel. In addition to possibly causing Judge McKelva's death, she also unsettles his immortality by disrupting the family, works, possessions, and memories that he leaves behind.

The second session began with a presentation on Pat Jalland's book *Death in the Victorian Family*. She describes death as a social act, and she conceptualizes the notion of the good death, the way most people would imagine their own ideal passing. In the Victorian period, the good death meant dying at an advanced age in one's own home surrounded by loved ones in a state of religious grace and with minimal pain and no violence. Most of my students agreed that this is how they would idealize their own deaths. This standard allowed us to construct a rubric for evaluating whether or not characters died a good death, and we discovered to no one's surprise that characters in southern literature rarely die a good death. Most of the characters in southern literature seem to die difficult, solitary, or painful deaths. Of all the books we read in the semester, Judge McElva's comes closest to meeting the criteria for a good death. In some respects, he dies well because he is older and surrounded with his remaining family, but Fay's childish tantrum complicates his passing, adding an element of violence and disruption to his death. This led a student to raise an excellent question: for whom is the death good, the deceased person or their family? We discussed this question for the remainder of the class. Many students felt that the purpose of the good death was to soothe the family's grief. To the individual, a good life is more important than a good death.

In the next class, a student presented on Jessica Mitford's *The American Way of Death Revisited*, which allowed us to interrogate the economic and material aspects of the death industry. Her book exposes the ways that death has been commercialized by funeral homes, cemeteries, conspicuous memorialization, and an array of business and political interests to capitalize on a family's grief after the loss of a loved one. This book led us to ask questions about death as a transaction and the commodification of grief, a set of questions that are relevant to the southern funeral customs represented in part 2 of *The Optimist's Daughter*. We focused our attention on the community of Mount Salus and the family dynamics that play out there during the Judge's funeral. The family gathers at the home for a wake where offerings of food are brought to the family to signify the community's shared grief. Then the Judge is buried in the town cemetery, but his grave is located in the new section of the cemetery near the interstate and away from the most prominent families in the community. My students observed that the divided cemetery and the interstate highway indicate the effects of modernity on the small town, whose population has dwindled as more people, like Laurel, move into cities. My students also brought up the symbolism of clocks and time in our discussion. There are several examples of clocks in the section, beginning with the grandfather clock in the family home, and the repeated references to clocks and time are an obvious symbol of mortality.

For the third class session, we discussed the incarnations of memory in part 3 of the book. As birds chatter in the branches, Laurel and her friends chat in the garden near Becky's roses. We discussed the way that Welty uses imagery to enhance the scene, and we teased out two patterns in this section. One of the patterns involved bird imagery, which culminates in the chimney swift trapped in the house, and the other pattern concerns memories attached to material objects. From her mother's roses, Laurel moves to her father's library, where she constructs a memorial version of him in her imagination that omits Fay, and later she reads through her mother's letters and confronts the image of her parents in her memory. As we discussed this section of the text, we wondered about how accurate and stable memory can be, and we proposed that memory is, in fact, dynamic and contingent. We wondered if these material items, as Becker suggests, construct immortality, and we worried that they do not. Immortality, my students argued, is an illusion.

For the last session, we discussed part 4 and returned to the lingering question about memory as a burden to frame our discussion of Laurel's late husband, Philip Hand. He died during the war when his ship sank, "left bodiless and graveless of a death made of water," and we compared his death to Judge McKelva's relatively good death (*Complete Novels* 979). The pattern of death and remembrance in the novel by now became clear; Mount Salus for Laurel is a mausoleum of memories to her father, her mother, her husband, her past, and the South. All of her memories coalesce around a breadboard that Philip carved for Laurel's mother that Fay uses as an ashtray, which angers Laurel. When she confronts Fay, Fay says, "The past isn't a thing to me. I belong to the future" (991). This comment reveals the underlying tension of the novel, and my students recognized that the novel's tension stemmed not from Judge McKelva's death directly but from the conflict between Laurel's past, which she has attempted to detach herself from in Chicago, and the future of her family and the South. We asked, as we read the final sentences of the novel, whether Laurel says good-bye to the past.

Several of my students wrote close readings of the bird in the house from section 3 of the novel (981–85). The recurring bird symbolism in the book charts a motif of memory as fleeting and elusive. They chirp and flit, distracting the reader during conversations between characters and chattering in the background during key scenes, but the chimney swift trapped in the house brings the bird symbolism unmistakably into focus. My students recognized that the bird has a symbolic meaning, but they disagreed about what it signified. Some gravitated toward fairly obvious readings that the bird symbolizes an elusive memory, and others suggested that the bird represents Laurel's attempts to detach herself from the past by figuratively chasing it away. One especially perceptive reading used the detail that Mr. Cheek, the handyman who attempts to catch the bird, "crows" (983) at Laurel to construct an interesting feminist reading of the book that suggests that the home was a patriarchal space—a metaphorical birdcage—that Laurel must vacate.

My students had a great deal of latitude in how they constructed their end of semester papers. The assignment required them to write an extended research-based analysis of one or more of the texts we read during the semester. Some students wrote about specific works, such as a fascinating essay about African American conjure traditions and Randall Kenan's *A Visitation of Spirits*, but others wrote papers that addressed multiple works. One in particular tackled the notion of a good death as an illusion, using *A Death in the Family*, *As I Lay Dying*, and *The Optimist's Daughter* to argue that the living judge the process of dying only to assuage their own fears of the unknown. Another student's paper analyzed books about death as processes of denying death. Her essay used Becker's theory and the clock symbolism in *The Optimist's Daughter* to suggest that a book about death is ultimately a vain attempt at constructing immortality.

Reading *The Optimist's Daughter* in this class allowed us to connect several issues that were central to the topic of death in southern literature. Becker's theory about the denial of death played an important role in our discussions as we wondered whether the artifacts and conversation that Laurel encounters in Mount Salus signify the structures of civilization that contribute to an illusion of immortality. If immortality exists, we wondered, is it a form of memory? The book also gave us a useful insight into the deathways of a middle-class family and to our own experiences with deathways in the contemporary South. Discussing the economics of death led to some fascinating conversations, for example, about the burial of Addie Bundren in *As I Lay Dying* as an illustration of the family's poverty, which contrasts with the middle-class expressions of grief that accompany Judge McKelva's obsequies. Most of the students in my class had attended several funerals, but few had thought of them from the critical perspective of the commercialization of death or the culture of memorialization. We were able to see the social function of death and the practices that accompany it, leading us to recognize that death is more about the living than the dead.

We were able to use these insights to interrogate the deathways represented in the other novels we read. Most of the novels we read incorporated some element of familial obligation as part of the death practices, but these were expressed differently in the early twentieth-century South depicted in *A Death in the Family* and in the rural South depicted in *As I Lay Dying*. I began the course with *A Death in the Family* to establish the effects of death on a strong family unit, and we were able to contrast that family structure with the dysfunctional families in *The Optimist's Daughter* and *As I Lay Dying*, and contrasting these novels allowed us to consider the ways that families operate as dynamic structures. The comparatively good death that Judge McElva dies in *The Optimist's Daughter* was also a useful counterpoint to the violent, complicated deaths in *Strange Fruit* and *A Lesson before Dying*. The unsettled family structure in *The Optimist's Daughter* offers instructive points of comparison with the resilient family structures in Gaines's novel, and we had a fascinating conversation about whether Jefferson dies a good death in *A Lesson before Dying*. Welty's realism also contrasted in interesting ways with the magical realism of *A Visitation of Spirits* and the historical realism of *The Resurrectionist*. Guinn's book is based on the grave robbers who supplied southern medical schools with corpses in the nineteenth century, and it elevates the conversation about death as commodification to another level, one where the body itself becomes a product.

The Optimist's Daughter works well in a course about death in the South because it reflects the changes taking place in the region through the lens of a small town situated within the greater context of the rapidly developing nation. In this respect, the book works extremely well in any number of contexts. Published at a time when the term "sunbelt" was coming into discourse to describe the economic development in the southeastern and southwestern United States, it illustrates the issues taking place as the post–civil rights movement era South urbanized and industrialized. Because Laurel lives in Chicago, the book also illustrates the effects of the great migration on white middle-class southerners, who, like their white working-class and African American counterparts, deserted the South in droves to seek better opportunities outside the region.[2] The book pairs exceptionally well with Peter Taylor's novel *A Summons to Memphis* to describe the complicated feelings that white southern expatriates felt toward the region, and the familial deaths in both of these books imply the metaphorical death of one incarnation of the South in the years after the civil rights movement. However, as current civil and political issues indicate, reports of the South's death have been greatly exaggerated.

Notes

1. As Bob Brinkmeyer argues in "New Orleans, Mardi Gras, and Eudora Welty's *The Optimist's Daughter*," the atmosphere of carnival as a disruptive spirit permeates the novel.
2. The syllabus for this course can be found at http://faculty.mercer.edu/davis_da/.

Works Cited

Becker, Ernest. *The Denial of Death*. 1973. New York: Free Press, 1997.
Brinkmeyer, Robert. "New Orleans, Mardi Gras, and Eudora Welty's *The Optimist's Daughter*." *Mississippi Quarterly* 44.4 (Fall 1991): 429–41.
Jalland, Pat. *Death in the Victorian Family*. New York: Oxford UP, 2000.
Mitford, Jessica. *The American Way of Death Revisited*. New York: Vintage, 2000.
Rozier, Travis. "'The Whole Solid Past': Memorial Objects and Consumer Culture in Eudora Welty's *The Optimist's Daughter*." *Southern Quarterly* 53.1 (Fall 2015): 125–39.
Welty, Eudora. *Complete Novels*. New York: Library of America, 1998.

Indigenizing Welty

—**Mae Miller Claxton,** Western Carolina University

In several panels on Native American literature that I have attended recently, the moderator has opened the session with a recognition of the indigenous inhabitants of that location, a reminder of histories and culture too often erased, appropriated, or just ignored. Teachers of Welty's work should provide similar reminders. After all, Welty, who noted that "fiction depends for its life on place," often reminds her readers of a place's earlier inhabitants (*Stories* 783). The problem, of course, is that most of us did not receive a thorough education in Native American history and literature. We don't know which resources will be helpful to us as instructors, and we need help planning courses that integrate historical and cultural contexts with literature. In this essay, I provide resources for the instructor who wishes to begin integrating Native American studies with the teaching of Welty's works. I also suggest a contemporary novel by Oklahoma Choctaw writer LeAnne Howe, *Shell Shaker*, as an effective pairing with Welty's *The Wide Net and Other Stories* and/or her novella *The Robber Bridegroom*. Incorporating Native American studies into our curricula requires some courage and preparation, but it repays in untold ways. In fact, we owe it to our students to provide this perspective so that we do not overlook what the indigenous inhabitants of our country have to teach us.

My perspective has been informed by my study of Welty and my own "place." I teach at Western Carolina University in Jackson County, North Carolina, near the Great Smoky Mountains National Park. At one end of our county, the Eastern Band of Cherokee Indians occupies 68,000 acres of land (originally 135,000), and its influence on the area is significant ("About Eastern Band"). Just outside my office building, near the site of a mound that was bulldozed in the 1950s, Dr. Jane Eastman, an archaeology professor, found artifacts likely dating back to the early archaic period, 8050–7900 BC. She and her students also found other evidence of a fairly sizable Cherokee village, including postholes for the wall of a house. Our official university website states that WCU was established in 1889, but the Cherokee have lived in the area for thousands of years—farming, fishing, and living their daily lives ("About Western"). As a way to increase my knowledge of Native American art, history, and culture, I have participated in two week-long workshops at the Museum of the Cherokee Indian, taken two classes in the Cherokee language, and done a lot of reading and visiting of Cherokee sites in the area.

Admittedly, most instructors do not have the resources available that I have had. On the other hand, for scholars new to indigenous studies, the "Native South" is an exciting, relatively new field of study with a presence at many conferences.[1] Influenced by twenty-first-century developments in southern studies, which moves away from previously drawn borders and strict racial binaries, this scholarship recognizes multiethnic identities and complex spaces where white, black, and Native Americans lived together (see Dolores Flores-Silva's and Keith Cartwright's essays in this volume).[2] At the 2008 Society for the Study of Southern Literature (SSSL) conference at William and Mary College, Native American writers Craig Womack, LeAnne Howe, and Allison Hedge Coke read from their work, and scholar Ellen Arnold presented a talk on "Teaching American Indian Literatures in the South" and passed out a sample five-to-six-week unit on Eastern Cherokee and Choctaw literature. At SSSL 2012, Eric Gary Anderson discussed "Indigenizing Southern Literature Classrooms," advocating for the inclusion of Native American texts in a class that might otherwise include Faulkner, Welty, and O'Connor.[3]

Although southern literary scholarship has just recently begun to acknowledge indigenous influences, Eudora Welty had an acute understanding of Native Americans' roles (specifically the Choctaw, Chickasaw, and Natchez) in Mississippi in the state's history and culture. Furthermore, her own art, especially her photography and writing, reflected these important influences. Welty wrote to her agent Diarmuid Russell as she began to consider the historical imaginative setting for her collection of stories *The Wide Net and Other Stories* and her novella *The Robber Bridegroom*: "Think of all the people who would be in my book—wonderful Indians to start with, and the Indian tales are beautiful and dramatic and very touching some of them" (*Author* 42). This collection of stories and Welty's novella are often taught in the classroom and contain a complex knowledge of history and a critical commentary on American westward expansion. Teachers interested in providing a new perspective on Welty should first consult two works that consider Native Americans in Welty's works. Michael Kreyling's 1979 essay "Clement and the

Indians: Pastoral and History in *The Robber Bridegroom*" and Annette Trefzer's chapter in her important book *Disturbing Indians: The Archaeology of Southern Fiction* (2007) both explore the role of Native Americans in Welty's Natchez Trace fiction. These two sources are a good place to start for teachers.

Another book worth consulting is *Mississippi: A Guide to the Magnolia State* (1938). This book, available in full text online, includes a surprising amount of information about Native American life in Mississippi, along with historical and geographical information about important indigenous sites in the state. Welty contributed two photographs to this book during her time working for the Works Progress Administration (WPA) in the 1930s. She also took at least one photograph entitled "Choctaw girls," which is part of the Eudora Welty Collection in the Mississippi Department of Archives and History in Jackson (Marrs 101). Welty was very well acquainted with the WPA *Guide*, published by the Federal Writers' Project, and it continues to be a very useful resource in the classroom. Instructors of the Natchez Trace fiction might also consider adding her essay "Some Notes on River Country," where Welty includes much of the history she uses in her fiction (*Stories* 760). Other useful resources are the history page of the Choctaw Nation website[4] and National Park Service website[5] on the Choctaw as part of the history of the Natchez Trace.

These resources show students that Welty knew her indigenous history and incorporated it skillfully into the creation of fiction. While providing students with information on the culture and history of Native Americans is valuable and meaningful, I would like to take one step further and suggest that teaching the perspective of Native American scholars on literature might be even more valuable, a perspective that should enter into all of our classrooms. "Peoplehood: A Model for the Extension of Sovereignty in American Indian Studies," by Tom Holm, J. Diane Pearson, and Ben Chavis, introduces students to a Native American perspective on the purpose of scholarship. Rather than viewing knowledge as an isolated pursuit that may lead to personal benefit, for example a raise, tenure, or a promotion, these scholars recognize that "the essence of Native American knowledge is the understanding of how things are interrelated and continuously interacting" (20). Thus, scholarship must always benefit the community, not just the individual. It must work toward an intellectual "sovereignty" for the group. This article posits a matrix with interlocking circles—language, sacred history, place/territory, and ceremonial cycle (or religion). The "peoplehood model" can be applied to Native American literature, but we should also apply it to non–Native American literature. How do Welty's works, for example, fit into this model? How does she explore these four categories in her works? These are productive discussions for all of the works we teach. I would even suggest that this volume fulfills the "peoplehood model" because these essays benefit the community of instructors.

LeAnne Howe's 2001 novel *Shell Shaker* provides an excellent pairing with Welty's Natchez Trace works because it explores the same history and many of the same themes, especially how the past influences the present. In addition, it supplies an example of how a Native American writer might fit within the "peoplehood" model. Adding this novel to the syllabus, in addition to supplying cultural and/or historical background, creates a new framework for a richer understanding of Welty's works.

Both writers view "story" and language as inherently powerful. Welty writes in the section titled "Listening" in her memoir, *One Writer's Beginnings*, "Long before I wrote stories, I listened for stories. Listening *for* them is something more acute than listening *to* them. I suppose it's an early form of participation in what goes on. Listening children know stories are *there*. When their elders sit and begin, children are just waiting and hoping for one to come out, like a mouse from its hole" (*Stories* 854). This description is a communal experience of language similar to the way Howe describes stories in "The Story of America: A Tribalography." Welty writes about children participating in stories as active listeners. Howe goes even further, suggesting the importance of story for the entire tribal community. She writes, "Native stories are power. They create people. They author tribes. America is a tribal creation story, a tribalography" ("Story" 29). In *Shell Shaker*, Tema Billy tries to explain this concept to her English husband, Borden Beane. He replies, "No, I don't understand that kind of irrational thinking. In essence you're saying that speech determines actions. Like God saying, 'let there be light,' and the lights come on" (36). Tema replies, "'Yes, that's the way it works'" (36). For Tema, who is Choctaw, words spoken aloud have incredible power.

Shell Shaker supplies an alternative narrative to the history portrayed in textbooks privileging the written word over oral storytelling. In *The Robber Bridegroom*, Welty constructs her own alternative text in which she documents, fictionally and sometimes fantastically, the spread of American colonialism and the resulting annihilation of Native Americans and institutionalization of slavery. Both works begin with stories, Welty's with Anglo-European fairy tales and American folktales and Howe's with traditional Choctaw stories.[6] In effect, Welty leaves her stories at the borders of the Mississippi River in Natchez, having documented the travel east to west. Howe continues the story into contemporary times with a movement back east for a more hopeful ending. She begins her work with life in a village before the arrival of Europeans: "There was once a road, an ancient trade route that began in the east.... Down this road came a terrible story" (1–2). Welty's collection *The Wide Net and*

Other Stories and *The Robber Bridegroom* document this same "terrible story" and its outcomes for the Choctaw, Chickasaw, and Natchez living in the area.

Another common theme for Welty and Howe is a complex use of time and chronology. One of my students on a discussion board post suggested that Howe blurs the lines between "story" and "history" by combining past with present. In her article, Howe defines the term "tribalography" as "the Native propensity for bringing things together, for making consensus, and for symbiotically connecting one thing to another" ("Story" 42). "Native stories," she writes, "pull all the elements together of the storyteller's tribe... and connect these in past, present, and future milieus" (42). Thus, the story of *Shell Shaker* begins in Oklahoma and ends on a sacred mound in Mississippi in a kind of reverse Trail of Tears, where past and present unite in order to restore balance and healing to a family and extended community. In a similar way, Welty in her Natchez Trace story "A Worn Path" combines past and present, taking the reader on a journey in the present but also reminding her audience of the violent histories of Native Americans and African Americans.[7] The journey on the "worn path" is a search for healing that intertwines past and present, similar to Howe's novel. Howe's complex intertwining of multiple journeys in *Shell Shaker* helps students understand similar themes and narrative strategies in Welty's Natchez Trace works.

Although the Natchez Trace stories lend themselves most readily to "indigenous" readings, other Welty settings spring to mind, for example, "Shellmound" of *Delta Wedding*, an indigenous reminder of Native American history in Mississippi and a site near Greenwood, Mississippi, named after a Chakchiuma, Choctaw, and Chickasaw battle. In addition, there are the fictional and geographical landscapes of *Losing Battles* (*Mississippi* 422).[8] All of us need to consider these "geographies" as we plan our courses. At WCU, we offer classes on native plants, the Cherokee language, basket making, and Cherokee history, among others. Our students research the importance of river cane in Cherokee culture and map fishing weirs on the Tuckasegee River. In my own classes in southern literature and Appalachian literature, I incorporate works by LeAnne Howe, Linda Hogan, Robert Conley, contemporary Qualla Boundary writers, and many others. Beyond just adding a few new books to my classes, though, "indigenizing" my own scholarship and teaching has completely transformed my own perspective on issues of language, region, and geography, and how a particular "place" impacts the art that emerges from it. Far from being lost or "removed," the culture, history, and art of the Native South should continue to inform our teaching.

The students in my classes often react with chagrin to what they have not been taught: "Why hasn't anyone told me about this?" One student in a recent graduate class wrote about the stories not told in his family about his own Native American roots: "I suppose I'm angry about that. I feel robbed of experience." In his remarkable book *The Truth about Stories: A Native Narrative*, Cherokee writer Thomas King begins each section with a similar description: "There is a story I know. It's about the earth and how it floats in space on the back of a turtle. I've heard this story many times, and each time someone tells the story, it changes" (121). Sometimes it's the audience that changes, sometimes the storyteller, sometimes the details or chronology. The point is that it's all about stories. He writes, "The truth about stories is that that's all we are" (2). At the end of the book, King reminds his readers that he is a storyteller and that he has now passed on his stories to them. It is their responsibility to figure out what to do with them: "Just don't say in the years to come that you would have lived *your* life differently if only you had heard this story. You've heard it now" (167). In her fiction, Welty constructs her own "tribalography," an alternative American narrative strongly influenced by her understanding of Native American history and culture. I believe that it is our responsibility as teachers to help students "hear the story" and decide what they want to do with it.

Notes

1. Examples would be the South Atlantic Modern Language Association (SAMLA), the Association for the Study of American Indian Literatures (ASAIL), and the Society for the Study of Southern Literature (SSSL). The 2016 theme for the annual Faulkner conference was "Faulkner and the Native South."

2. Two useful introductions to the "Native South" are in Taylor and Hobson et al. Instructors might also browse issues of the journal *Native South* and the November 2012 newsletter of the Society for the Study of Southern Literature (SSSL), volume 46, issue 2, the Native South issue.

3. See teaching resources at our website.

4. See https://www.choctawnation.com/history-culture/history.

5. See https://www.nps.gov/natr/learn/historyculture/choctaw.htm.

6. See Eyster's essay in this collection on folklore and fairy tales in Welty's fiction.

7. The *Mississippi Guide* includes a legend stating that the name of the Yazoo River comes from this battle and is an Indian word meaning "river of death" (422).

8. "A Worn Path" is included in the collection *A Curtain of Green, and Other Stories* but takes place along the Natchez Trace.

Works Cited

"About the Eastern Band of Cherokee Indians." *Cherokee Preservation Foundation*. Cherokee Preservation Foundation, 2014. Web. July 11, 2016.

"About Western Carolina." *Western Carolina University*. Western Carolina University, 2016. Web. July 11, 2016.

Anderson, Eric Gary. "Indigenizing Southern Literature Classrooms." Society for the Study of Southern Literature Conference, Vanderbilt University, Nashville, TN, 2012.

Arnold, Ellen. "Teaching American Indian Literatures in the South." Society for the Study of Southern Literature Conference, William and Mary College, Williamsburg, VA, 2008.

"Choctaw." *Natchez Trace Parkway*. National Park Service, n.d. Web. July 11, 2016.

"History." *Choctaw Nation*. Choctaw Nation, n.d. Web. July 11, 2016.

Hobson, Geary, Janet McAdams, and Kathryn Walkiewicz, eds. *The People Who Stayed: Southeastern Indian Writing after Removal*. Norman: U of Oklahoma P, 2010.

Holm, Tom, J. Diane Pearson, and Ben Chavis. "Peoplehood: A Model for the Extension of Sovereignty in American Indian Studies." *Wicazo Sa Review* 18.1 (2003): 7–24. Project MUSE. Web. August 3, 2016.

Howe, LeAnne. *Shell Shaker*. San Francisco: Aunt Lute Books, 2001.

———. "The Story of America: A Tribalography." *European Contributions to American Studies* 54 (2005): 17–38. *America: History & Life*. Web. July 8, 2016.

King, Thomas. *The Truth about Stories: A Native Narrative*. Minneapolis: U of Minnesota P, 2003. Indigenous Americas.

Kreyling, Michael. *Author and Agent: Eudora Welty and Diarmuid Russell*. New York: Farrar, 1991.

———. "Clement and the Indians: Pastoral and History in *The Robber Bridegroom*." *Eudora Welty* (1979): 25–45. *Essay and General Literature Retrospective (H. W. Wilson)*. Web. July 11, 2016.

Marrs, Suzanne. *The Welty Collection*. Jackson: UP of Mississippi, 1988.

Mississippi: A Guide to the Magnolia State. New York: Viking P, 1938. Internet Archive. Web.

Taylor, Melanie Benson. *Reconstructing the Native South: American Indian Literature and the Lost Cause*. Athens: U of Georgia P, 2011.

Trefzer, Annette. *Disturbing Indians: The Archaeology of Southern Fiction*. Tuscaloosa: U of Alabama P, 2007.

Welty, Eudora. *Complete Novels*. New York: Library of America, 1998.

———. *Stories, Essays, and Memoir*. Ed. Richard Ford and Michael Kreyling. New York: Library of America, 1998.

Taking *The Wide Net* to the Waters of *La Frontera* along Eudora Welty's Natchez Trace

—**Dolores Flores-Silva,** Roanoke College

When I teach my class in Chicano literature in the general education offerings at my home institution, a liberal arts college in Virginia, I face a number of problems in drawing students into the content, both the imagined and real spaces of the reading assignments. Similar problems can arise even when teaching Latin American literature courses in my modern languages department: how to motivate students to read with care, interest, recreative imagination? Students in our digital information age may have a stronger aversion to the alleged monotony of history than our own generations did. I insist on providing historical foundation behind the fiction I teach since most of my courses deal with historical movements and their repercussions in the modern era. Chicano/a identities and writings do not come from out of nowhere, ready for consumer airtime and downloading. My courses on Latin American cultures often challenge the conservative and nationalist ideologies of students whose educations have not pushed them to think from perspectives outside of mainstream US political and media currents. If we are to place any value in truly holistic humanistic studies, it is our mission to find ways to help students identify with the imagined worlds of texts and spaces where their sense of otherness can overwhelm them. One of my answers to this problem has been to ease my students southward in overland travel through a slightly more familiar (but still often otherly or othered) local South. No author serves me better in this than does Eudora Welty and her Natchez Trace fiction, which casts a truly wide net.

In order to ease my students' southern travels into the virtual spaces of fiction, I have launched my course on Chicano Literature with stories from Welty's *The Wide Net* (1943) and with references to her first novella, *The Robber Bridegroom* (1942). What, we might ask, could Eudora Welty have in common with Chicano (or "Latin") literature and cultural history? Welty's engagement with the Natchez Trace and Natchez itself is what makes her a writer of traceways of *la frontera*, a writer who reminds us that the US southwestern borderlands have a long history of shift and flow. The seemingly domestic/domesticated Welty helps me push students into topics that may make them feel uncomfortable and perspectives they haven't learned to value. Welty's wide array of representations can help us recognize and confront stereotypes of minorities that have been created and maintained by national and regional structures of power. For me, teaching a Chicano course and being a Mexican citizen presents a double difficulty.[1] Students often assume, from the first day, that I am going to be prejudiced against Anglo-Americans and the United States. Throughout the semester, I have to show that my only intention is that they consider more holistic and integral understandings of human society beyond the tiresome roles of victim and oppressor. The bottom line, as Welty stated in her preface to *The Collected Stories*, is that it is not easy "to try to enter into the mind, heart, and skin of a human being who is not," as she put it, "myself." Whether we are challenged to understand or empathize with the perspectives of "a man or a woman, old or young, with skin black or white [or brown], the primary challenge lies in making the jump itself," she asserts (*Stories* 829).

Because Welty's Natchez texts carry the resilient trace of old frontiers between New Spain (on the verge of becoming Mexico) and the fledgling United States, they serve me well in introducing students to the importance of historical context. Before we begin discussing Welty's fiction, my students read an online article, "Manuel Gayoso and Spanish Natchez" by Jack D. Elliott Jr., and they study maps of the boundaries between Spanish Louisiana, Spanish West Florida, and the United States in 1789 (just before the United States gained control of Natchez). We examine excerpts from a poem by Manuel Antonio Valdes (Mexico, 1787) celebrating Don Bernardo de Galvez's victories over the British at Natchez, Baton Rouge, Mobile, and Pensacola during the US Revolutionary War of Independence. I have students research the life of Galvez, who was Spanish governor of Louisiana and Florida Occidental before becoming the sixty-first viceroy of New Spain (one of the last rulers of colonial Mexico before independence in 1810). Students learn that Louisiana was an administrative district of the viceroyalty of New Spain from 1763 to 1802, taking in the territory to the west of the Mississippi, plus New Orleans and parts of West Florida, including Natchez. It was, in effect, a province of Mexico. As border spaces, Natchez and Louisiana were what Texas later became. The tales of outlaws, illicit trade, piracy, shifting alliances and questions of allegiance, documentation, and land title that emanate from the Old Natchez Trace all deal with motifs familiar to folk on both sides of the US/Mexican border.

Welty's Natchez helps me teach border histories and launch a study of changing maps and terrain. Her work introduces social landscapes of the plantation or hacienda, and her writing style offers an early formation of the marvelous real, or magical realism as we have come to know it. Welty was writing magical realism in the early 1940s, whether critics acknowledge it or not. Welty serves as a bridge to render my own souths—the souths of my Latin American and Chicano classes—less otherly, less alien, and more part of our shared world: a bridge I first glimpsed through José Limón's *American Encounters: Greater Mexico, the United States, and the Erotics of Culture* (1998).

I like to assign one or two stories from *The Wide Net* in their entirety and "sample" the rest of the stories via chunks of paragraphs or sentences from the vivid prose of each as they connect to the historical, stylistic, and contextual subject matter of my Chicano or Latin American courses. In this way, I put Welty in dialogue with writers such as Gloria Anzaldúa, Sandra Cisneros, and Rosario Castellanos as well as with Rosario Ferré (Puerto Rico) and Lydia Cabrera (Cuba and Miami) with whom Welty is read most richly.[2] I focus upon *The Wide Net*, a collection of eight stories set in the Mississippi region of Natchez and the Natchez Trace.

The collection's opening story, "First Love," allows me to introduce Welty's use of "the marvelous real" as the deaf narrator (in the 1807 world of Natchez frontier inns) moves beyond lip-reading to apprehend signification in the frosty air of winter breaths—so "marvelous to him when the infinite designs of speech became visible in formations on the air" (*Stories* 186)—and he is a guide as well to the love messages carved into a table in Spanish "for anyone to read who came knowing the language" (188). In the title story, "The Wide Net," Welty stretches her mythopoetic webbing to take in indigenous Mexican identifications of the rabbit and the moon in a tale that is the carnivalesque flip side of "La Llorona." Another story, "The Winds," carries wild soundtracks filled with children's chants to "Lady Moon" (262), sweeping us up into an equinoctial storm that blows everything together across borders: the white girls and their black nurses, "the hot tamale man" (260), the Catholic bells, and the protagonist's fascination with the outcast neighbor-girl Cornelia: "Thy name is Corn, and thou art like the ripe corn, beautiful Cornelia" (260). Here, we have entered the Hurricane-swept space of the Corn-mother, that

Gulf-passage to "the long times of the world" (265) where indigenous Mesoamerican cultures meet the Mississippian.

The final story, "At the Landing," for example, reminds us of the shifting of borders, as "the town was still called The Landing" even though "The river had gone, three miles away, beyond sight and smell," returning "only in flood" (292). The story's central character, Jenny Lockhart, grows up "between her mother's two paintings" hanging in the parlor: "'The Bird Fair' and 'The Massacre at Fort Rosalie'" (292). I ask my students to go online to seek historical information on this massacre at Fort Rosalie, and what they find is one of the most complete and bloody defeats ever inflicted by American Indians (the Natchez) upon European settlers in a colonial fort (over two hundred French dead in 1729 with many women, children, and slaves abducted). That the Natchez were soon massacred and nigh-eliminated—with their leader the Great Sun, his sub chiefs, and war chief Tattooed Serpent all killed or sold into slavery in St. Domingue in just over a year—is part of the unstated subtext of painting and story. And so too is a dark and mysterious magical realism working its currents through the story, through the body of a quiet, passive, obedient girl, in love with the idea of love itself, who would "let the touch be magical" (293). Welty's prose builds around a certain "innocence," a notion "that no kiss had ever brought love tenderly enough from mouth to mouth," a "delight" and "strange glow" in facing "a mystery that is in the other heart.... a fragile mystery [that] was in everyone and in herself," accompanied by a knowledge: "the secrecy of life was the terror of it" (296, 297).

The flood in "At the Landing" is a kind of carnival of death and flesh, of *carne* (meat) and the carnal, and Jenny partakes with a new hunger: "She ate eagerly, looking up at him while her teeth bit, to show him herself, her proud hunger, as if to please and flatter him with her original and now lost starvation" (305). "At the Landing" concludes with the falling of the floodwaters and the town's thick coating of silt, muck, and refuse. Scavengers find usable debris and even an old Spanish coin. With the fall of the floodwaters, we learn how the town has identified the object of Jenny's obsession—Floyd—not simply as "'the wild man'" but as one who "had the blood of a Natchez Indian, though the Natchez might be supposed to be all gone, massacred" (308). Mostly, however, Floyd is "just like all men ... something of an animal" (309). When Jenny seeks to join Floyd down along the fishermen's camps by the river where "[v]eil behind veil of long drying nets hung on all sides" amid the smell of campfires and cooked "fish and the wild meat" (311), she becomes the catch or female body trapped in these men's nets, in one of the most chilling scenes in all of literature, rendered all the more devastatingly through the veils of Welty's opaquely oracular prose.[3]

Here, Jenny Lockhart becomes the flesh/*carne* of the *barbacoa* rack that shows up again and again in texts of the Gulf region. Women along the gendered, racialized, nationalized borders of Latin American and Chicano/a writing (as well as in Welty's and Faulkner's Mississippi) are so often scripted as flesh for consumption, a spicy dish, as male carnal desire so often reduces women along our gulfs and borders of consciousness to mere *carne* (meat), in ways that show up not simply as the bycatch of the fishermen's nets in Welty, but repeatedly in the cantina women of Hollywood westerns, in the *casta* paintings engaged by Natasha Trethewey, in discussion of La Malinche/La Chingada/The Fucked (see Octavio Paz), and in the critiques of writers as various as Ferré and Anzaldúa, Sor Juana Inés de la Cruz, and Sandra Cisneros. My students come to see this, and they have connected such scenes in Welty (from *The Robber Bridegroom* to "At the Landing") to the way Sandra Cisneros scripts the death of the Awful Grandmother (and even the birth scene of the narrator) in *Caramelo*.

By the time my students have moved from Welty to Márquez and Ferré, or to Anzaldúa and Cisneros, they have gained a sense of the hauntings of history, the carnivalesque wonders (and reductions of folk to carnage) along cross-cultural frontiers, and the entrapments of patriarchal structures of machismo that conjoin haciendas with the plantations and paternalism of Uncle Sam, all in a prose often dreamlike and (sur)real. Welty's prose introduces them to the notion that we have been trained how to look—and especially not to look—at ourselves and each and every other. In her prose, they see that we end up looking at the very things we've been told are not fit for our shared sight, and we see this in a powerful woman's writing so often dismissed as domestic, quaintly southern, even demure. Welty also moves my students to see that we are not locked into the victim/oppressor relations we tend to conjure. By the time that students in my Chicano class have worked their way through our readings to finish with Sandra Cisneros's *Caramelo,* most of them have entered into a world of immigration, repatriation, and working visas, and they begin to develop ideas on how consumerism stretches the distance between their own society and those considered alien or other. Welty helps to make the jump to follow these worn paths. She opens up the fluidities of borders and history. She has us read life through other eyes and skins—to apprehend the cultivated domesticity and the unguessed wildness that exist between ourselves and our every signifying other.

Notes

1. Faculty who are not teaching Welty's work in a Latin American context (but who may have a student interested in writing an essay on Welty from this approach) would do well to read José Limón's *American Encounters*. In particular, I recommend the following two chapters of Limón's book: chapter 1: "The Other American South: Southern Culture and Greater Mexico" and chapter 4: "De Aca De Este Lado: Screening Domination and Desire."

2. Mexican American writer Gloria Anzaldúa (1942–2004) won international recognition with her book *Borderlands: La Frontera, The New Mestiza* (1987). Mexican American writer Sandra Cisneros (1954–), author of novels such as *The House on Mango Street* (1984) and *Caramelo* (2003), has been acclaimed for her innovative work in a number of literary genres. Mexican writer, essayist, and poet Rosario Castellanos (1925–1974) was one of the most representative literary voices of the twentieth century in Mexico. She is considered a precursor of Mexican feminism and wrote powerfully of hacienda-based asymmetries of power in her home state of Chiapas. Rosario Ferré (1938–2016) was one of the most prolific Puerto Rican writers who belonged to the so-called Generation of the '70s. She innovated with powerful representations of a declining planter class, strong voicings, and thematics of feminism, and a steady recognition of the agency of blacks in the creation of Puerto Rican national culture. Lydia Cabrera (1899–1991) was a Cuban anthropologist and writer well known for her Afro-Cuban tales and her ethnographic work. She published over one hundred books and was considered an expert in the study and practice of Santería and Afro-Cuban religions, traditions, and customs.

3. Among the fullest and most recent readings of "At the Landing" is chapter 5 of Harriet Pollack's wonderful book, *Eudora Welty's Fiction and Photography: The Body of the Other Woman* (Athens: U of Georgia P, 2016), especially pages 179–87.

Works Cited

Elliot, Jack D., Jr. "Manuel Gayoso and Spanish Natchez." *Mississippi History Now*. Mississippi Historical Society, 2015. Web. March 15, 2016.

Limón, José. *American Encounters: Greater Mexico, the United States, and the Erotics of Culture*. Austin: U of Texas P, 1998.

Paz, Octavio. *The Other Mexico: Critique of the Pyramid*. Trans. Lysander Kemp. New York: Grove P, 1972.

Welty, Eudora. *Stories, Essays, and Memoir*. Ed. Richard Ford and Michael Kreyling. New York: Library of America, 1998.

Woodward, Ralph Lee, ed. and trans. *Tribute to Don Bernardo de Galvez: Royal Patents and an Epic Ballad Honoring the Spanish Governor of Louisiana*. Baton Rouge and New Orleans, Historic New Orleans Collection. 1979.

III

"Lifting the Veil": Teaching Welty and African American Identity

> My wish, indeed my continuing passion, would be not to point the finger in judgment but to part a curtain, that invisible shadow that falls between people, the veil of indifference to each other's presence, each other's wonder, each other's human plight.
> —**Preface to *One Time, One Place: Mississippi in the Depression***

Teaching "A Curtain" in the Thick of Things

Welty and Race in Diverse Classrooms

—**Christin Marie Taylor,** Shenandoah University

Eudora Welty's "A Curtain of Green" may seem like an odd choice for teaching race and literary protest. Welty was not a protest writer in the traditional sense, and the narrative does not speak explicitly about race. What's more, novice and experienced readers alike find the story anticlimactic and weird, just plain weird. If pressed to offer comment, my undergraduates focus on Larkin's loss, coping, and quest for self. When questioned about the curious appearance and swift departure of Jamey, an African American hired hand, they have little to say. Yet Larkin's self-seeking hangs in the balance with this seemingly minor character. As the story builds to a climax, the space between them gets thick.

Welty mentioned "the thick" while recalling the moment she found herself as a storyteller. As a girl she had observed J.W., an African American youth, at work in her mother's garden. He was busy amidst the flowers when he said, "I wish there wasn't a rose in the world" (qtd. in Haltom, Brown, and Clay 68). Welty went on to explain, "As I saw him there without a name to his initials, wishing for a world without its roses, but caught in the thick of them ... it might have been the first time I knew the compulsion to step back and place myself at a story-teller's remove" (qtd. in Haltom, Brown, and Clay 68). Though Welty spoke of "the thick of them" colloquially, we could say "the thick" was not only a dense spread of roses but also the brambly brakes of segregation that shaped a carefully crafted society. By highlighting instances of "the thick" in "A Curtain of Green," we may help students explore the interaction between Larkin, Jamey, and the garden as Welty's meditation on race.

I taught "Curtain" for the first time in a "first-year experience" seminar on American Renaissance and Resistance. Many students were the first in their families to attend college, student athletes, or international students. I used poetry and prose to teach critical and creative analysis as we engaged our course theme.

Social movements organized the syllabus. "Curtain" appeared at the start of my unit on the civil rights movement, which ended with King's "Letter from Birmingham Jail." To this point in the semester, students had sailed through charged literature about political rebellion, racial oppression, and social change. They found Paul Laurence Dunbar's "Sympathy" accessible via metaphors of bondage and nature—the caged bird beats his chest and flaps his wings for freedom. The animal imagery in "If We Must Die" by Claude McKay—"If we must die, let it not be like hogs" (1) but "fighting back" (14)—provoked engaged discussion about bravery and patriotism. When we arrived at Welty's story, however, I was met with faint scowls and averted eyes. They seemed to feel betrayed.

In hindsight I realized students had not shied away from earlier discussions because they had a sure footing. Previous readings mapped onto their prior knowledge about the Jim Crow era. The writers' political stakes and even the messages behind metaphors of nature and race remained clear. Some students of color felt safe discussing racial topics with me because I resembled them in one way or another. Even if others did not identify with me or certain readings, they, too, enjoyed "speaking truth to power" by way of the texts. In sum, the reading experiences produced what students (and many readers) desired—an underdog, a happy ending, a sense of heightened awareness, and redemption.

"Curtain" has no champion, no victim. And Welty's writing style, as critic Harriet Pollack argues, is "opaque" (60). This opacity generates a narrative "thickness" that, like Larkin's garden, becomes difficult for undergraduates at any level to penetrate. Because of the story's difficulty, I now employ a learning-centered strategy in my first-year experience, women's, and American literature classes. These courses may differ in terms of students' comfort with writing and literary analysis and even classroom dynamics. However, the narrative distance, the near-beheading of Jamey, and an overwhelming prose style create a barrier that places students (and teachers) in "the thick."

I dedicate at least two class meetings to the task. I begin by acknowledging students' aversion with a free write: "Do you like this story?" "What do you think the story is about?" "How does the story make you feel?" Students hesitate to admit they dislike the piece, so I show a twitter hashtag about the entire story collection that reads in part, "#ACurtainofGreen blows" (Harris).

Awkward giggles begin to relieve the pressure the story places upon them, and students find they share an uncertainty about what to think or do. I hope they will eventually appreciate the productivity of uncertainty; a similar question lingers for Larkin. What is she to do?

I do not lecture at first (and sometimes not at all). I utilize a modified jigsaw method to teach content while allowing students to generate their own ideas instead. I put students in small groups. Each receives a handout with a set of questions, related images, background information, and instructions that will help them arrive at unique close readings and analyses. Once this group work concludes, we jigsaw—one representative from each group will merge to form new small groups.[1] Each student must teach his or her peers key information and explain the analysis decided upon in the previous group.

The jigsaw lends itself to a variety of literature and proves useful when students lack necessary prior knowledge or when an instructor wishes to cover a range of content in a condensed time frame. When classroom environments become polarized, overly quiet, or dominated by a few, this approach also recalibrates student interaction and in-class contributions through cooperative problem solving. In the case of "A Curtain of Green," students acquire knowledge, learn new approaches to literary analysis, and discern relationships between topics, such as women's history, genre, and tropes of nature, race, and space. Together, they ultimately arrive at arguments about the story's resistance, including, but not limited to, the ways Welty upsets legacies of plantation culture and compliance with racial segregation by disordering Larkin's place.

For most students, a story about an isolated white widow has little connection to modern civil rights. To promote understanding, some groups receive information about gender, class, and segregation. Historian Grace Elizabeth Hale demonstrates that in fiction and in practice, white women of the middle class were key in the maintenance of racial separation (93). Some students consider the ways "Curtain" interrogates white women's agency in the system. As Susan Donaldson argues, Larkin's place as "the mythic white woman . . . is maintained through constant surveillance and brutal violence" (59). One group locates markers of Larkin's class privilege as well as social forces that attempt to police her gendered position. Another examines how Larkin's work in an untidy garden suspends her role.

Students recognize gardening as a coping mechanism. The jigsaw helps them take another step: gardening allows Larkin to process the loss of a husband and allegorizes the loss of an established social order (and his death signifies that fall). After his passing, she assumes her duty as a widow in Larkin Hill—and by extension her place as the "new" bearer of old norms. But the narrative depicts an unraveling mantle. Shifting from a domestic lady to a domestic worker of sorts, Larkin "worked without stopping ... submerged all day among the thick, irregular ... plants" (*Stories* 131). Her gardening causes further reversals: "The servant would call her at dinnertime, and she would obey" (131). As Larkin's effort rises and her position declines, the garden becomes increasingly disordered and thicker.

Additional groups consider the garden's disorder in relation to plantation romance and race. The plantation and its domesticated landscape marked signs of white racial freedom and identity during the antebellum era. Postbellum fiction and popular culture evoked images of plantations to symbolically reassert the logic of Jim Crow. Provided with information about plantation symbolism, students look for ruptures. Larkin's garden overflows:

> It might seem that the extreme fertility of her garden formed at once a preoccupation and a challenge to Mrs Larkin. Only by ceaseless activity could she cope with the rich blackness of this soil. Only by cutting, separating, thinning and tying back in the clumps of flowers and bushes and vines could she have kept them from overreaching their boundaries.... And yet, Mrs Larkin rarely cut, separated, tied back.... (131)

Larkin does not separate her plants. Collapsing boundaries between types "without any regard for harmony of color" (131), Larkin's violation of color lines troubles the maintenance of segregation.

Welty deploys the sign of the "jungle" to underscore this violation. Larkin's garden "had the appearance of a sort of jungle" (131–32). The jungle signals the antithesis of the plantation's symbolic order, associated constructs of race, and an undoing. Larkin seems possessed by this undoing, in fact, increasingly desirous as the garden grows. Yet she exists alone in the garden save Jamey. Here, the space, the separation, and the difference between them gets thick.

Students expect developed characters and complex interactions, but Larkin's superficial intolerance of Jamey (including rage at "[a] look of docility in the Negro's back") and his simple, childlike characterization seem to merely echo tropes of a racist past (133). So other groups read Larkin and Jamey (both shaded "yellow") as a mirror pair (130, 133). Larkin works feverishly, unable to fend off the memory of her husband's death, a sign of her lack of control. Jamey functions as her mirror opposite. He appears "motionless" and "negligently stir[s] the dirt" (134). She attempts to prod him with a shout, but "her voice hardly carried in the dense garden" (134). He wears a slight, "rather deprecating smile" that disparages her fervor. And his absorption in an "impossible dream" (133), signifying a wish for the future, contrasts her entrapment in the tight grasp of the past.

Jamey's closeness and difference foil a shocking and shocked feminine whiteness. Looming over him with a garden tool and poised to "strike off" his head, Larkin wonders, "Was it not possible to compensate? to punish? to protest?" (134). It may appear Larkin longs for personal justice, a life in exchange for a too-soon-departed mate. Her near act also emblematizes a white feminine longing and a sense of urgency—for what remains unsaid. And Larkin lacks the power to stake a claim.

The narrative ends with Jamey briefly standing over Larkin before fleeing the garden, reflecting African American mobilization. At the same time, Larkin, who had fainted like a flower in the green, becomes a sleeper of sorts, marking white women's action latent. This ending suggests an undetermined destiny and presses students to seek answers to difficult questions. What did it mean and how did it feel to live as a propertied white woman or a propertyless black man caught up in a deliberately cultivated garden of segregation? How are oppression and freedom yoked? Where does agency reside?

These messy questions and other unpredictable inquiries make "A Curtain of Green" a risky medium for teaching race and social protest. The narrative's lack of clarity may cause unexpected shifts in the classroom. Students become discomfited because the narrative refuses to satisfy their expectations for what fiction should teach them about justice and race. The story offers no enlightenment or reward. Like the garden, matters of agency are "tangled" and "confusing" (130) because control, including our ability to determine Welty's message, remains fugitive in the text.

Welty's elusive portrayal of a widow in a garden captures the thickness of privilege, gender, and race, suggesting a need for "protest"—a term that appears just when it seems Larkin may commit a horrible act. She asks herself, "Was it not possible to compensate? to punish? to protest?" But the rain stops Mrs Larkin from "punishing" a black body; her relief does not come through violence. Welty's story suggests the need for a different kind of protest, but does not enact it. Instead, the garden subtext pushes students to think outside of binary oppositions, such as action and inaction, power and powerlessness, control and subjection, and black and white. Students have the benefit of Welty's aesthetic take on the messiness and difficulty of these seeming oppositions when they read new material, such as King's discussion of nonviolent direct action in "Letter from Birmingham Jail." Others look back and reconsider Welty's representation of a privileged white woman in relation to Dunbar's "caged bird," and some make new, unexpected claims about gender, power, nature, and race. Whether they carry with them a fond remembrance of Welty's "Curtain" or not, students are more comfortable with uncertainty when they move on to new texts. Most important, they have learned how to think through the thick of things.

Note

1. The jigsaw has taken on many uses in the classroom since its inception in 1971. The jigsaw seems particularly fitting for teaching "A Curtain of Green" because the method, originally created to lessen conflict following racial integration, helps ease tensions and foster community by providing students with a sense of common ground (Aronson).

Suggested Further Reading

Crews, Elizabeth. "Eudora Welty's 'A Curtain of Green': Overcoming Melancholia through Writing." *Eudora Welty Review* 2.1 (2010): 21–33.
Donaldson, Susan V. "Parting the Veil: Eudora Welty, Richard Wright, and the Crying Wounds of Jim Crow." *Eudora Welty, Whiteness, and Race.* Ed. Harriet Pollack. Athens: U of Georgia P, 2013. 48–72.
Kreyling, Michael. "Modernism in Welty's *A Curtain of Green and Other Stories*." *Southern Quarterly* 20.4 (1982): 40–53.

Works Cited and Consulted

Aronson, Elliot. *The Jigsaw Classroom.* Social Psychology Network, 2000–2016. Web. May 31, 2016.
Delvin, Albert J., ed. *Welty: A Life in Literature.* Jackson: UP of Mississippi, 2007.
Donaldson, Susan V. "Parting the Veil: Eudora Welty, Richard Wright, and the Crying Wounds of Jim Crow." *Eudora Welty, Whiteness, and Race.* Ed. Harriet Pollack. Athens: U of Georgia P, 2013. 48–72.
Dunbar, Paul Laurence. "Sympathy." *The Collected Poems of Paul Laurence Dunbar.* Ed. Joanne M. Braxton. Charlottesville: U of Virginia P, 1993. 102.
Hale, Grace Elizabeth. *Making Whiteness: The Culture of Segregation in the South, 1890–1940.* New York: Vintage, 1998.
Haltom, Susan, Jane Roy Brown, and Langdon Clay. *One Writer's Garden: Eudora Welty's Home Place.* Jackson: UP of Mississippi, 2011.
Harris, Emery. "I thought i just wasnt paying attention and then after 9 chapters I figured out each chapter is a different story." https://twitter.com/hashtag/ACurtainofGreen?src=hash blows." August 8, 2012, 5:13 p.m. Tweet.

McKay, Claude. "If We Must Die." *Complete Poems*. Ed. William Maxwell. Chicago: U of Illinois P, 2004. 177.

Outka, Paul. *Race and Nature: From Transcendentalism to the Harlem Renaissance*. New York: Palgrave, 2008.

Pollack, Harriet. "Words between Strangers: On Welty, Her Style, and Her Audience." *Welty: A Life in Literature*. Ed. Albert J. Delvin. Jackson: UP of Mississippi, 2007. 54–81.

Pollack, Harriet, ed. *Eudora Welty, Whiteness, and Race*. Athens: U of Georgia P, 2013.

Welty, Eudora. *Stories, Essays, and Memoir*. Ed. Richard Ford and Michael Kreyling. New York: Library of America, 1998.

Yaeger, Patricia. *Dirt and Desire: Reconstructing Southern Women's Writing, 1930–1990*. Chicago: U of Chicago P, 2000.

The Matter of Black Lives in American Literature

Welty's Nonfiction and Photography

—**Ebony Lumumba,** Tougaloo College

>There are famous and important writers whose work, one feels, would or could have been written by other people. Then there are those few whose work could only have been written by them. Miss Welty's work is in the latter category—it has her special clarity, her special beauty, her very special brilliance. The literature of this country is graced by her participation in it. She has certainly been a genuine education for me.
>—Toni Morrison[1]

From grassroots protestors to political pundits, the value of black life in America rests on the minds of many. Though popular, this conversation is not new. As an instructor at a historically black college, I am always considering how literature reflects or rejects black life as valuable. Thus, teaching American literature fills me with a certain anxiety. I often struggle with how to reasonably revise the canon and focus on stories of communities with which my students might more readily identify.

In my experience, the early American literary canon primarily focuses on texts and authors who represent a singular background and experience. Thus, students are inundated with readings that represent the ideal American as white, landowning, formally educated, and male. I find that the country's infamous history of the disenfranchisement of people of color and women lacks proper representation within the canon. As a result, many of my students struggle to connect with the texts traditionally included in such a course. Thus, I intentionally concentrate on an honest curriculum that allows students to read themselves and their ancestors beyond the marginalia of the texts and the larger society.

In order to foster a space where students feel connected to literature that is meant to represent their native land, I integrate traditionally canonical works as well as those written by women and writers of color. This is where Eudora Welty comes in. Welty may not stand out as the optimal choice in this pursuit. However, her work allows students to rethink the ways communities are represented by those writing from alternate cultural spaces—a worthwhile perspective in analyzing the narratives of any place.

Using Welty (in my rather ambitious aspiration) to de-canonize the American literary canon in the minds of my students relies on a mode of irony similar to Welty's use of the trope in many of her works. On the surface, it makes no sense to depend upon a white female writer to examine equitable inclusion of black life in American literature. However, Welty's unconventional approach (at times) to acknowledging black communities challenges my students to think beyond general representations of any community, especially their own. Literary scholars (many included in this collection) keenly address Welty's inclusion of black characters and culture in her fiction, nonfiction, and photography.[2]

In *Eudora Welty and Politics: Did the Writer Crusade?* Harriet Pollack and Suzanne Marrs acknowledge Welty's use of irony as a means of making covert commentary on racial injustice in the era and areas she inhabited. They assert that Welty applied irony "to bring into focus perspectives that should not go unseen, to expose myths and misconceptions, smugness and self-deception" (Pollack 224). This is exactly how I want my students to approach the canon of American literature—with a critical, "very searching" eye—a phrase Morrison used to describe Welty herself.[3]

Welty's acute ability to reflect alternate communities and her demonstration of female ingenuity separates her from many of her writing predecessors and contemporaries. To me, this is most present in her nonfiction and photography. My purpose for incorporating Welty in the study of American literature is to increase my students' connection with a canon that does not consider them as much as they are obligated to consider it. Ultimately, I hope to guide them in finding glimpses of themselves in "the literature of this country."[4]

In the very first weeks of class discussion, I encourage students to question why particular works might have become canonized and what function those narratives serve in understanding American culture. Our discussions are enhanced by referencing their course portfolios, which are composed of several short response papers (250 or more words) on each assigned text.

Their responses help them keep track of the connections between the various texts we engage in the course. In them, they must include two brief biographical facts about the author of each assigned reading (not shared in lecture) and respond to the following questions:

1. What is the community of focus in this work? Is there more than one? Support your answer with textual evidence.
2. How does this text correspond with the writing movement under which it falls? Be specific.
3. Does this text relate to that of a previously discussed author? If so, name the author and discuss the connection as you see it.

Last, students are asked to connect an aspect of the text to one of our three course sub-themes (freedom, revolution, nation-building). Once we've gotten to Welty, this exercise is complicated as students are asked to engage the photography as text.

These discussions and responses push students to reject surface readings of works they have likely encountered in their high school American literature courses. They no longer have to trust William Bradford's account of Plymouth Plantation or accept Emerson's ideas on the makeup of the American scholar. They are free to interrogate every author and his or her work.

My own interest in Welty's treatment of a different cultural community began with my introduction to her fiction with stories such as "A Worn Path" and expanded as I was introduced to her photography and nonfiction.[5] Thus, I find it useful to begin with Welty's "A Worn Path." Students are initially resistant to the author's descriptions of Phoenix Jackson and critique the characterization as reductive and racist. They often immediately compare Welty's lack of consideration for Jackson's humanity (as they see it) to the treatment of other marginalized communities from texts we've read earlier in the course. To them, she has further relegated blacks and women to the margins.

I find it beneficial to introduce Welty's photography at this moment in our discussion. In an era when students demand visual narratives (e.g., Twit pics, Instagram posts, Snap Chat, picture messaging, memes), it makes sense to introduce them to this aspect of Welty's creativity. Her photographs not only capture people living entirely disparate experiences from the writer and her community, they also illustrate her complex interaction with black communities. This is useful in complicating our study of the American literary canon.

Upon viewing images such as the bootlegger woman, the women dressed as birds in front of Farish Street Baptist Church, middle-aged midwife Ida M'Toy, the holiness church mothers, and other black subjects captured by Welty, students typically develop the particular stance of believing Welty to have been an unwelcomed voyeur to these communities.[6] This is when I introduce Welty's own words about what she saw as she photographed these people and their experiences.

Welty describes the elderly black woman in the heavy overcoat displayed in *One Time, One Place* as having a "heroic face ... full of meaning more truthful and more terrible and, I think, more noble than any generalization about people could have prepared me for or could describe for me now" (7). This comment (among others) helps to ground the class's perspective on Welty's opinion of her black photography subjects. The intersection of gender and race in Welty's photography and written work reveals her acknowledgment of marginal communities as worthy of focus and further complicates our class discussions.

Next, we look to the nonfiction narratives that seemingly accompany some of her images (e.g., the pageant birds, Ida M'Toy, etc.) and search for details of Welty's experience with the communities they depict. As we discuss and reference the responses students have written, it often becomes obvious that black life mattered to Welty. Yet, the question still remains—why? Some students, as perhaps I had initially, maintain their skepticism about Welty's intentions in capturing and narrating the experiences of the black people in the photos. Although they have read the foreword of *One Time, One Place*, where Welty shares sentiments such as, "And had I no shame as a white person for what message might lie in my pictures of black persons? No, I was too busy imagining myself into their lives to be open to any generalities," I typically have to push their analysis further by introducing more of the writer's nonfiction (5).

Being located in Welty's hometown of Jackson, Mississippi, provides us the luxury of being able to visit some of the places Welty photographed like Farish Street Baptist Church. During this visit, I ask students to consider how Welty (considering her race, class, and social position in the 1940s) might have been received in this community. They also reflect on whether someone like Welty might be welcomed or feel comfortable in this community today. Upon reading "A Pageant of Birds," students conduct a similar analysis to that of every other work we've engaged in the course. In general, this leads to their concluding that Maude Thompson occupies a considerable position in the action of the narrative. We then go back to "A Worn Path," and the class is encouraged to compare the way the real Maude Thompson was written to that of the fictional Phoenix Jackson. This exercise usually leads them to rethink their initial critique of the latter character and Welty.

Studied alongside Welty's photography, narratives such as "Ida M'Toy" (1942), "Pageant of Birds" (1943), and "Cindy and the Joyful Noise" (2014) reveal the author's point of view and the uniqueness of the lives of people consigned to the margins of social consideration.[7] Each of these texts focuses on real African American women Welty encountered. Ida M'Toy, Maude Thompson, the women in the bird pageant, and Cindy and her religious troupe would have likely never made it into the pages of the American literary canon had Welty not captured and written about their "special beauty."

Teaching Welty assists me in creating an environment of inclusion and thoughtful learning while focusing the course on how and why images of certain populations (e.g., African Americans, women) are generated in American literature. Welty's photography and nonfiction centered on the black lives she encountered achieve something quite different from some of the black characters in her fiction. Studied alongside her short stories and novels as well as those of other American literary icons, her photographs and nonfiction allow students to come to a more profound consideration of America's cultural fabric.

The use of these elements of Welty's canon creates an anthropologic experience for my students wherein they not only become familiar with American literary tradition, but the cultural implications of the field as well. They are not simply exposed to the stories of Welty's imagination; they are introduced to the impetus for some of those fictional characters—the real life black lives of Maude Thompson, Ida M'Toy, and others. This holistic approach to examining American authorship strengthens students' ability to analyze the canon and embed their unique perspectives into that analysis. I hope that Welty's "special clarity" in narrating the lives of these black women and their communities provides my students with a deeper understanding of their own worlds. Sure, it is ambitious, but so is the matter of equitably focusing American literature on a discussion and appreciation of black life.

Notes

1. Taken from Toni Morrison's introduction of Welty at the 1980 American Book Awards. Toni Morrison introduced Welty, who was unable to attend.

2. *Eudora Welty, Whiteness, and Race* (ed. Harriet Pollack, 2013) comprises twelve essays that vigorously examine and interrogate Welty's consideration of the black community in her work as well as her ideas regarding racial injustice. Susan V. Donaldson's assertion that Welty's work bears a likeness to Richard Wright's in the way it satirizes social unrest

pertaining to race, Rebecca Mark's position that "The Demonstrators" embodies political agency on the part of the black citizens of Holden, and Suzanne Marrs's concept of Welty employing racial slurs in her casual correspondence with intentional irony are joined by the works of Claxton, Eichelberger, Ford, Griffith, McMahand, McWhirter, Pollack, Watson, and Yaeger.

    3. In the Welty Collection housed at the Mississippi Department of Archives and History, there is a handwritten note from Toni Morrison to Welty. This note accompanied a copy of Morrison's introduction of the writer when she presented the 1980 National Medal of Literature to her in absentia. Morrison's note reads, "Change of pronouns. I thought I'd be on stage talking to you, looking into those very benevolent, very amused, and *very searching* (oh very searching) eyes of yours. love, Toni."

    4. Taken from Toni Morrison's introduction of Welty at the 1980 American Book Awards.

    5. As the 2013 Eudora Welty Research Fellow, I had the opportunity to peruse the entire Welty Collection housed at the Mississippi Department of Archives and History (MDAH). This research led to my presentation at MDAH and a subsequent article in the *Eudora Welty Review* titled, "'Caught in the Act of Living': Welty as a Voyeur and Witness of Black Life."

    6. These images are available in the Welty Collection at the Mississippi Department of Archives and History. Published collections of Welty's photography such as *One Time, One Place* (1971) and *Eudora Welty: Photographs* (1993) also exist as useful resources for examining Welty's visual art. The critical commentary that accompanies images such as "Colored Entrance," "Washwoman," "Making a Date," and "Dolls" published in *Eudora Welty and Politics* (2001) also proves beneficial to providing students with a means of initiating their critical engagement of the photographs and Welty.

    7. "Ida M'Toy," originally printed in *Accent* in 1942, is reprinted in *The Eye of the Story*. "Pageant of Birds," originally printed in the *New Republic* in 1943, is reprinted in *Eye* and in *Stories, Essays, and Memoir*. "Cindy and the Joyful Noise" was unpublished throughout Welty's life; it is now available in the *Eudora Welty Review*.

Works Cited

Lumumba, Ebony. "'Caught in the Act of Living': Welty as a Voyeur and Witness of Black Life." *Eudora Welty Review* 6 (2014): 193–208.
Morrison, Toni. Letter from Toni Morrison. 1980. Eudora Welty Collection. Mississippi Department of Archives and History. Jackson, MS.
Pollack, Harriet, ed. *Eudora Welty, Whiteness, and Race*. Athens: U of Georgia P, 2013.
Pollack, Harriet, and Suzanne Marrs, eds. *Eudora Welty and Politics: Did the Writer Crusade?* Baton Rouge: Louisiana State UP, 2001.
Welty, Eudora. "Cindy and the Joyful Noise." *Eudora Welty Review* 5 (2013): 19–26.
———. *The Eye of the Story: Selected Essays and Reviews*. New York: Random House, 1978.
———. *One Time, One Place*. New York: Random House, 1971.
———. *Stories, Essays, and Memoir*. Ed. Richard Ford and Michael Kreyling. New York: Library of America, 1998.

"Powerhouse" and the Challenge of African American Representation

Teaching Eudora Welty and Race in an American Literature Survey

—**Jacob Agner,** University of Mississippi

American literature surveys tend to clump Eudora Welty with the crowded school of southern gothic writers, which can cause a more singular understanding of her significance to fall by the wayside. For that reason, I teach Welty in my survey with regard to her exceptional attention to America's vexed legacies of racial representation. I use her 1941 short story, "Powerhouse," about a black musician performing for an all-white audience in Mississippi, as a text that self-consciously investigates ways in which racial identity has been constructed in American literature and addresses the complicated politics behind crossing the color line in fiction. Welty's sensitive rendering of Powerhouse serves as a key pivot in my survey, which on the one hand invites a recap of previous works' strategies of racial representation and signals on the other the survey's turn toward late-twentieth-century trends in multiculturalism and postmodernism. Teaching Welty's story about a black performer, in short, is an effective way of teaching the performativity of race as a social construct.

The way I teach race as a social construct is through the basic concept of literary representation. My lesson on "Powerhouse" starts out as an intervention of sorts, in which I state that reading about race (or class or gender) implies that such categories are not just biographical markers for characters and authors. Race can in fact be created anew by words on the page—only through a different kind of black and white. This is the challenge of representation, I explain, the re-presenting of reality through language. After this point, I heighten this challenge by discussing political concerns in the field of representation over who has the right to write about certain characters and situations. How far, and under what risks, can writers explore a perspective fundamentally different from theirs?

Eudora Welty is an interesting case study in this regard. A middle-class white southern woman from segregated Mississippi, Welty has been appreciated by African American author Toni Morrison for writing "about black people in a way that few white men have ever been able to write" (47). Morrison's claim leads me to two suppositions: (1) something behind Welty's strategies of racial representation has been deemed noteworthy by a writer of color, and (2) whatever Welty did as a white writer differentiates her from most white male writers. These two points, broad as they may be, work especially well within the framework of the survey, whose overview of canonical writers, many of them the "white men" Morrison evokes, invites the class to think comprehensively across the works.

Before I make these comparisons, however, I ask about "Powerhouse": what, in the story's language, does Powerhouse look like? Students will smile and say he is a large African American man, and this is a good moment to bring up images of Fats Waller and a clip or two from the 1943 musical, *Stormy Weather*, which features him playing, and explain how "Powerhouse" was inspired by Welty's seeing Waller live in Mississippi. But then I ask them a harder question: how else does the story, for the lack of a better term, describe Powerhouse's *blackness*? This is where the smiles falter. The opening paragraph of Welty's story has plenty of language about Powerhouse's physical appearance, but a lot of that language is compromised by incredibly troubling rhetoric: "You can't tell what he is," I recite, "'Nigger man'?—he looks more Asiatic, monkey, Jewish, Babylonian, Peruvian, fanatic, devil" (*Stories* 158). What is Welty's strategy in starting with a series of racial stereotypes? Why would she start there? I suggest here that Welty is exposing a problem in American literature in point of view and audience, which the rest of my lesson will contextualize.

From there I recall several stories by white male writers in the survey, such as Joel Chandler Harris's "The Wonderful Tar-Baby Story," Mark Twain's *Adventures of Huckleberry Finn*, and William Faulkner's "That Evening Sun" and reopen these works to an ongoing critical controversy. Despite the reputations these writers hold, their works have turned into sparring grounds for debate about their representations of characters of color.[1] Flipping through passages of Harris's phonetic dialect for Uncle Remus, Twain's liberal use of the descriptor "nigger" through Huck's voice, and Faulkner's use of Nancy's rape and incarceration for Quentin Compson's racial knowledge, I complicate such stories by considering whether their black characters are largely constituted by a literary tradition created by and for white America. These characters are reminders that, for centuries, open access to literary expression for African Americans was challenged by a dominant white culture that instituted forms of racial representation not necessarily representative of black people. To reinforce this point, I pull up slides with images of "tar babies," Little Black Sambo, Uncle Remus, Al Jolson in *The Jazz Singer*, and Hattie McDaniel's Mammy from *Gone with the Wind* and provide definitions of blackface minstrelsy and the plantation myth.[2] My purpose here is to show how the history of black representation has been laid with a minefield of *mis*representations, and many of America's canonical writers, either inadvertently or not, may be seen in line with this damaging tradition.

With this in mind, I return to descriptions of Powerhouse such as his "African feet of the greatest size" (158) and ask whether he figures into this tradition (158). One bright student, however, will call attention to the line, "This is a white dance" (158). I suggest this one line by Welty makes apparent something crucial in "Powerhouse" that the other works have taken for granted. The scene showcased in "Powerhouse"—a white audience observing a black performer—encapsulates an unaddressed point of view that has shaped a lot of American literature's racial representations. America's black characters may only be projections of what white American audiences want: "Is it possible that he could be this!" the audience exclaims in Welty's story, "When you have him there performing for you" (158). This makes us wonder how much of Powerhouse's show is tailored for this audience. When the opening narrator observes, "You know people on a stage—and people of a darker race" (158), Welty makes the connection that race is as much of a performance in the story as its song and dance numbers.

Now that the lesson has worked to position Welty against a white literary tradition of stereotyped black characters, I then ask if there are aspects of Powerhouse's performance that are not constructed for white pleasure. To assist this point, I place Welty in the survey near a lesson on the Harlem Renaissance, which teaches how 1920s and 1930s Harlem stoked an unprecedented explosion of African American creativity that made room for new forms of black expression in modern art.[3] I like to frame "Powerhouse" here as one of the first stories we read that was written in a "post–Harlem Renaissance" America, and I show that Welty was closer to this movement than most realize. Five years after Alain Locke's 1925 articulation of a "spiritual Coming of Age" for African Americans, Welty, too, was undergoing part of her own coming of age in New York City while attending business school. Though a white southerner, she witnessed firsthand Harlem's jazz and vaudeville shows in their zeitgeist.

I now offer a comparison to another literary tradition—twentieth-century African American literature. While the audience and location is different, the object of interest in "Powerhouse" is similar to poems like Claude McKay's "The Harlem Dancer" and Sterling Brown's "Ma Rainey," in which speakers are transfixed by powerful black performers who signify a range of complex emotions. Like McKay's dancer who suggests behind her "falsely smiling face" a "self [that] was not in that strange place" (13–14), Powerhouse also shows hints of disillusionment and frustration: "White dance, week night," Powerhouse lists at one point, "raining, Alligator, Mississippi, long ways from home" (164). And when Powerhouse quips to his band mates, "That ain't Lenox Avenue" (161), he refers to one of Harlem's famous streets, which Langston Hughes famously used as the setting for his benchmark poem, "The Weary Blues." Though the white audience says, "Powerhouse is not a show-off like the Harlem boys, not drunk, not crazy," he *is* one of those boys, bringing elements of the Harlem Renaissance in a reverse migration to Mississippi (158).

Another intriguing example of Welty's knowledge of black culture involves Powerhouse's tale about Uranus Knockwood, the character he says has been preying upon his wife while he's away from home.[4] I teach this story as a "toast" from the African American oral tradition. Toasts are lively and boasting forms of improvised storytelling that involve tales about conquering an adversary. Laced with profanity and sexual innuendo, toasts depict a different kind of black masculinity from white stereotypes—urban and edgy, ribald and violent.[5] "You know what happened to me," Powerhouse tells the crowd, "I got a telegram my wife is dead" (161). Blunt and apprehensive, Powerhouse can sound far different from jovial Uncle Remus. "What the hell was she trying to do?" he curses aloud (161). The detailed toast demonstrates how Welty as a white writer makes a significant effort in her fiction to accurately depict a black oral tradition that her white characters may have never even heard before: "Uranus Knockwood is the name signed," Powerhouse teases, "Ever heard of him?" (161).[6]

In this doubled way of reading Powerhouse, Welty suggests that traditions of representation and racial performance are culturally relative. Powerhouse can be one thing for one audience, something else for another. We especially learn this when Powerhouse announces halfway through the story, "It going to be intermission" and walks off stage (162). This intermission scene, I pause and emphasize, is the heart of Welty's project. Through the slightest point of view change, Welty does something extraordinary during the intermission. She leaves the white audience altogether in the dance hall and follows Powerhouse to the World Café, wherein we find segregated black community, the "hundred dark, ragged, silent, delighted Negroes" about to enjoy another version of the showman (163). Powerhouse performs the toast again, now for a black audience and receives a noticeably warmer reaction. Here I explain the magic trick Welty has pulled off: she has left the white point of view of her story and imagined a space just for black pleasure and interaction. I also emphasize the significance of this point-of-view change in our survey by asking the class to imagine how jarring a chapter like this would have been in *Huckleberry Finn* if Twain wrote it from Jim's perspective. Powerhouse's visit to the World Café, coupled with the emergence of the Harlem Renaissance, suggests no less than a changing worldview developing in the survey. The implied unilateral organization of American literature around a white point of view no longer encompasses the growing ethnographic multiplicities of American art forms and artists.

Thus once Powerhouse returns to the white audience for the story's finale, in which he sings, "Somebody loves me! Somebody loves me! I wonder who!" (170), there is a debate at hand. By the end of the lesson, I have shown the class two different Powerhouses, one a part of the literary tradition meant for white consumption, and the other a part of a new and avant-garde black coterie. I ask, then, who *does* love Powerhouse by the end? What legacy does he belong to? Is he a Harlem Renaissance modernist or an antiquated sellout? By the same token, does Welty as a white writer overcome the challenge of accurately constructing a convincing African American character without succumbing to racial stereotype? Answers to these can go either way in the lesson's last minutes, but the two overarching points I try to drive home here are that race is more of an externally constructed performance than a stable source of identity, and much of the literature in the rest of the survey will follow Powerhouse's and Welty's lead.

Notes

1. Current Norton editions include excerpts on the debate around race in *Adventures of Huckleberry Finn*, but additional online articles regarding the ways white writers have continued to stir controversies around racial representation can also be found in Coates, Kakutani, and Colby.

2. For online information on blackface minstrelsy and the plantation myth, see Huse and Sanders; and for a more benchmark reading on the complex relationship between white desire, black representation, and the minstrel show, see Lott.

3. For a short and helpful summary of the Harlem Renaissance and its relationship to European and American modernism, see Levenson, 259–66.

4. For an alternate discussion of Powerhouse's connections with the trickster figure from African American folklore called the "signifying monkey," see Bearden.

5. I also like to play to the class segments of Ruby Ray Moore's vulgar toast about Jody the Grinder, who, like Knockwood, is an infamous character known for sleeping with black men's wives.

6. For a fuller discussion on the ways in which Welty constructs black characters that seem to be audience-aware and separate from the stories they are a part of, see Pollack and McWhirter.

Works Cited

Bearden, Kenneth. "Monkeying Around: Welty's 'Powerhouse,' Blues-Jazz, and the Signifying Connection." *Southern Literary Journal* 31.2 (Spring 1999): 65–79.

Coates, Ta-Nehisi Paul. "Why 'Tar Baby' Is Such a Sticky Phrase." *Time*. Time Inc., August 1, 2006. Web. August 3, 2016.

Colby, Tanner. "Can a White Author Write Black Characters?" *Slate*. The Slate Group, September 19, 2012. Web. August 3, 2016.

Huse, Andy, and Simone Sanders. "Blackface." *History of Minstrelsy: From "Jump Jim Crow" to "The Jazz Singer."* University of South Florida Special & Digital Collections. 2012. Web. August 3, 2016.

———. "Plantation Nostalgia." *History of Minstrelsy: From "Jump Jim Crow" to "The Jazz Singer."* University of South Florida Special & Digital Collections. 2012. Web. August 3, 2016.

Kakutani, Michiko. "Light Out, Huck, They Still Want to Sivilize You." *New York Times*. The New York Times Company, January 6, 2011. Web. August 3, 2016.

Levenson, Michael. *Modernism*. New Haven, CT: Yale UP, 2011.

Locke, Alain. "Enter the New Negro." *Survey Graphic* 6.6 (March 1925): 631–34.

Lott, Eric. *Love and Theft: Blackface Minstrelsy and the American Working Class*. 20th Anniversary Edition. Oxford: Oxford UP, 2013.

McKay, Claude. "The Harlem Dancer." *The Norton Anthology of American Literature*. Gen. ed. Nina Baym. 8th ed. Vol. D. New York: Norton, 2011. 482.

McWhirter, David. "Secret Agents: Welty's African Americans." *Eudora Welty, Whiteness, and Race*. Ed. Harriet Pollack. Athens: U of Georgia P, 2013. 114–30.

Morrison, Toni. "Talk with Toni Morrison." Interview with Mel Watkins. *Conversations with Toni Morrison*. Ed. Danille Taylor-Guthrie. Jackson: UP of Mississippi, 1994. 43–47.

Pollack, Harriet. "Reading Welty on Whiteness and Race." *Eudora Welty, Whiteness, and Race*. Ed. Harriet Pollack. Athens: U of Georgia P, 2013. 1–22.

———. "Words between Strangers: On Welty, Her Style, and Her Audience." *Mississippi Quarterly* 39.3 (1986): 481–505.

Railton, Stephen. "Blackface Minstrelsy." *Mark Twain in His Times*. University of Virginia Library, n.d. Web. July 25, 2016.

Saloy, Mona Lisa. "The African American Toast Tradition." *Folklife in Louisiana: Louisiana's Living Traditions*. Louisiana Division of the Arts, n.d. Web. July 25, 2016.

Welty, Eudora. *The Eye of the Story: Selected Essays and Reviews*. New York: Vintage, 1979.

———. *Stories, Essays, and Memoir*. Ed. Richard Ford and Michael Kreyling. New York: Library of America, 1998.

"We Must Have Your History, You Know"

*African/Soul Survivals, Swallowed Lye,
and the Medicine-Journey of "A Worn Path"*

—**Keith Cartwright,** University of North Florida

Students know, consciously or intuitively, that they have swallowed a lot of "lye" in their schooling. Many of the most gifted among them—with healthy gag reflexes—dropped out of school and shape some of the conspicuous absences in our classrooms. We work with the diplomaed survivors: students on a path to success that they want to believe in and that they, more than ever, simultaneously question. Historicization offers one path to the treatment of popularly swallowed lies.[1] Myth, almost homeopathically, offers another. And it is from the intersections of history, myth, and ritual that I guide students on the medicine-journey of what may be Welty's most widely read story: "A Worn Path." Aspects of this path are familiar to older generations of readers who followed Odysseus into the underworld, the magi along the path of their star, Dante into his dark wood, Chaucer's pilgrims on the road to Canterbury, T. S. Eliot's speaker entering the waste land. Welty's medicine-journey does not necessarily depart from this path in the way it initiates readers into the deep time and space of a planet touched by counterculturally charged soul-animations out of Mississippi.

While there is indeed something universal about the journey of the phoenix in its morphing regenerations, there is also something historically specific about following a Jackson (Phoenix) through a space cleared violently by that frontier president whose face appears on the twenty-dollar bill. Written from Jackson, Mississippi, "A Worn Path" winds through raw spaces touched by plantation capitalism (see Beckert's *Empire of Cotton* and my own "Jackson's

Villes"). Readers follow its avatar, Phoenix Jackson, to initiate renewed respect for old apprehensions of the world and to fetch medicine to unblock our throats from the lies we've swallowed. I teach this approach to "A Worn Path" by reading the story in tandem with initiatory tales and rituals of the black Atlantic world. I guide students into a realm of what J. R. R. Tolkien called "fairy." The realm of fairy tale and fantastic escape in Welty's Mississippi converged with very real African spirits—of orisha, djinn, and marooning—and was convergent too with a realm of Choctaw (and older Mississippian) medicine, along deeply layered paths.

My students tend to like Tolkien's quest world of virtual reality through which they may follow various avatars. I encourage them to make rather similar journeys along the paths traveled by Africans and their descendants. They often balk at these paths into Afro-creole virtual realities (really, who wouldn't in the face of slave ships?), or they want to reduce everything they encounter to a message of well-rehearsed racial traumas and the enshrined struggle to overcome them—a path so worn they/we can hardly read it. I encourage them to follow Phoenix Jackson with the same empathy and openness they give to Tolkien or *Star Wars* as I send them from the reading experience of "A Worn Path" into the virtual muck of Zora Neale Hurston's *Their Eyes Were Watching God*, the satiric initiatory bush of Lydia Cabrera's *Afro-Cuban Tales*, the narrative sea changes of Paule Marshall's *Praisesong for the Widow*, or the textual medicine rites of Leslie Marmon Silko's *Ceremony*.

In teaching students to enter new kinds of readerly congregations, I am not primarily invested in teaching certain African "survivals" in the post-plantation world and then using traces of such "survivals" to argue for a mode of reading that links Welty to the syncretic shaping of a larger black Atlantic world. Yes, readers can learn to see things this way. But there are bigger fish to fry, and Welty offers pathways for opening our eyes more fully to becoming the *hippikats* (open-eyed folk) our Wolof-speaking Senegalese guides have called us to be. We can read like true hippies (or hipcats, hipsters, hip-hoppers), not by teaching a set of "survivals" but by attending to the practice of body-and-soul survival in a world intent upon zombification of disposable lives. The conclusion of my book *Sacral Grooves, Limbo Gateways* (2013) makes this case in its response to "A Worn Path," but what I have to say here is more attentive to the story's everyday use in our classrooms and to how we may guide students on the journey.

I open discussion of "A Worn Path" via a folktale of an orphan girl's initiation into womanhood that serves as a launching point of my courses in American, southern, African American, Caribbean, or Africana literatures.[2] It is a widespread Afro-diasporic tale of two girls sent into the wilderness to wash a dirty or blood-stained container. The first girl, the orphan, is not supposed to survive the ordeal, but she greets the bush-wonders she encounters with an incredible traveler's savvy, accepts the mentorship of a disfigured (one-armed, one-legged) wilderness crone, and receives her transformational gift of three eggs, bursting them one by one on the return home—with each egg revealing new riches. The second girl, the spoiled daughter of a second wife, is then sent into the wilderness to get her own gifts, displays a closed-minded narcissism in the bush, and refuses mentorship. She does not listen well to the instructions for bursting the eggs she receives, and unlooses a series of curses and torments that—in many tellings—kill her. This tale of entry into a terrifying and wondrous realm of the sublime, of two girls whose quest to wash bloody calabashes (first menses) sends them to receive their eggs from an initiating crone, traveled widely via the Atlantic slave trade. We may find many examples from which to launch our bush-journeys: beginning with a Senegalese (Wolof) tale and including versions from Louisiana to the Bahamas, St. Kitts, South Carolina, Grenada, St. Vincent, Dominica, Guadeloupe, Mexico, Haiti, and Florida. My *Sacral Grooves, Limbo Gateways* (2013) offers detailed readings of the tale and its variants (13–27). Among the best known examples is a prize-winning children's book, *The Talking Eggs* (Sans Souci and Pinkney,1989), based on a version of the narrative presented by past MLA president Alcée Fortier in Louisiana Creole (1895). A related tale from South Carolina shows us something of the stakes of engaging this realm in the classroom. In the South Carolina tale, an orphan girl sings a password song by the waterside, and a water-genie surfaces, feeding and caring for the girl on each visit until the stepfather follows along to kill the spirit with a single shotgun blast. That this particular tale was recorded by a student in a classroom on St. Helena Island (circa 1922) suggests the damage done by mainstream education to the matrices of survival tapped by Afro-creole mentors. My students get this. They know the vulnerabilities of the spirit to being "shot down" by an authority figure. We may spend only one day discussing "A Worn Path." But we spend days discussing the tales that build an interpretive context for our readings, and all of our readings take on a certain cumulative looping across the duration of the semester.

    Familiarity with the orphan initiation tale can raise the stakes of our readings of "A Worn Path." We can begin to understand that Phoenix Jackson is on a medicine-journey to foster the phoenix-egg of survival across generations. She encounters a number of challenges on her quest, greets them all, and pockets gifts (coins described in egg-language) as she fetches the healing medicine for a grandchild who has swallowed lye. Phoenix, born into slavery and "too old at the Surrender" (*Stories* 178) to have attended school (where the initiatory bush-spirit gets shotgun-blasted), carries an unsurrendered

Afro-diasporic authority and is thus able to initiate her grandson (and readers, including the fledgling author herself), thus restoring voice to spiritual children whose throats have been blocked by the curricular lies of white supremacy. We may begin to see that this is a story of soul-survival itself in a world where the spirit and any holistic claim to knowledge or humanity has been imperiled. The grandson of the story, the phoenix's reproductive egg, is—like Phoenix herself—not dead yet. And "A Worn Path" is both the quest and the medicine that let Welty herself lay claim to authorial voice in the final story of her first published collection.

A number of Afro-creole religious structures enable us to historicize this approach to Phoenix Jackson's journey. The foundations of Afro-Baptist faith in the United States go back to early praise house societies along the southeast coast, especially the Gullah/Geechee Sea Islands of South Carolina and Georgia. Members were initiated into praise house societies by undergoing a period of spiritual "travels" in a process also known as seeking. Undertaken under the mentorship of a spiritual parent, the "travel" called for transformational visions, dream interpretation, and the construction of a travel narrative to be essayed to the congregation for approval. In dialogue with the orphan folktales, I share with my students something of the process of Afro-Baptist travels as I describe them in *Sacral Grooves* (17–21, 39–41), and I have them read travel narratives of Gullah seekers collected in Lorenzo Dow Turner's *Africanisms in the Gullah Dialect* (1949), including Rosina Cohen's journey on behalf of a baby:

> If you seek religion, you compel to see that baby. And what is that baby? Your soul, your soul is the baby, you understand. And you got to go to him and ask, "Lord, I ain't see my baby this month." And you beg him and beg him; and at last when he give [it to] you, you wash it off nice and clean. Oh Lord! I so glad to have a baby. Oh, I run around, carry it to my leader; tell him.
>
> He say: "That's your soul; that's your soul. The baby is your soul. Don't let nobody fool you; the baby is your soul." (275)

This narrative helps us see that Phoenix travels on behalf of her own soul. As long as she continues, the soul lives and finds voice. We discuss the importance of ring shouts and sacred music in pulling minds, bodies, and souls together in spaces of white supremacy. And we listen to the coastal Georgia's McIntosh County Shouters, as well as to a performance of "That Old Time Religion" by Julia Dawson on the "Florida Memory" collection, to prepare students to consider Phoenix's scarecrow dance, her confident strut and step in the face of ghosts.

After the travel and the shout, it is a third part of the Afro-Atlantic ritual complex—the saraka (or saracca) rite—that most energizes my teaching of "A Worn Path." Across the black Atlantic world, communities and individuals receive the blessings of the ancestors by setting ritual "tables" for the children, the ancestors' freshest representatives on earth. Saraka is a sacrificial expenditure that bestows blessings to the degree that the role of service to coming generations is fostered and made real. I have participated in saraka ceremonies in Senegal and have read—in the WPA text, *Drums and Shadows*—about their continuation in post-slavery coastal Georgia among descendants of Senegambian Muslims. Made on key days of the Muslim calendar or as a thanksgiving to the ancestors for blessings received, sweetened "saraka" cakes (from Arabic *sadaqa*, to make sacrifice, give charity) have been distributed in rites of "feeding the children" throughout West Africa's diaspora along with other offerings of saraka/saracca in Georgia, Trinidad, Grenada, and Carriacou (see Cartwright 43–44, 63). Merle Collins's film *Saracca and Nation* (2008) offers a great resource for this ethos that Phoenix Jackson's journey embodies, and which we find in Mexico's Day of the Dead, the Gulf South's All Saints' rites, and even faintly in Halloween—when spirits masquerade from house to house for treats.

Like their teachers, students wonder how Welty may have received this saraka medicine and its Afro-Atlantic sense for sacrifice or charity. I show them that traces of it traveled from the Sea Islands to white Mississippi households, as we can see in Judith Sensibar's account of the Sea Island Creole formations that shaped William Faulkner through the woman he knew as "Mammy Callie": Caroline Barr (34–125). We can take the time to see that something of it percolated into Welty's consciousness via the black churches of Jackson (even in pageants of the birds), via the vibrant musical culture of the black South, and via the cultural vitality of New Orleans. Ultimately, my own teaching does not point to transmissions of individual African "survivals" across plantation spaces. The whole notion of African survivals carries with it the assumption that African consciousness was never intended to survive, never imagined by the master class to have value. For this reason, we do not speak of European "survivals," nor do we employ the terms "Eurosouthern" or "Euro-American" as we do "African American." These kinds of discussions bring us to the larger stakes of our reading and practice.

Wendy Belcher's notion of "discursive possession" provides one tool for understanding the agency of Africans and African practices within canonical "Western" texts. Using spirit possession as a "way of thinking about asymmetrical relationships between subjectivities," Belcher shows how African discourse might "animate" a white author's text: "In this folk paradigm, spiritual possession is a loss of control that results in an openness to difference, a penetrability." If Welty saw her imaginative task to be "to try to enter into the mind, heart, and skin of a human being who is not myself" (829), why should readers be surprised that entry and agency might cut both ways across color and gender lines in her texts or that her own mind, heart, and skin might be entered by others? Imagination's survival calls for an ability to move across borders between self and other. The cultural repertoire of African descendants nurtured this ability—as a matter of daily survival—better than did the blockages (never total) of white supremacy. Facing the task of empathic understanding, Welty understood that "the primary challenge lies in making the jump itself" (829). Everything we do in the classroom focuses on this primary challenge: making the jump, or even fostering ways in which the flows of our own consciousness may be jumped in productive, medicinal readings.

With the reorientation that "A Worn Path" provides, students and teachers can make the journey with Phoenix Jackson as she ponders becoming Osain—the one-armed and one-legged initiatory spirit of the Yoruba/Afro-Atlantic bush, maimed from having guided so many initiatory journeys, and often identified with birds (see Thompson 42–51). We move past "dead trees, like black men with one arm ... standing in the purple stalks of the withered cotton field" (173) and pass with Phoenix through the barbed wire blocking our path, a bit uneasy about not having the money to "pay for having her arm or leg sawed off if she got caught fast where she was" (173). What we see is that nothing will stop this movement to fetch the medicine, that getting caught fast where we are is not an option. We dance with the scarecrow ghosts "in a little strutting way" (173), and our hands come to pocket the hunter's dropped nickel "with the grace and care they would have in lifting an egg from under a setting hen" (175). Our feet know where to take us as we travel to Natchez, ascend the building with its framed diplomas of accreditation, and face clinical authority as a "charity case" (177). But we (through Phoenix) are the ones bringing another authority—or another reading—to the clinic. When told to "Speak up" since "We must have your history, you know" (177), we begin to sense that the clinic, the school, the university, have all been incapable of "having" or understanding our holistic history. Phoenix indeed carries an unsurrendered knowledge on her mission to fetch medicine for a grandson whose "[t]hroat never heals" from having "[s]wallowed lye" (178). Her saraka-work tends to all of us who have swallowed the lies of history.

This story's steady presence in American Lit classrooms and anthologies likely animated other important medicine work that followed, as my syllabi often move to address. For example, Leslie Marmon Silko sent Tayo on a journey beyond the booze that "was medicine for the anger that made him hurt ...

medicine for ... choked-up throats" (37). Silko's *Ceremony* offers treatment: "as long as people believed the lies, they would never be able to see what had been done to them or what they were doing to each other" (177), and we see too that "If the white people never looked beyond the lie, then they would never be able to understand how they had been used by the witchery" (177). In "What You Pawn I Will Redeem," Sherman Alexie shows himself to be a spiritual and literary descendant of Welty and Silko as he features a grandson, Jackson Jackson, on his medicine-journey to redeem the pawned inheritance of the dead grandmother. He reverses Phoenix Jackson's medicine-journey and signifies upon the homelessness wrought (and writ large) by Andrew Jackson. Silko and Alexie show the signs of having followed Phoenix and Eudora—and having mastered the jump—before taking up their own literary medicine journeys. Teachers of Welty can help Eudora's new readers begin making the jump with Phoenix and allowing something of Phoenix's spirit to make the jump into us, as Welty surely did in letting her text serve as the spirit's host.

Notes

1. For a literal (and more historicized) response to the "swallowed lye" of this story, see Melissa Deakins Stang, "Parting the Curtain on Lye Poisoning in 'A Worn Path,'" *Eudora Welty Review* 1 (2009): 13–24.

2. I teach Welty's story in a wide array of course offerings: American literature surveys, courses on southern literature or hemispheric postplantation literatures, courses in Caribbean writing, and in a senior seminar titled "Myth, Fable, and Fantasy." In most classes we discuss "A Worn Path" in a single day. But we do so after having already spent days of discussion on the folktales and other materials that I use to contextualize the mythic and fabulous elements of this story. As with the folktales, we keep going back to Welty's story long after the one-day discussion of it. My practice in the classroom calls for recursiveness, intertextual loopings, and reading and rereading (via class discussion and writing) across the semester's duration.

Works Cited

Alexie, Sherman. *Ten Little Indians*. New York: Grove, 2004.
Beckert, Sven. *Empire of Cotton: A Global History*. New York: Knopf, 2014.
Belcher, Wendy Laura. "Discursive Possession." *Ideas of the Decade: The 2014–2015 Report on the State of the Discipline of Comparative Literature*. ACLA, December 11, 2014. Web. March 23, 2016.
Cartwright, Keith. "Jackson's Villes, Squares, and Frontiers of Democracy." *The Oxford Handbook of the Literature of the US South*. Ed. Barbara Ladd and Fred Hobson. New York: Oxford UP, 2016.

———. *Sacral Grooves, Limbo Gateways: Travels in Deep Southern Time, Circum-Caribbean Space, Afro-Creole Authority*. Athens: U of Georgia P, 2013.
Collins, Merle. *Saracca and Nation: African Memory and Re-creation in Grenada and Carriacou*. 2008. Video.
Dawson, Julia. "That Old Time Religion." Florida Memory. State Library and Archives of Florida, n.d. Web.
Drums and Shadows. Georgia Writers' Project. Work Projects Administration. 1940. http://www.sacred-texts.com/afr/das/
Fortier, Alcée. *Louisiana Folk-Tales in French Dialect and English Translation*. New York: American Folklore Society, 1895.
San Souci, Robert D., and Jerry Pinkney, illustrator. *The Talking Eggs*. New York: Dial, 1989.
Sensibar, Judith. *Faulkner and Love: The Women Who Shaped His Life*. New Haven, CT: Yale UP, 2009.
Silko, Leslie Marmon. *Ceremony*. New York: Penguin, 2006.
Thompson, Robert Farris. *Flash of the Spirit: African and Afro-American Art and Philosophy*. New York: Vintage, 1984.
Tolkien, J. R. R. *On Fairy Stories*. Ed. Verlyn Flieger and Douglas A. Anderson. New York: HarperCollins, 2014.
Turner, Lorenzo Dow. *Africanisms in the Gullah Dialect*. 1949. Columbia: USC P, 2002.
Welty, Eudora. *Stories, Essays, and Memoir*. Ed. Richard Ford and Michael Kreyling. New York: Library of America, 1998.

IV

"Learning to See": Bodies in Welty's Texts

The human face and the human body are eloquent in themselves, and stubborn and wayward, and a snapshot is a moment's glimpse (as a story may be a long look, a growing contemplation) into what never stops moving, never ceases to express for itself something of our common feeling. Every feeling waits upon its gesture. Then when it does come, how unpredictable it turns out to be, after all.
—**Preface to *One Time, One Place: Mississippi in the Depression***

Picturing Difference and Disability in Our Classrooms

—Keri Watson, University of Central Florida

Although best remembered for her stories, Eudora Welty also took candid, yet complex, photographs of Mississippi.[1] Many of these images were published in *One Time, One Place* (1971), *Photographs* (1989), and *Eudora Welty as Photographer* (2009), but Welty's photographs of the 1939 Mississippi State Fair have not garnered the attention they deserve. Moreover, few scholars have addressed ways to use Welty's photographs in the classroom. As I will show, Welty's fair photographs, several of which feature the large painted banners used to advertise the human attractions of the sideshow, present important insight into Welty's stories, many of which also include characters with physical and cognitive disabilities.[2] Welty's photographs, like her stories, do not just humorously document life in Mississippi, they also challenge the anxiety that surrounded disability during the Great Depression. This subversive quality makes them well suited for those interested in teaching diversity and demonstrating to students the ways in which ableism, like racism and sexism, is socially constructed.[3]

During the 1930s, people with disabilities faced segregation and oppression. Considered by the medical and political establishments as "unfit" for normal roles in society, disabled people were excluded from jobs provided by the New Deal's Works Progress Administration programs, which, according to the WPA's Worker Handbook, were reserved for "able-bodied" Americans "certified by a local agency." "Ugly laws," which made it illegal for people with visible disabilities to be seen in public, were passed across the country, many of which were not repealed until the 1970s (Longmore and Goldberger 894). Twenty-eight states adopted statutes that sought sterilization, marriage restriction, and institutionalization of the disabled, and eugenicists advocated euthanasia for disabled infants. People with disabilities were systematically incarcerated and subject to deportation under immigration law (Carey 52). Following the increased demand for segregated housing brought on by prejudicial medical diagnoses and public discrimination, states began building residential institutions at a rapid pace.

Visual and material culture of the 1930s reinforced discrimination against people with disabilities. Most notably, the photographs taken under the auspices of the Farm Security Administration ignored those with impairments, and popular films and literature perpetuated stereotypes by portraying people with disabilities as villains or victims. Lon Chaney starred in a series of films, such as *The Blackbird* (1926) and *Tell It to the Marines* (1926), where bodily difference signaled interior derangement, and writers, such as William Faulkner and John Steinbeck, used disabled characters, such as Benjy and Lennie, as ciphers for economic hardship. As literary historian Thomas Fahy argued, Depression-era writers made "the damaged body a metaphor for unbearable loss—a tangible sign for the eroding impact of unrelenting poverty, hunger, and unemployment" (15).

In contrast, the sideshow, although not without its issues, offered people with disabilities the opportunity to make a decent living and challenge stereotypes. As theorized by Rosemarie Garland-Thomson, Rachel Adams, and Robert Bogdan, the sideshow presented performers a stage on which to invert societal roles and confront viewers' assumptions about people with bodily or cognitive differences. At the same time, the sideshow, set up in a liminal space within the already transient state fair, was a place where visitors' fantasies of aggression and superiority could be safely played out and their sense of normality could be both constructed and reassured (Cohen 17). Recognizing its contradictory nature and subversive potential, Welty looked to the sideshow as a viable and compelling subject for her work. Humorous and engaging, her photographs of sideshow banners investigate human psychology and exaggerate the disparity between the real and imagined. As Welty said in *Photographs*, "My taking the freak *posters*—not the human beings—was because they were a whole school of naïve folk art. And, of course, totally unrelated to what you saw inside the tent. The posters show bystanders being suddenly horrified at a man who could twist himself like a snake. They are all looking with hands drawn back and shrieking, and *they* were all perfectly dressed, probably wearing evening clothes" (xix). Welty recognized that the gawkers were as much a part of the spectacle of the sideshow as the performance itself.

To demonstrate how the sideshow was a complicated and dynamic space of identity negotiation, show students Welty's photographs *Hypnotized* and

Hypnotist (figs. 1 and 2). When presenting the photographs, it is helpful to employ Visual Thinking Strategies (VTS), an inquiry-based learning pedagogy developed by Abigail Housen and Philip Yenawine. In VTS, students are asked to look carefully at works of art, talk about what they see, support their ideas with evidence, and listen to and consider the views of others. In order to lead the class through an analysis of the photographs, students are asked: "What's going on in these pictures? What do you see that makes you say that, and what more can you find?" As students offer their interpretations, point at the areas being discussed and paraphrase their comments in a neutral way. For instance, students may notice the painted banners in the background of *Hypnotized*. Under the lighted sign for India, a banner depicts a young, idealized Odar wearing a turban, cape, and harem pants conjuring a curvaceous flying goddess with a snake-charming pipe. Ask the students to describe what they see in the painted banners and on the stage. Point out the figures standing on the stage in *Hypnotist*. Students may notice that in this photograph Welty has revealed the real Odar as a bald middle-aged man and the female performer as a modern woman with a bobbed hairstyle and a belly dancer costume. Ask students if they can find other incongruities between the banners' advertisements and the performers on the stage. Perhaps they will notice the man dressed in the cap and gown of graduation. They may be interested to learn that the sideshow used this costume to both legitimate the performances and to satirize authority figures such as clergy, judges, and professors. Viewing the photographs next to one another helps students recognize the illusory and constructed nature of the sideshow and illustrates that gaffes are plain to see, if they know where to look.

Once they have established the sideshow as a performative space, pair Welty's photograph of a banner advertising the "Mule Face Woman" with her photograph of "Twisto the Rubberman" to explain the ways in which gender and race are conflated with disability (figs. 3 and 4).[4] Use these images to lead students through either VTS or a "think-pair-share" exercise during which they have ten minutes to quietly look at the photographs and write a compare-and-contrast essay. In "think-pair-share," students should then be given about five minutes to share their essays with another student. After this, the essays and photographs can be discussed as a class. Students might notice that the "Mule Face Woman" is depicted as an exotic mule/human hybrid reclining on a chaise lounge and that the signifiers of femaleness are inscribed on the body through the sheer, bias-cut dress, crystal jewelry, and alluring pose. If students have read Zora Neale Hurston, remind them that in *Mules and Men*, mules are used allegorically to symbolize labor, stubbornness, and mischief, whereas in *Their Eyes Were Watching God* Matt Boner's mule symbolized social status.

The human/animal hybrid of the banner can be read as embodying societal anxiety over miscegenation, which is further echoed in the mule, the result of horse/donkey interbreeding. The hybrid dislocates the identifying signs of species, gender, and race; it forces the viewer to interrogate the space between human and animal, male and female, and black and white, as well as the societal prohibitions that consistently reinforce differences and separations. Ask the students to think about how gender is represented differently in the two banners. The "Mule Face Woman" lacks a human head, reason, and mobility, but "Twisto" yields superhuman power over his contorted body. Twisto has broad shoulders, a svelte physique, and a fully articulated head complete with curly hair, arched eyebrows, and an animated face. He grins broadly at the viewer, and the twist of his torso as well as his right hand direct the viewer's attention to three young ladies who gaze admiringly at him over the railing. Once students have had a chance to discuss the images, invite them to consider how Welty's photographs of sideshow banners relate to her short stories.

Like the sideshow, Welty used her fiction to investigate identity performance and upend normative expectations. For instance, "Lily Daw and the Three Ladies" and "Keela, the Outcast Indian Maiden," which Welty wrote while she was covering the 1939 Mississippi State Fair as a writer for the WPA, include characters who seem respectable but whose actions betray their prejudices. In "Lily Daw and the Three Ladies," Mrs. Carson, Mrs. Watts, and Aimee Slocum conspire to send the cognitively impaired Lily to the state mental institution to prevent her from running away with a traveling circus performer. The "ladies" attempt to steal Lily's agency, but Welty comically exposes their bias while simultaneously celebrating Lily's independence and challenging readers' assumptions about sexual desire in people with intellectual disabilities. Similarly, in "Keela, the Outcast Indian Maiden," Lee Roy, a disabled black man who dressed as a Native American woman and ate the heads off live chickens for a traveling sideshow, is the hero of the story, while Steve, a white carnival barker, and Max, a white juke-joint owner, are revealed as racist and unstable. As Rebecca Mark contends, Welty used performance to allow the title character to project "the image of the tethered carnival freak/geek back on white liberal readers as an image of their own narcissistic racism" (25). Through the guise of Keela, Lee Roy crosses the boundaries of species, gender, culture, and race, and like Lee Roy, the story does not go where the reader expects; instead it challenges assumptions, stereotypes, and white privilege. Lily and Lee Roy are not limited by their minds or bodies; instead they are disabled by society. Discussing Welty's use of disability, as well as gender and race, in these stories alongside her photographs of the 1939 Mississippi State Fair helps students visualize disability as a social construction, and

Picturing Difference and Disability in Our Classrooms

Figure 1. Welty, *Hypnotized*, State Fair, Jackson, 1939. Copyright © 1939 Eudora Welty, LLC.

Figure 2. Welty, *Hypnotist*, State Fair, Jackson, 1939. Copyright © 1939 Eudora Welty, LLC.

Figure 3. Welty, *Sideshow*, State Fair, Jackson, 1939. Copyright © 1939 Eudora Welty, LLC.

Figure 4. Welty, *Sideshow*, State Fair, Jackson, 1939. Copyright © 1939 Eudora Welty, LLC.

I have found that students were receptive to these types of exercises because they help illustrate the socially constructed nature of gendered, raced, and abled identities. Rather than lecturing about the photographs and their relationship to Welty's biography, inquiry-based learning encourages students to lead the discussion.

Whereas disability was not part of the American experience as imagined by the New Deal, the sideshow subverted expectations and cultivated a space where difference could be celebrated. Like the sideshow, which reveals that difference is arbitrary, Welty's photographs and stories acknowledge and explore the variations in human experience. The sideshow's banners, divorced from their referents and couched in humor and parody, may embody 1930s anxieties over disabilities, but Welty's photographs of them draw attention to the absurdity of prejudice. Although Welty was unable to transgress the boundaries of the real world that prevented her from entering the sideshow's tent, she used her art—both her photography and fiction—to create timeless, appealing, and hilarious characters who transgress raced, gendered, and abled identities. Leading students through a comparative analysis of Welty's fair photographs, animated by discussion of "Lily Daw and the Three Ladies" and "Keela, the Outcast Indian Maiden," introduces students to disability studies and cultivates a deeper understanding of Welty's work.

Notes

1. For more on Welty's photography, see Turner and Harding, Pollack and Marrs, Prenshaw, and McHaney.

2. Several of Welty's stories, such as "The Key," "Why I Live at the P.O.," "Keela, the Outcast Indian Maiden," and "Lily Daw and the Three Ladies," include characters with disabilities.

3. For more on ableism, see Campbell, Longmore and Umansky, and Shapiro.

4. You also could use Welty's photograph of "The Headless Girl," which uses misogyny to exaggerate the power relationship between men and women and to medicalize the woman who has "lost her head" as a hysterical and beheaded corpse.

Works Cited

Adams, Rachel. *Sideshow U.S.A.: Freaks and the American Cultural Imagination*. Chicago: U of Chicago P, 2001.

Barilleaux, René Paul. *Passionate Observer: Eudora Welty among Artists of the Thirties*. Jackson: Mississippi Museum of Art, 2002.

Bogdan, Robert, et al. *Freak Show: Presenting Human Oddities for Amusement and Profit.* Chicago: U of Chicago P, 1990.

Campbell, Fiona K. *Contours of Ableism: The Production of Disability and Abledness.* New York: Palgrave Macmillan, 2009.

Carey, Allison C. *On the Margins of Citizenship: Intellectual Disability and Civil Rights in Twentieth-Century America.* Philadelphia: Temple UP, 2009.

Cohen, Jeffrey Jerome. *Monster Theory, Reading Culture.* Minneapolis: U of Minnesota P, 1996.

Fahy, Thomas. "Worn, Damaged Bodies in Literature and Photography of the Great Depression." *Journal of American Culture* 26 (2003): 2–16.

Garland-Thomson, Rosemarie. *Freakery: Cultural Spectacles of the Extraordinary Body.* New York: New York UP, 1996.

Housen, Abigail. "Aesthetic Thought, Critical Thinking and Transfer." *Arts and Learning Journal* 18 (2002): 99–132.

Longmore, Paul K., and David Goldberger. "The League of the Physically Handicapped and the Great Depression: A Case Study in the New Disability History." *Journal of American History* 87 (2000): 888–922.

Longmore, Paul K., and Lauri Umansky. *The New Disability History: American Perspectives.* New York: New York UP, 2001.

McHaney, Pearl. *Eudora Welty as Photographer.* Jackson: UP of Mississippi, 2009.

Mark, Rebecca. "Carnival Geeks and Voodoun Healing: The Performance of White Guilt and African-American Empowerment in Eudora Welty's 'Keela, the Outcast Indian Maiden.'" *Mississippi Quarterly* 62.1 (2009): 13–34.

Pollack, Harriet, and Suzanne Marrs. *Eudora Welty and Politics: Did the Writer Crusade?* Baton Rouge: Louisiana State UP, 2001.

Prenshaw, Peggy Whitman. *Eudora Welty: Critical Essays.* Jackson: UP of Mississippi, 1979.

Shapiro, Joseph P. *No Pity, People with Disabilities Forging a New Civil Rights Movement.* New York: Random House, 1993.

Turner, W. Craig, and Lee Emling Harding. *Critical Essays on Eudora Welty.* Boston: G. K. Hall, 1989.

Welty, Eudora. *Photographs.* Jackson: UP of Mississippi, 1989.

Welty, Eudora. *Stories, Essays, and Memoir.* Ed. Richard Ford and Michael Kreyling. New York: Library of America, 1998.

WPA Workers' Handbook. Records of the Works Progress Administration. 1936. National Archives.

Queering Welty's Male Bodies in the Undergraduate Classroom

—**Gary Richards**, University of Mary Washington

Over the past two decades, I have taught Eudora Welty's fiction in a variety of undergraduate courses, including introductions to fiction for non-English majors, surveys of southern literature for English majors, and courses on southern women's writing cross-listed in both English and women's and gender studies, and in all of these, her fiction has enriched the endeavors. Even in a course narrowly focused on southern writers' representations of Europe, "Going to Naples" worked beautifully alongside texts such as Mark Twain's *Innocents Abroad* and Elizabeth Spencer's "The Light in the Piazza." Recently, however, as I renewed my efforts to have students understand and meaningfully participate in discourses of sexuality, I have been teaching Welty in three primary venues: surveys of southern literature and modern US fiction geared for English majors and first-year seminars on sexuality in southern literature geared for non-English majors during their first semester in college.

In the survey of southern literature, I remain convinced of the benefits and convenience of an anthology and typically opt for Norton's *The Literature of the American South*. Insofar as I want students to read widely within the anthology, this limits my options for Welty to "A Curtain of Green" and "Where Is the Voice Coming From?" both of which bring specific rewards and liabilities. In the other two venues, I break free of anthologies and have students buy *The Collected Stories of Eudora Welty*, an inexpensive paperback that maximizes options when fine-tuning syllabi and implicitly invites students to explore Welty beyond class discussion. Still, even with these options, I find myself repeatedly assigning, within a variable grouping of four or five Welty stories, two of her best-known and most accessible ones, "The Wide

Net" and "Why I Live at the P.O.," since they allow for, among other things, nuanced explorations of male homosociality and queer male bodies while appealing even to beginning college students.

Other texts by Welty, of course, more overtly negotiate male same-sex desire, with "Music from Spain," featuring Eugene MacLain's homoerotically inflected journey *"because he wanted another love"* (*Stories* 476), being perhaps the most prominent. I rarely teach "Music," however, for a variety of reasons, including the story's length (especially as compared to the brief early stories), the lack of a propulsive plot, and the lyricism that some students find tedious. Moreover, because I typically want the class's texts by Welty to centralize the South as a region, I forego "Music" because she sets the story in San Francisco and uses Eugene's Californian exile to minimize his regional identity. Finally, with this setting, Welty's story unwittingly participates in a broader literary project that relegates male same-sex desire to East and West Coast metropolitan centers such as New York and San Francisco and implies that southerners of the 1930s and 1940s could act upon this desire only outside their indigenous region.

In contrast, the accessible "The Wide Net" and "Why I Live at the P.O." have marked early to mid-twentieth-century settings in the small-town South and thus allow students to refine their thinking about sexuality within a specifically regional context. This is especially important in the first-year seminar where the focus on regionalized sexuality supersedes that on the literary texts, an inversion of the situation in typical literary surveys. I organize the course around topics in sexuality and have each student give a substantive presentation on a topic before the class explores a text using that topic as a frame. (Such pairings include bestiality and James Dickey's "The Sheep-Child," childhood sexuality and Dorothy Allison's *Bastard out of Carolina*, and sadomasochism and Tennessee Williams's "Desire and the Black Masseur.") Central among these topics is homosociality, a term with which students are often not familiar, even if they usually recognize the concept once discussion begins. After a student presents the topic, I provide Eve Sedgwick's classic definition from *Between Men* (if the student has not) and direct the class to the various homosocial institutions that govern human relationships: homes, dormitories, public restrooms, sports teams, religious organizations, sororities and fraternities, and so on. Conversation segues into how these structures can discipline heterosexual desire and activity yet ironically foster slippage into even more "deviant" sexualities, such as homoeroticism, homosexuality, and situational homosexuality. Students have already read Richard Wright's "Big Boy Leaves Home," which allows me to cite that story's opening sections for familiar examples of male homosociality.

With the concept thus defined and exemplified, "The Wide Net" becomes a fantastic text to pair with male homosociality. This is not, of course, the only pairing that would work with Welty within this pedagogical configuration. One iteration of the class, for instance, fruitfully paired white female sexuality with "Lily Daw and the Three Ladies," "Petrified Man," and "Why I Live at the P.O.," all of which allowed students to explore female homosociality and its policing of female sexuality. However, "The Wide Net" is truly a hymn to male homosociality that begs students to consider how Welty juxtaposes it with heterosexual marriage and procreation. Students can interrogate how Hazel's pregnancy functions and why she chooses to react as she does when her husband "went out with two of the boys down the road and stayed out all night" (204). Students can in turn grapple with how the men largely relegate her disappearance to an excuse for the audacious homosocial rituals that follow and what Welty may suggest with her ultimate celebration of William Wallace and Hazel's heterosexual foreplay, complete with "a little tap and slap" (226) that rivals the opening scene of Zora Neale Hurston's "The Gilded Six-Bits" for exuberance. Likewise, students can debate the nature of the central bond between William Wallace and Virgil and tease out the fault lines in the broader intergenerational, interracial, and interclassed structure of the expedition. Moreover, students can contemplate how these relationships are potentially bonded through the misogyny suggested by the gendered critique of Hazel's actions as "a woman's trick" (206) that "has kept one woman from talking a while" (211), the dismissal of Edna Earle's dim intellect, and the demonization of Hazel's mother. Finally, in our age when male same-sex couples often function in strict homosocial enclaves and reproduce, adopt, and/or raise children via means that minimize women, students can think about how Welty anticipates this behavior. What is the potential significance of her imagining men and boys who repeatedly transform traditional feminine roles at the exclusion of women, as when Sam wears the "string of lady's beads [...] around his head, with a knot over his forehead and loops around his ears" (216), and the Malone brothers take up a surrogate adopted child in "their alligator, tossing it in the air, even, like a father tossing his child" (222)?

For many of these same reasons, "The Wide Net" also works nicely in the modern US fiction course, especially if one seeks, as I do, to provide students an intimated genealogy of representations of male homosociality and homosexuality that showcases their subtle differences. In the most recent version of this class, students read "The Wide Net" in a cluster of Welty stories after, among other texts, Ernest Hemingway's *The Sun Also Rises*, Hurston's *Jonah's Gourd Vine*, and John Steinbeck's *Of Mice and Men* but before Gore Vidal's *The City and the Pillar* and its overt depictions of queer sexuality. As I hoped, students immediately drew parallels between the relationship between William Wallace and Virgil and that between Jake Barnes and Bill Gorton in Hemingway's novel, but the final examination forced students to think even more intertextually, asking them in one of several short essay questions to compare and contrast at least four writers' explorations of male homosociality and its potential slippage into male homosexuality.

One could easily embed a similar structure within a standard survey of southern literature. A particularly southern genealogy of male homosociality might position Welty's representations alongside, say, the relationships of Roderick Usher and the narrator in Edgar Allan Poe's "The Fall of the House of Usher," Huck and Jim aboard their raft in Twain's *Adventures of Huckleberry Finn*, Brick and Skipper in Williams's *Cat on a Hot Tin Roof*, and Baby Harper and Cecil in Monique Truong's *Bitter in the Mouth*. Thanks to the proliferation of queer southern literary studies over the last two decades, a range of secondary resources is readily available, with the book-length studies by Michael Bibler, John Howard, Tison Pugh, Benjamin Wise, and myself, among others, particularly useful. Although these studies do not necessarily centralize Welty, they nevertheless offer models of how southern writers of varied sexual identities have negotiated same-sex relations, whether homosexual or homosocial, within specifically regionalized contexts.

Finally, "The Wide Net" is pedagogically useful in inviting students to consider biographical contexts, which almost invariably change students' perceptions about the story's homosociality. With its prominent dedication to John Fraiser Robinson, the story prompts a discussion of Welty's vexed romantic relationship with him; the role that World War II may have played in his ultimate gayness; Welty's closeness with coteries of gay men in Jackson, New York, and elsewhere; and her affinity—stylistically and personally—with LGBT writers, including E. M. Forster, Virginia Woolf, and Reynolds Price. These ripples of amplification in turn squarely position Welty within global queer modernism and the long shadows it throws across the twentieth century and thus provides yet another point of entry for students, scholars, and lay readers who, without an understanding of regionally granulated queerness, might overlook how pertinent Welty's texts can be within this literary tradition.

Although "Why I Live at the P.O." does not take up male sexuality as its central concern, as "The Wide Net" does, the earlier story nevertheless also assists in this granulation. With queer representations, especially as tied to gender performance, amply circulating in twenty-first-century culture, students have few problems reading cross-dressing Uncle Rondo, clad in "one of Stella-Rondo's flesh-colored kimonos, all cut on the bias" (59), as a queer male body. Especially in the first-year seminar, where I attempt to give students basic critical concepts and terminologies related to gender and sexuality, this representation invites discussion and definition of cross-dressing, fetishism, transvestism, transsexual identity and embodiment, and other trans issues. But I also push students to consider the very specific role that the kimono plays in setting up Uncle Rondo as a surrogate for his niece. Already linked by a shared name, he and Stella-Rondo now share intimate apparel, the item that most closely links her to her husband and his desires. As she reminds Sister, the kimono "happens to be part of my trousseau, and Mr Whitaker took several dozen photographs of me in it" (61). Therefore, when Uncle Rondo puts on the negligee, he is not simply in generic female drag, but is dressed as his niece when she is most sexually provocative. What, I pose to students, might this reveal about Uncle Rondo's sexuality, especially given his seeming disinterest in heterosexual love and marriage? Might a third member of the family have been surreptitiously or unconsciously vying for Joe Whitaker's affections?

Welty reinforces this parallel between Uncle Rondo and his nieces with his multiple other transgressions of masculinity. His flair for the dramatic—beyond sporting the kimono—rivals Sister's, as when he drunkenly hisses: "'Sister,' he says, 'get out of my way, I'm poisoned'" (59). Moreover, he faces the ensuing moment not with manly stoicism but rather with desperation and weakness, "*pleading* with [Papa-Daddy] to slow down the hammock, it was making him as dizzy as a witch to watch it" (60). And when critiqued for his cross-dressing, Uncle Rondo behaves as petulantly as either of his nieces, anticipating the childish behavior of Sister in the last paragraph. "Uncle Rondo spills out all the ketchup and jumps out of his chair and tears off the kimono and throws it down on the dirty floor and puts his foot on it" (64).

I also ask students to consider how Uncle Rondo's periodic consumption of chemicals may relate to his performances of gender and sexuality. Is this an instance of recreational drug use associated with a queer subculture? Is it a means to escape an insufferable family during a "whole day in this house with nothing to do" (64)? And what of the ritual being enacted "every single Fourth of July as sure as shooting" (59)? If this holiday has consistently been linked to Sister's personal declaration of independence, might it not also be linked to Uncle Rondo's? Finally, pointing to Mama's speculation about Joe Whitaker, "I believed to my soul he drank *chemicals*" (63), I ask students the potential significance of the story's only other drug user being the man who now seems intent upon abandoning all trappings of heterosexual marriage.

With this groundwork laid, I conclude by pushing students to consider Sister's treatment of this queerness as absolutely unexceptional, as when she blandly dismisses her uncle's perverse behavior: "He's Mama's only brother and is a good case of a one-track mind. Ask anybody. A certified pharmacist"

(60). I then ask students to theorize what, if any, social and political commentary Welty may be making with this acceptance. Out of this process, students inevitably develop a fuller understanding of a seemingly minor character who has been connected with multiple forms of queerness throughout the story. Perhaps even more important, these forms are strikingly different from the male homosociality of "The Wide Net," and students can then see in these two Welty stories one of the hallmarks of—to me—a great writer: the ability to represent a range of nuanced sexualities with intelligence, sympathy, and humor.

Works Cited

Andrews, William L., ed. *The Literature of the American South*. New York: Norton, 1998.

Bibler, Michael. *Cotton's Queer Relations: Same-Sex Intimacy and the Literature of the Southern Plantation, 1936–1968*. Charlottesville: U of Virginia P, 2009.

Howard, John. *Men like That: A Southern Queer History*. Chicago: U of Chicago P, 1999.

Pugh, Tison. *Precious Perversions: Humor, Homosexuality, and the Southern Literary Canon*. Baton Rouge: Louisiana State UP, 2016.

———. *Queer Chivalry: Medievalism and the Myth of White Masculinity in Southern Literature*. Baton Rouge: Louisiana State UP, 2013.

Richards, Gary. *Lovers and Beloveds: Sexual Otherness in Southern Fiction, 1936–1961*. Baton Rouge: Louisiana State UP, 2005.

Sedgwick, Eve Kosofsky. *Between Men: English Literature and Male Homosocial Desire*. New York: Columbia UP, 1985.

Welty, Eudora. *Stories, Essays, and Memoir*. Ed. Richard Ford and Michael Kreyling. New York: Library of America, 1998.

Wise, Benjamin E. *William Alexander Percy: The Curious Life of a Mississippi Planter and Sexual Freethinker*. Chapel Hill: U of North Carolina P, 2012.

Loch of the Rape

Welty Stories and Sexual Violence

—**Michael Kreyling,** Vanderbilt University

> I would rather submit a story to the test of its outside world, to show what it was doing and how it went about it, than to the method of critical analysis which would pick the story up by its heels (as if it had swallowed a button) to examine the writing process as analysis in reverse, as though a story—or any system of feeling—could be more accessible to understanding for being hung upside down.
> —*Stories* 774–75

We teach Eudora Welty's fiction because we've been good at finding "buttons" of literary-critical insight and at training our students to do likewise. But sometimes we and our students inhabit different worlds: ours on the "inside" where the buttons are, the students' on the "outside" where the raw experience is.

It is typical of Welty to liken her fiction to a "system of feeling," an inside world, where disturbances in the outside world, everyday trauma large and small, fade from the radar. Think of teaching *Delta Wedding*, for example, in the charged atmosphere of "Black Lives Matter." What was local color for generations of students and teachers—cotton fields, knife-wielding fieldworkers, Pinchy "coming through"—is abruptly the foreground; the carceral plantation, exploited black labor, "the help's" stifled voice. Troy Flavin, once a demigod of renewal and rebirth, is now just one more iteration of "the man."

Critical race studies, however, is not my theme here, although it very well could be.[1] Instead, I want to make some brief comments about the relationship in Welty's fiction between the outside world of sexual violence and the inside frame, the "system of feeling," that mutes the trauma: overwhelmingly, but not exclusively, tropes of Greek and Roman myth. My reasons are twofold. In my own teaching and writing I have often taken tropes of sexual violence in Welty as "buttons" first, working from the inside (their mythic configurations) and belatedly arriving in the outside world. I have sometimes been embarrassed by presenting sexual violence in figural camouflage when its effects are traumatic facts in my own students' lives.[2]

I was prodded to think about this issue when *The National Intimate Partner and Sexual Violence Survey* (2010) made headlines, prompting several colleges and universities to consider monitoring what goes on in their classrooms. Opposition to "trigger warnings" was a reflex to me: Literature is not life experience; the trauma therein is a representation of an experience, not the real thing. Pope's "The Rape of the Lock" does not relate an actual rape; students should be able to separate the word from the thing. In any case, Pope's poem is *just* about snipping a lock of a woman's hair.

Some of the friction between those who favor trigger warnings and those who oppose them comes, it seems to me, from the chasm between the literary language we as teachers and critics are used to and the flat-line STEM-like language of the *NISVS*. Here are two excerpts from the "Executive Summary" of *NISVS*:

> Sexual violence, stalking, and intimate partner violence are major public health problems in the United States. Many survivors of these forms of violence can experience physical injury, mental health consequences such as depression, anxiety, low self-esteem, and suicide attempts, and other health consequences such as gastrointestinal disorders, substance abuse, sexually transmitted diseases, and gynecological or pregnancy complications. These consequences can lead to hospitalization, disability, or death. (*NISVS* 1)

The report goes on to recommend:

> Prevention efforts should start early by promoting healthy, respectful relationships in families, by fostering healthy parent-child relationships, and developing positive family dynamics and emotionally supportive environments. These environments provide a strong foundation for children, help them to adopt positive interactions based on respect and trust, and foster effective and non-violent communication and conflict resolution in their peer and dating relationships. It is equally important to continue addressing the beliefs, attitudes and messages that are deeply embedded in our social structures and that create a climate that condones sexual violence, stalking, and intimate partner violence. For example, this can be done through norms change, changing policies and enforcing existing

policies against violence, and promoting bystander approaches to prevent violence before it happens. (*NISVS* 4)

NISVS prose is denuded of figurative language; there is no "system of feeling" here, only stripped-down communication. It is clear to the point of tautology: foundations must be strengthened; norms condoning intimate partner violence must be changed. Of course these must be our individual and social goals. Most of us bristle at being told the obvious in lifeless language. As teachers of literature we'll dismiss the medium before we even get to the message. I did.

Stylistics aside, *NISVS* data suggest that sexual trauma is more widespread among our students than some teachers (myself included) might imagine. Researchers for *NISVS* surveyed a random sample of the public for instances of "rape, stalking, or violence by a romantic or sexual partner" and found that 36.7 percent of women surveyed and 28.5 percent of men had suffered such trauma. Forty-eight percent of women surveyed had experienced "psychological aggression" by an intimate partner: being called names such as "ugly," "fat," "crazy," or "stupid" (*NISVS* 46). Newer technologies such as social media, which distinguish our classrooms from those of past years, make such sexual violence as stalking and "expressive aggression" (name-calling) easier and more widespread. Even presidents-elect do it. The border between texting and acting has, sometimes tragically, proven difficult to police.

What does it mean, then, that many of our students will, statistically, have been victims of the kinds of trauma frequently depicted in reading we assign? In "A Piece of News," one of Welty's earliest stories, the central character, Ruby Fisher, fantasizes about being shot by her husband for an infidelity she might or might not have committed. "Petrified Man," although read by Welty and others as a comic *tour de force*, is after all about a serial rapist. "Flowers for Marjorie" turns on an act of "intimate partner violence" when Howard, a Mississippian out of work in Depression-era New York City, stabs his pregnant partner Marjorie (*Stories* 123). Or perhaps Howard is lost in a surrealist fugue, exhausted by his hunt for work, and there is no Marjorie at all. Still, in the traumatized classroom it might not matter whether the victim is real or hallucinated, cushioned by a comic voice or presented without stylistic deflection.

The Robber Bridegroom (1942) is a direct case in point. The novella's folktale accessories muted, the text resonates with "rape, stalking, or violence by a romantic or sexual partner." In the second chapter, the ingénue Rosamond is confronted on the Natchez Trace by the bandit Jamie Lockhart. Lockhart relieves Rosamond of everything she is carrying, including, layer by layer, her clothes. There the romantic partner stops, offering Rosamond a choice:

"Shall I kill you with my little dirk, to save your name, or will you go home naked?" (*Novels* 26).⁴ Rosamond, a self-reliant young woman, chooses to go home naked. The next day the two meet again, and stylistic flourish obscures the act. "The wild plum trees were like rolling smoke between him and the river, but he broke the branches and the plums rained down as he carried her under. He stopped and laid her on the ground, where, straight below, the river flowed as slow as sand, and robbed her of that which he had left the day before" (*Complete Novels* 33).⁵ What is Rosamond's relationship to the cohort of US women (one in five, according to *NISVS*) who have suffered rape? Or to the 79.6 percent of those women who have experienced rape before the age of twenty-five? Or to the 42.2 percent of those who experienced their first "completed rape" before the age of eighteen? (*NISVS* 2). Lest "the wild plum trees" befog the sexual violence in the novella, let us remember that Little Harp, Lockhart's *doppelganger*, kidnaps an Indian woman, drugs her, cuts off a finger, then throws "the girl across the long table, among the plates and all, where the remains of all the meals lay where they were left, with knives and forks sticking in them, and flung himself upon her before their eyes" (*Complete Novels* 63–64). The Indian girl does not survive Harp's assault; being raped is the last we hear of her: "and it was true: she was dead" (64). This unnamed Indian woman becomes a statistic, and no plum trees decorate what happens to her. Why not make the Welty classroom the site where these two ways of representing intimate partner violence, the literary and the statistical, compete for our attention and comment?

When I project the text of *NISVS* on the classroom screen, eyes roll and bodies slouch. My students have heard it all before, they tell me: in mandatory, first-year orientation; in residence-hall discussion groups. They are high achievers; they know the correct answers; they move beyond the obvious. But, when I've asked them to use *NISVS* jargon to re-explain the fiction I've just presented in its literary complexity, something like "education" happens. Students begin to see that every discourse obfuscates experience in its own peculiar way: STEM jargon buries the individual in the data set and drains away emotion, literary language tends to conceal raw experience in imagery and metaphor.

The most effective text for exploring contesting claims of data and metaphor has been "Moon Lake." In fact, all the stories in *The Golden Apples*, beginning with "Shower of Gold," are primed for this teaching strategy because of the heavy (almost overdetermined) layer of Greek and Roman myth Welty applied to character and plot. A shower of gold, the collection's opening metaphor, is the metaphor that occludes intimate partner violence inflicted by Zeus upon Danae. Rape is not the way the Zeus-Danae myth has been represented in classical texts, or in paintings by Rembrandt, Correggio, and Klimt. Nor in Welty. Danae is never a statistic in the raw count of spousal desertion, the hardships of single-mother parenting, or any of the social behaviors that might touch the actual experiences of the people in the classroom. Why not look at her that way?

"Moon Lake" is a harsher test of this classroom gambit because it surprisingly unfolds with stronger language than my students hear in their campus sexuality sessions. I have warned my students that, if this story were a film, it would probably be rated R. "Moon Lake" begins with the "Boy Scout and Life Saver" (Loch Morrison) presiding over a summer camp of town and orphan girls like a phallic avatar. "Sometimes he swung in the trees; Nina Carmichael in particular would hear him crashing in the foliage somewhere when she was lying rigid in siesta" (*Stories* 412). Both Loch's adolescent Tarzanic behavior and Nina's rigid anticipation of his threat provide "Moon Lake" with sexualized premonitions: in the text's "system of feeling," sex operates as the ominous hum of future violence.

The just-barely-unspoken plea against violation continues. The girls are paraded to Moon Lake for a morning swim "while the Boy Scout, waiting at the lake, watched them go in" (414). This male gaze could inflict visual trauma, for the girls have to strip to their "underbodies" under his eye. One of the orphans, Easter, stands out. Welty accords her a physical description rich in metaphor (417–18), but punctuated with a reminder of a physical check on literary allusion: "She had started her breasts" (418). And so a rhythm to the story sets in: flights of rich, allusive prose pinned to the sexualized female body in jeopardy. In the classroom, I have exploited the clash of these discourses by asking students to render Easter's (or any of the girls') experiences in *NISVS* language.

Easter, tickled by an errant boy, plummets into Moon Lake, fails to surface, and is wrestled to shore by the Boy Scout. Trained in the pre-CPR Holger-Nielsen Method of artificial respiration, Loch flings Easter's body atop a picnic table and, in a scene nearly identical to the one in *The Robber Bridegroom* in which the Indian girl is raped and killed (*Novels* 64), goes to work:

> The Boy Scout reached in and gouged out her mouth with his hand, an unbelievable act. She did not alter. He lifted up, screwed his toes, and with a groan of his own fell upon her and drove up and down upon her, into her, gouging the heels of his hands into her ribs again and again. (441)

When Easter does not respond, the Boy Scout becomes more brutal: "On the table, the Boy Scout spat, and took a fresh appraisal of Easter. He reached for a hold on her hair and pulled her head back. No longer were her lips faintly parted—her mouth was open. It gaped" (443). The scene on the picnic table merges rough sex with traces of Medusa on Easter's unconscious face, sexual violence yoked to metaphor. Inside the text, the audience for the violence on the picnic table is composed of women camp counselors, girl campers, the matron who has organized the outing, and a male hunter (Ran MacLain, it turns out, with dog and gun). No one intervenes, although the matron does express the wish that the Boy Scout "be put out of business" (442). The women seem mesmerized by the mimed sexual assault. It is, one of them cryptically remarks, "what he [the Boy Scout—and all men] came for" (442). Trigger warnings have been issued for far less suggestive material.

The challenge of reading and teaching Welty texts like these is, paradoxically, both familiar and new. That is, the text and subtext of sexual embodiment in Welty has long been a topic of critical discussion as one of the "system[s] of feeling" in her stories. In "Writing and Analyzing a Story," Welty, writing from the critical sector of her brain, seems to have taken an absolutist stance: as "system[s] of feeling," stories are free standing and inviolate ("there the story is"). But we no longer teach in classrooms where Welty's "system[s] of feeling" are wholly contained within the text, if we ever did.

We should not, however, let concern over sexual violence shut down discussion of literary discourse, nor let *NISVS*-like language be the only medium of communication. Let's put Welty's stories into dialogue with STEM-like, automated language. I'll bet that the two together do a more effective job of communicating the jagged trauma of sexual violence, and sensitizing us to dismantle its power, than either could do separately.

Notes

1. See Harriet Pollack, ed. *Eudora Welty, Whiteness, and Race* (Athens: University of Georgia Press, 2013).

2. As I worked on this essay, the Vanderbilt University student newspaper carried this headline story: "Breaking Down the Sexual Assault Survey," *Vanderbilt Hustler* January 27, 2016: 2. Online at www.vanderbilthustler.com. The graphic: 28 percent of female undergraduates reported a sexual assault.

3. http://www.cdc.gov/violenceprevention/pdf/nisvs_report2010-a.pdf.

4. Change one consonant in "dirk" and the sexually violent subtext of Lockhart's threat is overt. Another "button."

5. If your students' attention flags, introduce them to *The Fantasticks*, book by Harvey Schmidt, lyrics by Tom Jones. The musical opened off-Broadway in 1960 and was revived in 2006 and 2010. Let them listen to the "Rape Ballet" number, altered (after controversy) to "Abduction Ballet."

Works Cited

"Breaking Down the Sexual Assault Survey." *Vanderbilt Hustler* 128.3 (January 27, 2016): 2. www.vanderbilthustler.com.

"Campus Sexual Violence Resource List." *Sexual Assault Awareness Month*. National Sexual Violence Resource Center, 2016. Web. August 10, 2016. http://www.nsvrc.org/saam/campus-resource-list#Stats.

"National Intimate Partner and Sexual Violence Report." *The National Intimate Partner and Sexual Violence Survey*. CDC, 2010. Web. August 10, 2016.

Welty, Eudora. *Complete Novels*. New York: Library of America, 1998.

———. *Stories, Essays, and Memoir*. Ed. Richard Ford and Michael Kreyling. New York: Library of America, 1998.

Welty's Place in the Undergraduate Theory Classroom

—**Annette Trefzer,** University of Mississippi

Eudora Welty's short stories hold great theoretical promise and pedagogical appeal because they require close attention from undergraduate readers. Her stories, marked by textual complexity and subtlety of plot and humor, often seem to withhold rather than offer a sense of illumination. Granted, literary theory can also be a puzzling and mystifying experience, and teaching Welty alongside those who have penned theoretical manifestos may seem to compound the difficulty. But, as I will show, literary theory can help students confront the "obstacles" in Welty's stories, and the stories, in turn, can offer a range of questions and problems for reexamination as they highlight the blind spots of various theoretical lenses.

In a four-to-six-week teaching unit, I pair theoretical and literary texts as follows: We start with the formalist method of "close reading" and Welty's "A Piece of News," followed by feminism and theories of sexuality paired with "A Curtain of Green" and "Petrified Man," and end up with disability studies as illustrated in Welty's first short-story collection. I will suggest how students begin to engage with literary criticism and the terminology of literary theory as they explore Welty's stories, and, in turn, how sensitivity to Welty's use of language can enrich their own sense of interpretive control and joy.

Eudora Welty's emergence on the literary scene coincides with the publication of perhaps the most influential fiction textbook in American classrooms, Cleanth Brooks and Robert Penn Warren's *Understanding Fiction* (1943), a book that yielded methodological influence for several decades. Welty's story, "A Piece of News," appears under the title "How Plot Reveals," and as Brooks writes, "at first glance this story may seem to be no story at all—merely a trivial incident" (143). Of course, Brooks is asking about the meaning of plot, what Welty calls the "Why" of the story in her essay "Looking at Short Stories." Why does Ruby come in drenched from the rain? Why does she identify with the Ruby Fisher of the newspaper article? Why does she enjoy imagining herself dead, shot in the heart by her husband, Clyde? Why is she filled with excitement when he returns home? Why does Clyde put the newspaper into the fire? These plot questions, among many, ask about characterization, motivation, and theme. As Welty writes, "characters in the plot connect us with the vastness of our secret life, which is endlessly explorable. This is their role. What happens to them is what they have been put here to show" ("Looking" 90).

What the story shows is answered differently by different readers in the classroom. Many of my students—attuned to the roles of gender and sexuality in fiction—are quick to point out that Ruby's daydream is connected to her loneliness and lack of sexual fulfillment in her marriage and that therefore she goes "hitchhiking," a euphemism for her sexual adventure with the traveling salesman. They point out that when Clyde comes home, he "poked at Ruby with the butt of his gun," a gesture possibly hinting at domestic violence underscored by repeated reports of "slap[ping] at her" (twice), "spank[ing] her good-humoredly," and threatening to "smack the livin devil outa you" (*Stories* 20). The presence of a violent patriarchal force, both real and imagined in the daydream, is undercut by the ambiguous characterization of Clyde as at once violent and good-humored, explosive and meek, bold and afraid. This ambiguity corresponds to a similar ambiguity about Ruby, who is both sexually constrained *and* emancipated, submissive to her husband and yet autonomous. When students arrive at these gripping paradoxes, they are ready to consult with the critics.

I introduce Carol Hollenbaugh's short 1974 essay "Ruby Fisher and Her Demon Lover," an essay responding directly to Brooks and Warren's interpretation of the story. We compare the two critical commentaries: the New Critical analysis draws attention to the textual body and "the authority which the written word carries," whereas Hollenbaugh pays attention to Ruby's awakening pleasure in her female body. Combining sexuality and textuality in her chapter "Alice Can" in *Honey-Mad Women*, Patricia Yaeger accomplishes two important pedagogical goals: first, she makes explicit an argument about women's relationship to language and access to texts such as newspapers that some of my students intuited, and second, her fine-grained interpretation of "A Piece of News" is an exemplary illustration of the close reading technique in the service of feminist criticism. Yaeger asks, what theory of language does Welty's story embody? And she answers that it is a feminist language because when the newspaper meets the imprint of Ruby's female body, the alphabet changes (123).

This discussion leads straight to the heart of feminist theory and much Welty criticism from the early 1970s on. In my introduction to feminism in the theory seminar, I make a distinction between American and French feminism: the first group, including Nina Baym, Sandra Gilbert, and Susan Gubar, are interested in rethinking the canon, rereading images of women in fiction (written by both men and women) and reevaluating the experience of women; the second group, including Luce Irigaray and Hélène Cixous, influenced by psychoanalysis, are interested in the dynamics of identity formation, especially the body and its relation to language. We read Nina Baym's "Melodramas of Beset Manhood" to address questions of canonicity or, as she dramatically states: "how theories of American fiction exclude women authors" and then proceed to the second chapter of Gilbert and Gubar's *Madwoman in the Attic* where they ask, "what does it mean to be a women writer in a culture whose fundamental definitions of literary authority are [...] both overtly and covertly patriarchal?" (1532). How does one read strategies of "evasion and concealment" in women's fiction? (1534). How does one trace "subversive pictures behind socially acceptable facades?" (1539).

Following Gilbert and Gubar, I encourage students to be on the lookout for images of confinement and expressions of a split female self, caught between convention and self-realization. I pair this discussion of what Toril Moi calls "images of women in fiction" criticism with an analysis of Welty's "A Curtain of Green." Here students note the isolation of Mrs. Larkin in her garden, her confinement "within the border of hedge, like a high wall," her invisibility as she is "submerged" among her plants (130). And yet, she is watched by neighbors looking down on her in judgment from their upstairs windows: "Just to what end Mrs. Larkin worked so strenuously in her garden, her neighbors could not see" (131). But the students can: they propose that her garden work is a method for managing her grief, that the garden is an image for her own fertile womb, or her confused and angry mind; that she attempts to control nature with her vigorous hoeing and ironically tends that which killed her husband. One female student asked shyly: "in feminist criticism, are we allowed to say that she is 'crazy?'" This question returns us to the figure of the "madwoman in the attic" and a careful analysis of the narrative voice and perspective inviting us to judge Mrs. Larkin. Mrs. Larkin is a split figure, vulnerable and strong, victim and potential victimizer, an artist who uses the garden both to express and to camouflage herself, silent until her own voice begins to "part the hedge" drawn tightly around her heart. Her angry cry for "Jamey!" (133) ruptures her isolation and acknowledges her loneliness. Uttered in fierce accusation and desperation, the name of her young black helper is the only word Mrs. Larkin ever speaks directly, and it is reciprocated by Jamey's cry "Miss Lark! Miss Lark!" a new name that calls her back to life without her married title (136). Our discussion of why Welty wanted to accomplish this transformation through a black character, and what the symbolic, economic, and sociohistorical dimensions of this relationship are, leads the class to discuss racially marked bodies and gender roles in the South of the 1930s.

In our study of French feminist criticism, the idea that language as an instrument of patriarchy is not a neutral medium but one that prevents women from expressing themselves physically and intellectually is taken up by Luce Irigaray and Hélène Cixous. Students read Cixous's "The Laugh of the Medusa" and discuss her claim that woman has been "kept in the dark about herself"—a phrase that strikes back at Freud's sexist and racist characterization of women as "the Dark Continent." We examine her claim that writing is "the locus where the repression of women has been perpetuated" (245) and question the idea of "écriture feminine" as a text that "cannot fail to be more than subversive" (252). Although most students usually find the text "dated" because they want to believe that today's women are no longer barred from access to writing and that the sexual opposition that structures phallogocentrism has all but disappeared, some are intrigued by a kind of writing beyond logic and in purposeful opposition to grammar and the rules of reason. Is it really possible to write through a gendered body? And what about the figure of the Medusa?

Welty's story "Petrified Man" is an excellent match for this discussion. Patricia Yaeger asks, "How should we read phallic imagery when it is incorporated within women's texts? If the phallus is, as Lacan suggests, the central signifier of patriarchal culture, is the woman writer who gives phallic imagery a prominent place in her fictions reinstating our culture's patriarchal orientations?" ("The Case" 431). Welty's story certainly contains phallic imagery as it revolves around women's gossip in a beauty parlor and the discovery of the sideshow figure of the "petrified man," a man hard as stone, who is revealed to be a criminal wanted for the rape of four women in California. The petrified man stands in stark contrast to the domesticated husbands of the women in the salon: Mrs. Fletcher admits that "Mr. Fletcher can't do a thing with me" (25). In the intimate space of the women's beauty parlor, explicitly coded in lavender as a hyper-feminine environment, women are not only talking about their lack of sexual fulfillment, but they are actively reconstituting pleasure. The salon motto is "to give the lady what she was after" (31) and when Leota sends Mrs. Fletcher to the hair dryer, she asks "You can turn yourself on, can't you?" (30).

In light of Luce Irigaray's theory of self-sufficient female sexuality which students read in a small excerpt from *This Sex Which Is Not One,* it becomes clear that Welty's story critiques the phallus and the "desire to force entry, to penetrate" (259). As one student pointed out, the character of Billy Boy, whose probable birth name is William, could also be nicknamed "Willie" with obvious phallic reference! He has penetrated the female space, an act glossed by Irigaray as "a violent break-in: the brutal separation of the two lips by a violating penis." The physical penetration of Leota's "purse" is followed by linguistic violence as Billy Boy reinserts himself between the lips of the women in conversation in an attempt to trump their wits: "if you're so smart, why ain't you rich?" (36). This final patriarchal challenge to the power of women opens into a discussion of the complicated intersections between women's sexual, social, and economic power.

From the feminist deconstruction of the patriarchal male/female binary and the reconstruction of woman not as "lack" but as a fully viable self-sufficient female body, we move into a discussion of normative bodies and sexualities. I begin this segment on disability studies with a quick discussion of terminology: what are the implications of the terms "handicap," "disabled," or "people with disabilities"—what use is proper, better, best? What language to use is important because it can help us recognize people with disabilities with a sense of personhood and humanity. I also ask what counts as a disability, and what are the boundaries of this term? Without going too far into the foundations of medical, social, and legal models for helping with definitional clarity, we quickly realize that disability is best understood not as a "given" but as socially constructed. The American Disability Act (1990) specifies physical, cognitive, and sensory disabilities, or any impairment that limits at least one life activity. I also like to point out the magnitude of an issue that seems often invisible. According to the World Health Organization report of 2011, one billion people around the world, roughly 17 percent of the total global population, suffers from a disability (Hall 6). So, disability is not a marginal issue nor is it strictly a question about who is able-bodied and who isn't. In one way, everyone is temporarily able-bodied as becoming disabled is an aspect of identity as we grow older. Thus, disability and ability are not stable but fluid. Students quickly catch on to the ways ability is always "aspirational" as we admire quarterbacks and cheerleaders for bodily performances most of us cannot match.

At this point, students read the first chapter of Alice Hall's *Literature and Disability,* and they are quick to mention examples: Benjy in Faulkner's *The Sound and the Fury* and Hulga in O'Connor's "Good Country People," as well as characters in Welty's stories: Lily Daw and her xylophone player; Keela, the

Outcast Indian Maiden; Clytie; and Ellie and Albert Morgan. We discuss how to extend the disability focus from characters to themes and metaphors following Ato Quayson's suggestion that "we consider the plot of social deformation as it is tied to some form of physical or mental deformation to be relevant to the discussion of all literary texts" (in Hall). And, building on Alice Hall's guiding questions for her book, we ask: how do literature and theory present and/or challenge ideas of the "normal"? Students also read an excerpt from Robert McRuer's article "Compulsory Able-Bodiedness and Queer/Disabled Existence," a theory that interrogates the idea of the "normal." McRuer creates an intersection between disability studies and queer studies to show that heterosexuality functions like able-bodiedness in the sense that both concepts are presumed to be an invisible, unspecified, and "normal" standard. Furthermore, these terms are "compulsory"—a term students comprehend best when they begin to define it as mandatory, obligatory, or required by law. McRuer's argument is that "the system of compulsory able-bodiedness that produces disability is thoroughly interwoven with the system of compulsory heterosexuality that produces queerness; that—in fact—compulsory heterosexuality is contingent on compulsory able-bodiedness and vice versa" (354).

It is astonishing how many stories in Welty's first collection center on a character who is disabled: think of Ruby Fisher, who was "slow all her life"; Lily Daw, who "wasn't bright"; Little Lee Roy, who is "clubfooted" and on crutches; Ellie and Albert Morgan, who are deaf; Lily's xylophone player who is also deaf; Clytie Farr, whose "wits were all leaving her"; and the bickering old ladies in the nursing home. Think of R. J. Bowman's illness and heart failure, and more broadly of the disabling conditions of poverty in "Flowers for Marjorie" and "The Whistle," or the handicap of being black during Jim Crow such as suffered by Powerhouse and Phoenix Jackson. For Welty, whose disabled characters are often read as "grotesques," disability signifies on social "normality"; disability makes visible the problem with so-called norms and standards of southern communities. Part of the disability discourse in Welty's fiction is her interest in "freaks" and the "freak show" as venues that scapegoat individuals and produce as spectacles that which is "abject." We are reminded not only of Lily's visit to the "tent show" and Little Lee Roy's sideshow performance as the live chicken-eating Keela, the Outcast Indian Maiden, but of the performance of the Petrified Man in "the travelin' freak show" where nonstandard bodies are exhibited as "human oddities" and pygmies and the dead fetuses of "twins in a bottle" warn of human monstrosity.

In all of Welty's stories, the disabled body is subjected to a gazing subject positioned as "normal" (and normative) as in "A Memory" where the narrator observes the "unnaturally white and fatly aware" obese mountain of a woman with a loud "continuous laugh," another monstrous Medusa figure (95). But each story reverses the places of able-bodied and disabled by revealing the flaws—moral, social, and sexual—of those representing the apparently normative framework. Welty's critique in "A Memory" is directed at the female narrator who "felt a peak of horror" at seeing the woman's huge breasts (97) and the older boy's "protrusions" from his bathing suit (95). Linking lack of grace with lack of intelligence, the narrator judges harshly that "such people were called 'common'" (94), thus revealing her own sexual anxieties and class prejudices which turn lower-class bodies into monstrous exhibitions disturbing her enjoyment of a "normal" environment and heterosexual romance. In "Lily Daw and the Three Ladies," Welty offers a tantalizing glimpse not so much of Lily, who manifests a cognitive difference—she is quite smart in bargaining for items for her hope chest—but of a socially disabled community attempting to lock away a young woman for fear of her budding sexuality. Lily's sexuality is pathologized, linked to her disability, and thus opposed to what McRuer terms "compulsory heterosexuality." Thus there is something "queer" about Lily's sexuality and her desire to marry the perfumed deaf sideshow musician.

As students continue to explore the different ways in which Welty's stories articulate a critique of normalcy, they study Lennard Davis's overview of the history of normalcy and Rosemarie Garland-Thomson's introduction to the concept of the "normate." What I find particularly helpful in my classroom discussions about the intersections between able-bodiedness and heterosexuality is that a number of students not initially sympathetic to queer theory recognize nevertheless the discursive and sociohistorical construction of hegemonic ideas of the "normal" body and of heterosexuality. What we accomplish then is to show that the apparently "normal" is neither fixed nor without a history, and Welty's short stories provide a rich array of examples for such queer perspectives as they engage in imagining bodies that function differently.

I hope to have shown with a few examples from Welty's work the intersections where theory meets practical literary criticism and where fiction articulates positions that help students understand literary theory in turn. As students build their theoretical repertoire from formalism to disability studies (using the tools of psychoanalytic theory, critical race studies, and materialist and cultural studies, not discussed here) they begin to understand that contemporary criticism is not purely "formalist" or "feminist" but often a complex intersectional enterprise. As they widen their critical lenses, they also perceive the possibilities of rereading Welty's stories from different angles and with different results. We do not base our analysis on a single theoretical approach because theory itself is a site of change as it responds to shifting perceptions of identity and textuality, politics and history, culture and literature itself. For Welty literature and criticism are "separate gifts" (773), and yet, "[c]riticism is indeed an art, as a story is, but the story is to some degree a vision" (775). In my class, the purpose of literary theory is to help students attain Welty's vision.

Works Cited

Baym, Nina. "Melodramas of Beset Manhood: How Theories of American Fiction Exclude Women Authors." In Richter, 1519–30.
Brooks, Cleanth, and Robert Penn Warren. *Understanding Fiction*. New York: Appleton-Century-Crofts, 1943.
Cixous, Hélène. "The Laugh of the Medusa." In Parker, 242–56.
Davis, Lennard J. *Bending Over Backwards: Disability, Dismodernism and Other Difficult Positions*. New York: New York UP, 2002.
Garland-Thomson, Rosemarie. *Extraordinary Bodies: Figuring Physical Disability in American Culture and Literature*. New York: Columbia UP, 1997.
Gilbert, Sandra M., and Susan Gubar. "Infection in the Sentence: The Woman Writer and the Anxiety of Authorship." In Richter, 1531–44.
Hall, Alice. *Literature and Disability*. Florence: Routledge, 2015.
Hollenbaugh, Carol. "Ruby Fisher and Her Demon Lover." *Notes on Mississippi Writers* 7.2 (Fall 1974): 63–68.
Irigaray, Luce. "This Sex Which Is Not One." In Parker, 257–62.
McRuer, Robert. "Compulsory Able-Bodiedness and Queer/Disabled Existence." In Parker, 353–63.
Moi, Toril. "'Images of Women' Criticism." In Parker, 263–68.
Parker, Robert Dale. *Critical Theory: A Reader for Literary and Cultural Studies*. New York: Oxford UP, 2012.
Richter, David H. *The Critical Tradition: Classic Texts and Contemporary Trends*. Boston: Bedford, 2007.
Welty, Eudora. "Looking at Short Stories." *The Eye of the Story: Selected Essays and Reviews*. New York: Vintage Books, 1979. 85–106.
———. *Stories, Essays, and Memoir*. Ed. Richard Ford and Michael Kreyling. New York: Library of America, 1998.
Yaeger, Patricia. "The Case of the Dangling Signifier: Phallic Imagery in Eudora Welty's 'Moon Lake.'" *Twentieth Century Literature* 28.4 (Winter 1982): 431–52.
———. *Honey-Mad Women: Emancipatory Strategies in Women's Writing*. New York: Columbia UP, 1988.

V

Worldly Welty: International and Transcultural Contexts

American, deliberately regional in her settings, she "belongs," in
the narrow sense, to no particular nation or continent, having
found a means of communication which spans oceans.
—**Elizabeth Bowen**, *Eudora Welty: The Contemporary Reviews* (94)

Teaching Welty and/in Modernism

—**David McWhirter,** Texas A&M University

Despite her frequently acknowledged indebtedness to key predecessors—Yeats, Forster, and especially Woolf—and her regular intertextual engagements with these and other modernist writers (including Eliot, Joyce, Faulkner, and Hemingway), Eudora Welty has never figured very prominently in mainstream accounts of Anglo-American modernism.[1] The reasons for this neglect are, I think, several. Unsurprisingly, given the author's own stress on the importance of place in fiction, Welty's southernness and the narratives and values traditionally attached to that region have tended to shape and bound both the questions asked and the answers reached by scholars, and the frameworks within which she is taught. Her most widely anthologized stories ("A Worn Path"; "Petrified Man"; "Why I Live at the P.O."), all culled from her earliest volume of stories, have worked to pigeonhole her as a regional or local color writer, a judgment reinforced by the persistence of what biographer Suzanne Marrs calls "the mythic Eudora" (xviii), the provincial, "sheltered" spinster whose life was spent "in the quiet of a house in a quiet Mississippi town" (qtd. in Marrs xiii). This version of Welty also reflects the broader ways in which southern literary studies has traditionally configured the US South as an exceptional space of resistance to modernity, mass culture, and the nation itself.

Yet if Welty's modernism has too often been missed or distorted by those whom Paul Bové once dubbed "professional southernists" (116), it is equally true that the focus of much (although by no means all) of her fiction on rural and small-town Mississippi has worked to marginalize her in currently dominant modernist studies accounts that link modernism almost exclusively to the experience of *urban* life. Recent historicist and cultural studies trends in modernist studies, which emphasize modernist artists' consciousness "of their historical entanglements, their place within an epoch of accelerating social *modernization*" (Levenson 2), have tended to redirect critical attention toward the shock of the new as experienced in the explosively growing cities of late nineteenth- and early twentieth-century Europe and America.[2] The destabilizing, "disembedding" processes of social modernization—including changing attitudes toward gender, sexuality, class and ethnicity, the rise of consumerism and mass culture, and the emergence of new communication and transportation technologies and new media—were, by this account, most acutely felt in the modern metropolis theorized by thinkers like Simmel and Benjamin.[3] Indeed, as David Davis has recently argued, the very idea of a regional or rural or southern modernism such as Welty might be understood to have practiced would seem to be at odds with the dominant urban-centered paradigm of an aesthetic modernism centrally defined as a response to the upheavals of historical modernity. It hasn't helped that existing accounts of "southern modernism" were largely derived from the southern Agrarians and Fugitives, who promulgated a reactionary (and, within modernist studies, now decidedly out-of-fashion) strand of American modernism that fiercely resisted the changes brought by historical modernity and with which Welty, I argue, in fact had little in common.

In this essay I focus briefly on the challenges and rewards of teaching Welty in a junior-level class on Anglo-American modernism, populated mostly by English majors, where her 1949 story sequence *The Golden Apples* appears alongside texts by several of the modernist writers who most influenced her and to whom her work most directly responds. I regularly include Welty's fiction in syllabi for a variety of classes I teach, ranging from entry-level Introduction to Literature and American Literature survey courses to more advanced courses focused on "Life and Literature of the American South" and Mississippi Writing. But teaching Welty through the prism of contemporary modernist studies, and in the context of writers such as Conrad, Woolf, Eliot, Lawrence, Yeats, Richard Wright, Moore, Dorothy Richardson, Jean Toomer, H. D., Faulkner, and Cather, can help students apprehend Welty, not only as a southern writer, but as a full-blown international modernist in her own right, one moreover profoundly responsive to the circumstances of *southern modernity*—that is, to the historical processes of modernization that were transforming the US South, as well as the West's metropolitan centers, in the early twentieth century. *The Golden Apples*, which traces the small-town life of Morgana, Mississippi, from approximately 1904 (the date of James Vardaman's first gubernatorial inauguration, attended by Fate Rainey and—apparently!—King MacLain) to the late 1940s, *does* offer a counterpoint to urban-focused texts such as Conrad's *The Secret Agent* (often my starting point for this class),

Eliot's "Prufrock" and *The Waste Land*, Woolf's *Mrs. Dalloway*, or Richardson's *The Tunnel*. Indeed, with the important (and revealing) exception of "Music from Spain," a day-in-the-life-of-the-modern-city narrative demonstrably in direct conversation with *Mrs. Dalloway* and Joyce's *Ulysses*, the stories in *The Golden Apples* transpire in a landscape that might at first glance appear to be immune from the disorientations and displacements that metropolitan modernists variously deplored (Conrad, Eliot) and welcomed (Richardson, Woolf). But where traditional southern studies approaches might classify Welty's text as non- or even anti-modern, there is abundant evidence to suggest that the modernism Welty practices in her short-story sequence (a genre, not incidentally, that is itself quintessentially modernist) constitutes a fully aware, even celebratory engagement with the modernizing South it depicts.

Given Welty's characteristically oblique representational strategies, students often have trouble recognizing the dense historical specificity delineated in *The Golden Apples*. But Morgana is anything *but* a timeless, ahistorical place, the non- or pre-modern setting students (and their professors) sometimes take it to be. I thus ask students to keep a running timeline (start class each day by asking a student or two to provide a couple of the items they've noted) of the historical events, large and small, that Welty (in a manner that recalls Woolf's evocation, rather than presentation, of World War I in *Mrs. Dalloway*) consistently registers, however indirectly, in her text. These events subtly mark the seismic changes—social, political, technological, cultural—shaking rural Mississippi in the early twentieth century. In "June Recital," for example, Cassie Morrison recalls Virgie's brother Victor Rainey, "who was going to be killed in the [first world] war" (*Stories* 354); years later, in "The Wanderers," Virgie herself thinks of Cassie's brother Loch—"always polite, 'too good,' 'too young,' people said when he went to war," in this case World War II. Ask students to look up the notorious racist Vardaman (a whole other historical context there!), the significance of Billy Sunday (whose "visit to town" prompts "Mr. Nesbitt and the Men's Bible Class" to sponsor the orphans' attendance at the Moon Lake summer camp [412]), or the history of clear-cut logging in Depression-era Mississippi, alluded to by Katie Rainey, who "felt the world tremble; day and night the loggers went by, to and from Morgan's Woods" (516). With some encouragement—in Welty, the first pedagogical principle is that everything is in the details—students will also note some crucial technological changes: the difference between those logging trucks, or the powerful coupe driven by the middle-aged Virgie in "The Wanderers," and the blue wagon (with a "new flower in his horse's hat each day" [337]) that Katie's milkman father once slowly drove through Morgana making deliveries; "the day the airplane flew over with a lady in it" (335), viewed by Loch through his father's prized telescope; the air-conditioning ("Stay Cool at the Bijou. Enjoy Typhoons of Alaskan Breezes"—Texans get the importance of this!) introduced at the movie theater where Virgie provides musical accompaniment to the latest cinematic releases; the telephone service that both connects and separates Ran MacLain from his mother in "The Whole World Knows" ("The Lord never meant us all to separate," Snowdie tells him over the phone line. "To go and be cut off. One from the other, off in some little room" [464].)

How does Welty feel about the changes sweeping though Morgana? This question becomes even more crucial when students are urged to recognize that the apparently insular local culture portrayed in *The Golden Apples* is in fact permeated by other modernizing and globalizing currents of consumerism and mass media, currents that Eliot and others saw as contributing to modernity's fragmented, ruined, deracinated landscape, but which Welty, like many other modernists, saw as fascinating, vital aspects of modern culture that provided a vehicle for exploring previously unarticulated or prohibited possibilities and desires—especially for her women characters. As Maria DiBattista has noted, modernist writers inevitably regarded these new, popular cultural forms (the popular press, the cinema, music hall, advertising) as "an inalienable part of modern life, hence unavoidable subject matter whose forms as well as content might be assimilated or reworked, playfully imitated or seriously criticized" (4–5). Thus when I teach my class on modernism, I work to contextualize the putatively "high culture" experimental literature of the period not only in relation to developments in the visual arts—for example, in this instance, the surrealist art to which, as more than one critic has noted, Welty was signally attracted—but also to the emerging media and cultural productions of what Miriam Hansen has called "vernacular modernism": advertising, fashion, and consumer culture; mass-circulation magazines and newspapers; the cinema; radio, the Victrola, and popular music.[4] I ask students to watch for manifestations of this "other modernism" in our literary texts, to evaluate varied literary responses to the new forms of mass culture produced in and by modernity, and to consider the ways in which particular authors viewed such phenomena as threatening (as in Andreas Huyssen's famous formulation of "mass culture" as "modernism's other" [44]) or as an enabling expressive and cultural resource.

Ask students to look up a sampling of the range of cultural references in *The Golden Apples* (an in-class, get-out-your-phone Internet assignment will do the trick)—from Yeats's "Leda and the Swan," *Fantasia on Beethoven's Ruins of Athens* and "Perseus with the head of the Medusa" (554) to Rudolph Valentino and Lillian Gish, *The Cabinet of Doctor Caligari*, Billikin Shoes, Sweet Dreams Mosquito Oil, *The Re-Creation of Brian Kent* (the racy romance novel passed around by the campers in "Moon Lake"), and Blind Boy Fuller's "Rocks in My Bed Number Two" (Eugene recalls "an old Negro" in Morgana who, whenever he "was in trouble at home," would walk into the Morgana record store to ask that it be played [498]). Students will quickly see that in Morgana, where the distinctly southern folkways Welty clearly cherished (think of the rhymed fable of "Sir Rabbit" that "went through Mattie Will's head" [411] at the conclusion of her story) exist side-by-side with elements of modernist high culture (the Yeats poem "The Song of the Wandering Aengus" that "passed through [Cassie Morrison's] head, through her body" at the end of "June Recital" [399]) and the proliferating productions of mass culture, the regional and the national, the local and the global, tradition and modernity, high and low cultures are always already and inextricably intertwined. As I have argued elsewhere, in fact, the cinema in particular—in the early twentieth century an increasingly dominant cultural form abhorred and feared by some modernists (Lawrence) and embraced by others (notably H. D. and Richardson)—functions for Welty and especially for the girls of her fictional Morgana as a much-needed extension of experiential space, an alternative language for articulating racialized fears and desires connected to sexuality, and as the site for a new kind of gendered, public sphere, at once local and global, proper to the specific modernity of the supposedly "non-modern" space known as "the South" ("Welty Goes to the Movies").

Reconsidering Welty's aesthetic and representational practices in this light, and through the historicizing lens of the new modernist studies, as a complex set of responses to unfolding modernization processes as they transpired in a specific, local context (how exactly does it matter, for example, that the movie theaters regularly patronized by Morgana's girls were strictly racially segregated? how does Cassie Morrison's movie-going experience differ from Bigger Thomas's?) can help us, and our students, to recognize in *The Golden Apples* a modernism distinct not only from the reactionary, antimodern Agrarian modernist paradigm with which Welty has too often been mistakenly affiliated, but also from the work of modernists whose vision was shaped primarily by the landscapes of Paris, London, or New York. Placing and teaching Welty in the company of the modernists she admired and influenced and sometimes directly challenged also provides our students an opportunity to rethink and complicate the accepted critical narratives and analyses of modernism. Welty helps to show us that *all* modernisms, including those practiced in transnational spaces located outside the Euro-American sphere to which my own course is necessarily if regrettably restricted, are inevitably local, whether they are based in modernity's burgeoning metropolitan centers or at its peripheries, regional spaces like the American South, but also nonwestern, colonial, and postcolonial terrains. Inserting Welty into the modernist canon, reading her next to other women writers like Woolf and Richardson as well as figures like Conrad, Eliot, and Lawrence, can help strengthen our awareness of the very different ways in which men and women, and people of varying social classes, experienced modernization. And teaching Welty and/in modernism can also produce some surprising, occasionally counterintuitive insights regarding affinities and antagonisms among the writers in question: a recognition, for example, that Cather, another American regionalist modernist with whom Welty is often aligned, offers in *The Professor's House* (1925) a devastating critique of a feminized consumer culture that has far more in common with *The Waste Land* than with anything in *The Golden Apples*; or that Welty's inclusive, rich fusion of folk, high, and mass culture sources and references in *her* modernist masterpiece bears a striking, and pedagogically productive, resemblance to Jean Toomer's similar balancing act between African American folk roots and Afro-modern urban culture in *Cane* (1923).

In closing, I gesture toward what is for our students one of the most identifiably "modernist" and (children of *Star Wars*, *Harry Potter*, and *Game of Thrones* that they are) appealing aspects of *The Golden Apples*—the multiple, shifting, intertextual web of mythic references and allusions woven into the fabric of the sequence. What happens to still-pervasive, if now highly suspect, models of myth criticism, from Eliot's "mythical method" (483) to Jung's and Campbell's archetypes to Levi-Strauss's deep structuralism, when we introduce Welty's unique practice in this regard into the field of other modernist texts that extensively deploy myth? Teaching Welty as a modernist can help us to reopen questions ignored or foreclosed by the new modernist studies' historicist biases: questions, in this instance, about how and to what ends mythic allusion and patterning function in texts as diverse as Joyce's *Ulysses*, Woolf's *The Waves*, Toomer's *Cane*, Faulkner's *Absalom, Absalom!*, Chopin's *The Awakening*, Lawrence's *St. Mawr*, Cather's *The Professor's House*, H. D.'s *Helen in Egypt*, and Eliot's *Waste Land*. I ask students—sometimes through discussion, sometimes by way of an in-class writing assignment—to compare specific deployments of myth in our texts: the figure of Tiresias in Eliot and Toomer, for example, or the use of Greek tragedy in Faulkner, Cather, and H. D. Inserting Welty, whose "mythical method" differs radically from Eliot's essentialist and anti-historicist paradigm, is in fact continuous with her rich imagination of historical possibility, into such an exercise (ask the class to compare Yeats's "Leda and the Swan"—especially if they've read it earlier in the semester—to Welty's evocation of the poem in "Sir Rabbit"[5]) demonstrates once again how a modernism that includes Eudora Welty not only can enrich students' appreciation of Welty's achievement, but expand and complicate their understanding of modernism itself.

Notes

1. A partial list of such intertextual readings might include Patricia Yaeger's study of "Sir Rabbit" as a dialogue with Yeats's "Leda and the Swan," Rebecca Mark's interpretation of "Music from Spain" as an "answer" to Joyce's *Ulysses* (175–231), my own reading of "The Wide Net" as a response to Hemingway's "Big Two-Hearted River" ("Fish Stories"), and Peter Schmidt's analysis of "Asphodel" as a systematic send-up of Faulkner's *Absalom, Absalom!* (129–35). See also Suzan Harrison's book-length study of Welty's engagements with Woolf, who was, according to Welty, "the one who opened the door" (*Conversations* 82).

2. Recent anthologies edited by Levenson and Bradshaw/Dettmar offer helpful overviews of new developments in modernist studies.

3. Sociologist Anthony Giddens speaks of "the disembedding of social systems" in modernity, the "'lifting out' of social relations from local contexts of interaction and their restructuring across indefinite spans of time-space" (21).

4. For discussions of Welty's affinities with surrealism, see Fuller and McHaney.

5. For a guide, see Yaeger's brilliant reading of this intertextual relation.

Works Cited

Bové, Paul A. *Mastering Discourse: The Politics of Intellectual Culture.* Durham, NC: Duke UP, 1992.

Bradshaw, David, and Kevin J. H. Dettmar, eds. *A Companion to Modernist Literature and Culture.* Oxford: Wiley-Blackwell, 2008.

Davis, David A. "The Irony of Southern Modernism." *Journal of American Studies* 49.3 (2015): 457–74.

DiBattista, Maria, and Lucy MacDiarmid. *High and Low Modernisms: Literature and Culture, 1889–1939.* New York: Oxford UP, 1996.

Eliot, T. S. "Ulysses, Order, and Myth." *Dial* 75 (1923): 482–83.

Fuller, Stephen M. *Eudora Welty and Surrealism.* Jackson: UP of Mississippi, 2013.

Giddens, Anthony. *The Consequences of Modernity.* Stanford: Stanford UP, 1990.

Hansen, Miriam Bratu. "The Mass Production of the Senses: Classical Cinema and Vernacular Modernism." *Disciplining Modernism.* Ed. Pamela L. Caughie. New York: Palgrave Macmillan, 2009. 242–50.

Harrison, Suzan. *Eudora Welty and Virginia Woolf: Gender, Genre, and Influence.* Baton Rouge: Louisiana State UP, 1997.

Huyssen, Andreas. *After the Great Divide: Modernism, Mass Culture, Postmodernism.* Bloomington: Indiana UP, 1987.

Levenson, Michael H. "Introduction." *The Cambridge Companion to Modernism*. Ed. Michael Levenson. Cambridge: Cambridge UP, 2011.

Mark, Rebecca. *The Dragon's Blood: Feminist Intertextuality in Eudora Welty's* The Golden Apples. Jackson: UP of Mississippi, 1994.

Marrs, Suzanne. *Eudora Welty: A Biography*. New York: Harcourt, 2005.

McHaney, Pearl. "Forays into the Surreal: Eudora Welty's 'The Winds' and 'A Sketching Trip' and Joseph Cornell." *Miranda* 7 (2012): n.p.

McWhirter, David. "Eudora Welty Goes to the Movies: Modernism, Regionalism, Global Media." *Modern Fiction Studies* 55.1 (2009): 68–91.

———. "Fish Stories: Revising Masculine Ritual in Eudora Welty's 'The Wide Net.'" *Mississippi Quarterly* 62.3 (2009): 35–59.

Pollack, Harriet. *Eudora Welty's Fiction and Photography: The Body of the Other Woman*. Athens: U of Georgia P, 2016.

Schmidt, Peter. *The Heart of the Story: Eudora Welty's Short Fiction*. Jackson: UP of Mississippi, 1991.

Welty, Eudora. *Stories, Essays, and Memoir*. Ed. Richard Ford and Michael Kreyling. New York: Library of America, 1998.

———. *Conversations with Eudora Welty*. Ed. Peggy Whitman Prenshaw. Jackson: UP of Mississippi, 1984.

Yaeger, Patricia. "Because a Fire Was in My Head: Eudora Welty and the Dialogic Imagination." *PMLA* 99 (1984): 955–73.

Post Southern and International

Teaching Welty's Cosmopolitanism in "Going to Naples"

—**Stephen M. Fuller,** Middle Georgia State University

Positioning the writing of Eudora Welty outside the South, both as a location and as a category of inquiry, imposes an obligation that turns out to offer teachers emancipation. Almost exclusively a resident of Jackson, Mississippi, where she was born and raised, and author of many texts evoking southern locations, Welty somewhat inadvertently contributed to establishing and disseminating the idea that the region defined the woman and the literature that she produced. During the course of her long life, her reputation as a chronicler of an especially southern way of life assumed in scholarship and pedagogy proportions that overshadowed her work's explicit interest in life outside the South, in cities such as New York and San Francisco and countries such as Italy, Greece, Great Britain, and Ireland. Over time, this distorting overlay came to obscure the richer picture beneath, one revealing a life that included extensive travel and the creation of a considerable corpus of photographs and literary works that evince a profound supra-regional and supra-national curiosity. Isolating her approach to characterization in stories without southern settings or individuals, like *The Bride of the Innisfallen*'s "Going to Naples," for example, suggests Welty's post-southern internationalism, an interest evident in depicting women at odds with received portrayals of femininity often reproduced by male peers. Additionally, and perhaps more subversively, narratives like this one also challenge received reading habits—in particular, the assumptions and practices of New Criticism, the purportedly apolitical and ahistoric method of literary analysis that dominated American universities during most of her writing life, exercised a controlling influence over southern studies, and remains alive in the academy today. Teaching stories like "Going to Naples," perhaps too often ignored in commentaries and classrooms, presents notable opportunities for teachers to move beyond New Critical frameworks by inserting Welty's fiction into courses on global and post-southern Souths, international modernism, women in multicultural and gender contexts, and any aspect of critical theory.

Travel forms a central theme in Welty's life, a reality easily demonstrated to students by drawing their attention to Welty's memoir, *One Writer's Beginnings*; her photography, especially *Eudora Welty: Photographs*; and nearly any part of Suzanne Marrs's critical biography, *Eudora Welty: A Biography*, a narrative replete with examples of the writer in motion. In childhood, for example, arduous car rides from Mississippi to West Virginia, her mother's home state, and Ohio, her father's, revealed life beyond state boundaries (Welty 884–914), ones that she crossed repeatedly as she aged, relocating first to Wisconsin and then New York to pursue university learning. Keen early in life to pursue photography as an interest and perhaps as a career, she took pictures of these travels, a habit she continued to cultivate when she went with friends to Mexico in 1937 and later when she traveled widely in Mississippi for the Works Progress Administration. Regular visits to New York City and lengthy stays in San Francisco in 1946 and 1947 broadened a worldly outlook that enlarged again when she first traveled to Europe in 1949 (Marrs, *Eudora* 20–210). The widely available *Eudora Welty: Photographs* records some of the pictures that she took on these adventures outside the South. Visiting England to deliver a lecture at Cambridge University in the middle fifties, she visited Monk's House (xxiii), the country home of British modernist Virginia Woolf, a writer whose experimental prose exercised a powerful influence over Welty as she developed her fiction. Her international modernity is emblematized in the picture of Woolf's cottage, taken at a time when Leonard, Woolf's husband, still lived there (Marrs, *What* 90–91). Traveling solo to England and Cambridge took boldness, but her initiative to locate Woolf's home in a rural nook of the nation should satisfy many doubts regarding the depth of Welty's fascination not only with her modernist forebear but with places and cultures radically different from her own. Those who know the facts of Welty's life would then hesitate to dispute Salman Rushdie's verdict on first meeting her in the 1970s: "I thought she might be this little old provincial lady, and instead she was really tall, and she was incredibly cosmopolitan and articulate" (qtd. in Charles).

Among all of the narratives with international locations in *The Bride of the Innisfallen*, "Going to Naples" supplies one of the most powerful examples of Welty's intent to break with convention in order to reset her audience's "horizon of expectations" (Jauss 22) which may misleadingly associate Welty only with the South and/or with a static view of femininity. It concerns Gabriella, an eighteen-year-old New Yorker, whose mother has forced her literally screaming onboard the liner *Pomona*, bound for Naples where marriage awaits. Neither a southerner nor a woman depicted in a southern social context, Gabriella seems the product of a writer's conscious effort to strip away region as a central factor in the portrayal of a captivating protagonist. In fact, no region at all pertains because most of the action occurs on the high seas, where regional and national laws give way to those followed in international waters. Within this context, one that unmoors character from region, the story develops a reassessment of femininity by portraying a young woman inveighing against marriage and the mother insisting on it. In these respects, Gabriella challenges the depiction of women found in the novels and short stories of the canonical male writers of her era. For example, how many women found in the works of William Faulkner, Tennessee Williams, Richard Wright, Ernest Hemingway, or F. Scott Fitzgerald ever cross national or even regional boundaries? And when they do cross, does a narrow archetype of femininity prevail? Welty may well have endured a significant loss of critical esteem because, as Gordon Hutner observes in his survey of American domestic fiction, writers such as she "were scarcely recognized as participating in the new era of American fiction which supposedly came of age in time of war" since "there was a pronounced effort to liken new male writers to the 1920s novelists who became famous as postwar novelists: Fitzgerald, Hemingway, Dos Passos, and Faulkner. Unsurprisingly, many new authors were found wanting by comparison" (503).

A subtler and probably more threatening challenge to many students' reading patterns comes in the form of the philosophical attitude predominating in the narrative, one that suggests great impatience with New Critical interpretive strategies. So deeply did these theories of literary analysis penetrate American academic and cultural life that their legacy, despite the widespread rise of counterbalancing theories, continues to exert a powerful influence over the type of reading strategies promulgated at high schools and universities, a fact that especially hampers teaching Welty, whose style students frequently fault as too elliptical, under-edited, and excessively fond of miscellaneous detail. The writing of experimental short stories of avant-garde daring forms at least one consequence of Welty's intention to break with established patterns for prose narratives. In fact, the boldness of Welty's artistic challenge in "Going to Naples" prefigures the call for revolution in writing associated with many poststructuralists, perhaps especially with the work of French theoretician Hélène Cixous, a figure whose writing complements Welty's in the classroom.

Her landmark essay "The Laugh of the Medusa," not incidentally recycling a key figure of Welty's symbolic universe, passionately urges writers to reinvent their craft by producing texts marked by femininity. By femininity, Cixous does not necessarily mean writing by women or even about women but writing that occupies a position between gender categories, a place that for historical reasons women especially have assumed. "It is impossible to *define* a feminine practice of writing," she avers,

> and this is an impossibility that will remain, for this practice never can be theorized, enclosed, coded—which doesn't mean that it doesn't exist. But it will always surpass the discourse that regulates the phallocentric system; it does and will take place in areas other than those subordinated to philosophico-theoretical domination. It will be conceived of only by subjects who are breakers of automatisms, by peripheral figures that no authority can ever subjugate. (2046)

Alongside other works of Welty's, "Going to Naples" takes its place as a text written to discredit the New Critical discourse and in doing so makes the author a breaker of critical habits that view form as a force severing texts from history. On the contrary, Welty's formal experimentalism inserts her work into history; thus, the patterns of formlessness in "Going to Naples" maintain a political argument regarding the maligned feminine other akin to Cixous's. This courageous position, one that may have imposed a considerable artistic cost during Welty's life, may also explain her historic reputation as a regionalist laboring in the margins of modern literature, when noted experimentalists such as James Joyce have always enjoyed center ground. In fact, an effective way to highlight this sort of affinity may include teaching a text such as "Going to Naples" in a course on global modernism and/or postmodernism. For instance, putting Welty side-by-side with Joyce (whom Cixous valorized), Faulkner, Woolf, and Lawrence opens up a discussion of how each capitalizes on the use of narrative formlessness as a method for breaking with established patterns in fiction and creating new ones.

Practically, Welty's narrative demands that teachers and students reorder their assumptions by violating their horizons of expectation regarding the political significance of literary form. For example, "Going to Naples" furnishes only the barest of plotlines, so it disappoints readers searching for this sort of comforting structure. Characterization and theme, too, present challenges to audiences used to finding in these elements the full expression and measure of a writer's ability. In these three respects, the narrative makes the following overtures: a young woman departs New York City on the *Pomona* bound for Italy, where her overbearing mother hopes to find her single daughter a husband; Gabriella, a boisterous, adventurous, and independent woman, discovers a friend and potential romantic partner in Aldo Scampo, a tolerant and amiable demobilized soldier, who travels to Rome to study music; finally, plot and characterization ally to assert themes, such as the conflict inherent to questions of desire and gender. However, these assertions remain gestures somewhat unpursued as Welty goes about developing the story more subtly in the areas of point of view, symbol, and setting, aspects of her craft that lend themselves more readily to describing experiences that Cixous might define as those in which language surpasses the "phallocentric system." For example, the story strongly challenges preformed notions of order and stability with its use of free indirect discourse and symbols of subversive femininity, as represented by La Zìngara and Miss Crosby. Moreover, readers should take care not to underestimate how potently the absence of a fixed setting and/or the presence of a continually transforming one generate a context urging reform and validating change.

Reframing Welty in contexts post southern, international, and cosmopolitan can open views of her work previously closed. The views extend in many directions but rely on scholars lifting her work out of its regional framework and positioning it within broader currents of American and/or international modernism and postmodernism. My study, *Eudora Welty and Surrealism*, performs this act by stressing how thoroughly surrealist ideas penetrated American culture and how readily Welty assimilated these theories of an international avant-garde. Furthermore, new views of her work must also situate themselves explicitly in the context of critical theory, an act that lays bare assumptions underpinning what teachers claim they know about literature. While New Critical methods of the kind used in Michael Kreyling's *Eudora Welty's Achievement of Order* brought lasting insights, educators should also recognize the interpretive potential of feminist and psychoanalytic discourses, ones deployed to excellent effect by Dawn Trouard, for example. As a strategy in my classes on critical theory, I typically ask that students juxtapose older with more recent approaches to assessments of stories like "Going to Naples"; newer readings, for instance, blend strains of French and Anglo-American feminisms. To these in my experience successful strategies, teachers might also wed assessments pursued less frequently in Welty studies, such as those with a marked materialist and/or ecocritical frame of reference. Perhaps the greatest advantage resulting from teaching Welty through enlarged post-southern critical contexts, maybe especially to students of southern backgrounds, comes when readers acquire a deeper appreciation for the fundamental part played by continually shifting movements of history, culture, and politics in shaping literary as well as personal identities.

Works Cited

Charles, Ron. "Rushdie to Be First Speaker in Lecture Series Honoring Eudora Welty." *Washington Post*. The Washington Post, February 16, 2016. Web.

Cixous, Hélène. "The Laugh of the Medusa." Rpt. in *The Norton Anthology of Theory and Criticism*. Ed. Vincent B. Leitch et al. New York: Norton, 2001. 2039–56.

Fuller, Stephen M. *Eudora Welty and Surrealism*. Jackson: UP of Mississippi, 2013.

Hutner, Gordon. "Modern Domestic Realism in America: 1950–1970." *The Cambridge History of American Women's Literature*. Ed. Dale Bauer. Cambridge: Cambridge UP, 2012. 501–14.

Jauss, Hans Robert. *Toward an Aesthetic of Reception*. Trans. Timothy Bahti. Minneapolis: U of Minnesota P, 1982.

Kreyling, Michael. *Eudora Welty's Achievement of Order*. Baton Rouge: Louisiana State UP, 1980.

Marrs, Suzanne. *Eudora Welty: A Biography*. Orlando: Harcourt, 2005.

Marrs, Suzanne, ed. *What There Is to Say We Have Said: The Correspondence of Eudora Welty and William Maxwell*. Boston: Houghton, 2011.

Trouard, Dawn. "Welty's Anti-Ode to Nightingales: Gabriella's Southern Passage." *Mississippi Quarterly* 50.4 (1997). *Literature Resource Center*. Web.

Welty, Eudora. *Eudora Welty: Photographs*. Jackson: UP of Mississippi, 1989.

———. *Stories, Essays, and Memoir*. Ed. Richard Ford and Michael Kreyling. New York: Library of America, 1998.

Umbrellas and Bottles

Teaching Welty's Mythology in the Hong Kong Classroom

—**Stuart Christie,** Hong Kong Baptist University

> One of the best messages I get through the reading of *The Robber Bridegroom* is this: Love can override truths.
> —**Nicola**

Critics have consistently given credit to Eudora Welty's writing for having voiced a particularly regional sensibility: that of the American South. Far too few, however, have acknowledged her work as a gift to the world or to readers from outside the United States. As my students and I learned while reading Welty in Hong Kong, the People's Republic of China, her core literary values—the imagination at play, creative inspiration, and moral independence—can correlate to local predicaments facing readers in vastly different times and places. My experience teaching Eudora Welty in Hong Kong may also offer some indication of how "real world implications" impact the teaching of literature in classrooms well beyond the historical context of the American civil rights movement Welty wrote within, and as applicable to a variety of contexts and issues important to the present and future, ranging from transgender access to bathrooms to #BlackLivesMatter to the importance of sustaining the environment.

Another time, another place. The test of Welty's continued pertinacity, my students and I discovered, was not only her established value as a writer rooted exclusively in the American literary canon, but her timeliness and relevance beyond it. Welty's stories became suddenly applicable, in ways we had not anticipated, to issues and themes erupting in Hong Kong through the autumn of 2014. We read Welty's works against the backdrop of massive student involvement in the Hong Kong "Umbrella Movement" as it was called in the popular press locally and around the world. Student groups were key stakeholders in the 2014 protests designed to push the Hong Kong government to adhere to the pledged timeline of Article 45 in the Basic Law (香港基本法第四十五條). Jointly ratified by the People's Republic and the ex-ruler of colonial Hong Kong, Great Britain, Article 45 has been subject to controversial interpretation on all sides. For many, although certainly not all, of my students, Article 45 guaranteed universal suffrage to Hong Kong citizens by 2017. The Hong Kong government's apparent refusal to meet this established timeline sparked citywide protests, including a coordinated call to boycott all university classes commencing September 26, 2014. A degree of uncertainty arose across the days that followed as to how, or if, my teaching colleagues and I should continue teaching. I chose to honor all sides of the debate by not canceling the class. Nor did I penalize those students who chose to support the protest. (I required them, instead, to complete and submit assignments remotely.)

By the end of September 2014, there was palpable tension among those students, many holding conflicting viewpoints, who had continued to attend class. I made an attempt to diffuse it by seeking to offer Welty's myth-making as a practical example of how a good writer enjoins dialogue across different worldviews. Our classroom community, I warned, was a microcosm of the wider Hong Kong society: if we fail to communicate respectfully within these walls, we must surely fail to do so outside them. And although I did not require it, such a pressing context obviously permitted that interested students could reframe Welty's works in close proximity to what was happening on the streets. How can and should foreign (Anglophone) literature continue to matter to Chinese students at such challenging times? What is the impact of a foreign literature, if any, apart from the immediacy of the context in which it is read?

For the great majority of my students—mostly Hong Kong women, coming from recently middle- or lower-middle income backgrounds—"worlding" Welty had initially involved something far simpler. At the start of term, Welty's myth-making had seemed to offer merely the somewhat vague critique of an abstract realism, loosely conceived by us as "things as they stand in the world." Upon conclusion of the protests and the abandonment of the student boycott on November 19, 2014, some nine weeks later, my students' interpretation of Welty's stories had come to mean something completely different, mindful of a reality that had become much harder and more truthful, potentially threatening, and all too suddenly "real." Given new life during a time of profound existential crisis for Hong Kong society, Welty's stories had been completely transformed. In what follows, I focus briefly upon my students' "realization" of the mythical properties of everyday objects, which Welty stories demonstrate, as well as upon their search for consensus in the classroom, a search that builds community rather than divides it.

To the best of my knowledge, Eudora Welty has not been taught in Hong Kong before; if so, but sparingly, as a very small part of a survey course on American literary modernism or genre (i.e., the short story). Our seminar focused exclusively on five short stories, *The Robber Bridegroom*, and selected photographs taken during Welty's brief time at the Works Progress Administration (WPA). The course's primary semester-long teaching and learning activity (TLA) required students to build toward a "Hong Kong Mythology" created, storyboarded, and eventually filmed in groups. In addition to the storyboard, interim assessments contributing toward the final group video included a "Hong Kong Other" image-reading exercise (where students applied what I understand to be Welty's method as a photographer; i.e., using images to recover and interpret the gazes and perspectives of human subjects not widely understood or appreciated by the mainstream society); as well as a group-authored exegesis, reflecting upon which TLA outcomes had succeeded and which remained unachieved to date. The roll-out of these formative elements for the TLA, with interim assessments uploaded via our university's online student learning system and concluding with a final-project exhibition on the final day of class, provided the assessment framework. It was my job to provide the overall approach and enough substantive content so that my students could successfully address (and eventually meet) the course's stated learning outcomes.

Initially, I had offered a fairly straightforward and thematic approach to Welty's use of myth as adapted to her southern (American) context. What did her myth-making amount to in that context, and what literary purposes did it serve? Taking Welty's "Livvie" as our first example, my students and I observed how the story elevates everyday predicaments faced by African American Mississippians allusively, via references to classical (Greek) mythology and visual art. Rewriting the myth of Persephone to bracket the patriarchal power wielded by the characters Solomon and Cash, Welty empowers Livvie as an agent whose story is transformed from one of patriarchal containment to matriarchal sovereignty. Jamie Lockhart, in *The Robber Bridegroom*, was another popular example of how Welty's mythologizing transforms mere characterization into a catalyzing plot dynamic. Unlocking his heart's desires, Jamie's character transgresses existing boundaries in language and meaning, as well as what one "ought" or should do in any given situation.

Whether responding to Livvie's becoming or to Jamie's subversive narrative potential, my students' imaginations were activated, in the form of what Julia Eichelberger describes as "authorizing or celebrating their desires for more than is possible" in the world (Correspondence). By inviting my students to search for creative ways to apply Welty's myth-making to their own immediate context, the "Hong Kong Mythology" project also sought to transcend the limits of that context by transforming—localizing—a "foreign" literature as it was conventionally defined. (With an attempt to make Hong Kong's ethnic minorities more visible to my students, I had offered, for example, some basic statistics around life opportunities for African Americans in the rural South prior to 1960 and a "case study" of the career and activism of Medgar Evers.) Perhaps not surprisingly, my students began to look away from Welty's pages, searching for mythical potentials, invisible subjects, and analogies found in the Hong Kong world around them. They began to scout for the hidden immanence, as-yet-undiscovered, found in everyday objects. As they increasingly bought into the idea of unearthing the mythical potential hidden in everyday Hong Kong life, my students responded very positively to Welty's modeling of how an authentic locale—the commitment to local language, idiom, and place—is transformed by the energies of the universal meaning. Local contexts can also illustrate values anyone, anywhere, can understand and connect to. Using such a localized lens, instructors anywhere in the world can teach Welty's myths much as I did, by inviting their students to search for hidden potentials and analogies in their own immediate vicinity and as far from the constraints and "reality" of the American South as the imagination can allow.

After late September, it also appeared inevitable that the Umbrella Movement would intrude upon our dialogue and, at times, transform it. The TLA assessment sequence was already in process; some student groups, both present in class and in absentia, accordingly recalibrated their "Hong Kong Mythologies" data findings. Even as they occupied the protest sites, many of my students found ready material at hand as they prepared their storyboards. Formerly inert, everyday objects became illuminated by the collective mythological imagination. They began to realize the diverse signifying properties—symbolic, ideological, iconic—of such objects; and, seeking to apply Welty's method, my students began to observe how portable and humanizing mythical values can be across diverse contexts and languages. As in the epigram to this essay, the power of Welty's myths for many of my students lay in the displacement of hard truths in favor of the imagining of a happier future.

Inspired by E. M. Forster's short stories, Welty's mythical quietism held solid and magical realms equally sacred. Welty embeds the transcendent in the everyday without poisoning the capacity of either, as we saw in some of Welty's photographs. We looked, for example, at "Sunday Morning," Welty's fetching image of an African American girl in her Sunday best, holding a broad umbrella against the sun (fig. 1). The photograph is famous for the play of oppositions that the black-and-white medium only accentuates—dark and light together enjoin aspects of vulnerability and protection that the umbrella gathers to itself.

The diverse uses of the umbrella as a mythically realized object became all too clear once the Umbrella Movement gathered force. Early on, student protestors had used the umbrella only functionally, shielding themselves from the blows of police batons and pepper spray. As the occupy zones took on a more permanent

Figure 1. Welty, *Sunday Morning*. Ca. 1935. Copyright © 1935 Eudora Welty, LLC.

Figure 2. Cat and umbrella. Artwork by shino. (http://www.loftwork.com/portfolios/shino/archive/392523).

Figure 3. Umbrella signage. Photograph by Flora Yau.

aspect, students signified the "yellow umbrella," ubiquitously and variously, as protest aesthetic: as an emblem of protection (fig. 2), iconicity transformed by function as umbrellas became crafted into zip-up tents or as a surface to write on (fig. 3).

Inspiration now traveled rapidly in both directions, from Welty's text to Hong Kong context and back again. My students and I began to isolate earlier examples within the Welty corpus where a single object may serve to propagate an entire imaginary. My students and I had routinely observed how myth demands the transformation of realism, which, we supposed, takes the materiality of object-status for granted. In a well-known interview, Welty had recalled, for example, that "Livvie" was inspired by the photograph of a bottle tree (fig. 4) she had taken for the WPA (Prenshaw 91). Could not any everyday object once mythologized, we speculated, also encompass and sustain a world?

In "Livvie," the bottle tree serves not only as a symbol linking everyday use to a particular belief or worldview—as a spirit-catcher protecting African American homes from evil spirits, for example—but also inhabits "real" and mythical significance concurrently. Baby Marie, the friendly, traveling saleswoman, crosses the threshold into Solomon and Livvie's house with ease;

Teaching Welty's Mythology in the Hong Kong Classroom

Figure 4. Welty, *Bottle Trees*. Copyright © 1941 Eudora Welty, LLC.

Figure 5. The Water Bottle Umbrella. Photograph by Janet Lau.

Cash, the intended, must break the bottles on the tree before he can enter to incite Livvie's desire. My students reported that the Umbrella Movement had inspired a bottle tree, too, fashioned from the empty bottles of drinking water that had been used, on more turbulent nights, to wash pepper spray and tear gas from protesters' eyes (fig. 5).

As the protests intensified, however, our own discussion grew fractious as the world outside forced its way into our learning sanctuary. Sensibly, given the circumstances, my students began to debate the value of aesthetics versus politics. Always respectful, they began to call my own pedagogy to account, arguing that myths should depict not only foreign (English-language) literary practices but also validate claims defined by the Hong Kong context uniquely. In requesting the extension of a paper deadline, Nicola wrote: "It is very nice of Welty and Christie to voice out [on behalf of] the powerless, but [...] the powerless take the responsibility to fight for themselves as well" (fig. 6).

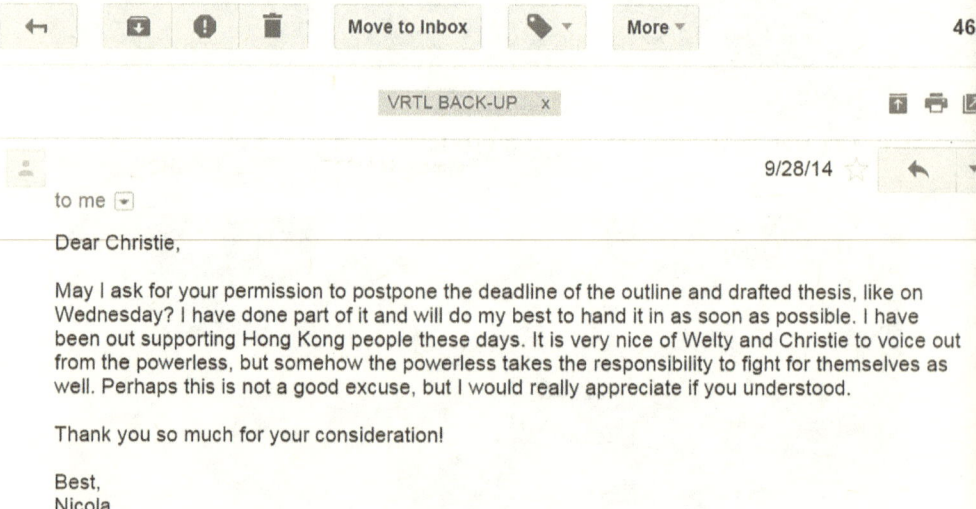

Figure 6. E-mail from Nicola.

Another student, Johnson, also informed me that he would be stepping away from class (fig. 7). In his letter to me and other professors, he made a thoughtful, if firm, critique of academic study in the context of "civil disobedience" and the "great stories and myths of a city."

As we progressed through the semester-long "Hong Kong Mythology" project, most students eventually came to understand the subtlety and real-world

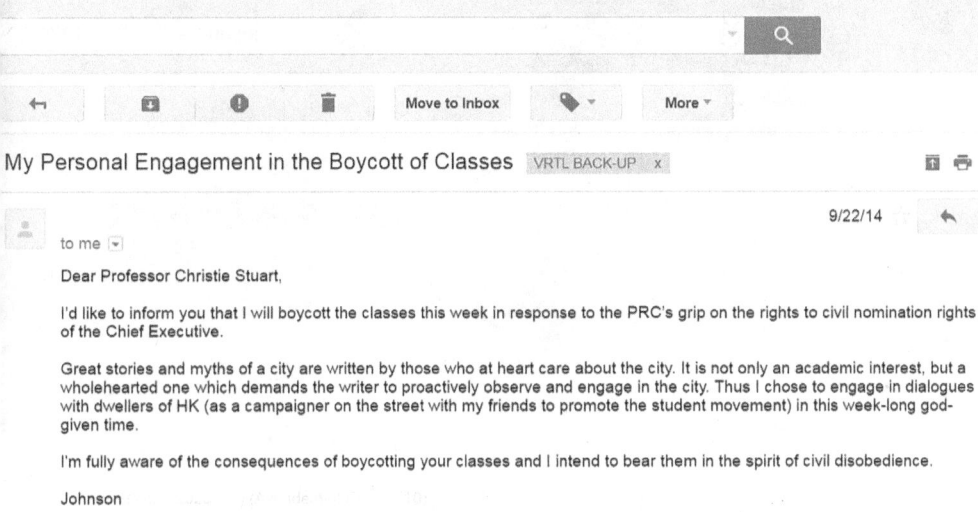

Figure 7. Letter from Johnson.

impact of Welty's myth-making, including its utility when making a present critique of reality, during what Johnson had aptly called Hong Kong's "god-given time." The photo-capture, storyboarding, and pre-filming elements of the TLA were satisfactorily completed by all student groups, more or less on time, and afforded sufficient scope linking Welty's own textual practice to the Hong Kong situation.

One group's storyboard comes instantly to mind. It begins in separation and ends aspirationally, with pro-establishment (blue ribbon) and pro-occupy (yellow ribbon) characters reaching consensus—the love of their home, a free and democratic Hong Kong—in a shared landscape of local recognition (fig. 8).

These concluding panels illustrate beautifully an outcome for teaching Eudora Welty in Hong Kong none of us could have predicted, and one, I suspect, which would have pleased the writer herself. As the semester drew to a close, my students began to internalize the power of myth to critique "things as they stand" in their society. Having observed how myth transforms everyday objects, they began, rightly, to regard *themselves* as mythical objects, each unique, world-forming, and alive to Hong Kong's unfolding story.

As the Umbrella Movement passed into history, my students struggled to accept that their protest would ultimately be defined by the lack of a political outcome. Still, for my part, I argued that it was precisely at such moments (for some, despairing) that the search for narrative outlets, distinct from

Figure 8. Blue-yellow ribbon harmony. Created by Anna, Karen, and Janet (Group 5).

history, becomes most crucial and prescient. Time and time again my students and I had repeated a phrase that Welty's stories had inspired in us: "if we can imagine it, is already real." What perhaps my students hadn't counted on—what had happened in the meantime during the protests and the process of completing their projects—was the collective benefit of what was occurring *inside* our classroom, as they committed to what might be called the process of consensus-based discovery. Students developed increasing respect for each other's positions despite, and probably because of, opposing views. The urgency of context had given collective focus to my Hong Kong students' mythologies and provided a workable basis for understanding how myth-making can build understanding across cultural and linguistic divides. And, for all the brilliance of my students' final projects, I was even prouder of that unintended learning outcome they had achieved collectively in class: the eventual appreciation of democracy in action, including the embrace of dissent, as it inheres in respectful group dynamics.

My Hong Kong students rightly felt—and continue to feel—that they are on the frontline of a globalizing process that the People's Republic of China now controls. They, Hong Kong's future leaders, were uniquely situated, and exposed, when seeking to imagine sustaining mythologies for twenty-first-century Hong Kong. I again quote Nicola's words extracted it from an in-class assessment:

> This was the time of our "Umbrella Movement," the first harmonious and loving protest that bound our people together and constructed new public and cultural spaces for Hong Kongers. It was the first protest in Hong Kong history in which the faith in humanity was, if not restored, then not reduced.

The wisdom of the comment lies in its appreciation of a contest for humanity bound by the double negative, a contest whose process is not yet entirely sustaining, not yet entirely destructive. Welty's myth-making created precarious space for my Hong Kong students to imagine their reality productively and otherwise. Across multiple data-types, and expanding conventional notions of the "literary," Welty's photographs, correspondence, and her emphasis upon compassion were particularly inspiring for my students who found (and redirected) imaginative resources in Welty's stories I couldn't possibly have expected. In Welty's words, "The transitory more and more becomes one with the beautiful" (*A Writer's Eye* 223). My students, too, were brave and beautiful in their transitory, god-given time. I dedicate this to them.

Works Cited

Eichelberger, Julia. Correspondence with author. April 4, 2016. Online.
Prenshaw, Peggy Whitman, ed. *More Conversations with Eudora Welty*. Jackson: UP of Mississippi, 1996.
Welty, Eudora. *Complete Novels*. New York: Library of America, 1998.
———. *Stories, Essays, and Memoir*. Ed. Richard Ford and Michael Kreyling. New York: Library of America, 1998.
———. *A Writer's Eye: Collected Book Reviews*. Ed. Pearl McHaney. Jackson: UP of Mississippi, 1994.

Transcontinental Welty

*Teaching Welty with South African Writers
Nadine Gordimer and Sindiwe Magona*

—**Pearl Amelia McHaney,** Georgia State University

In 1954, at the height of the Cold War, Eudora Welty addressed high school and college teachers as well as a general audience at an American Studies Conference in Cambridge, England. She articulated her position as a world citizen by describing the human condition:

> Mutual understanding in the world being nearly always, as now, at low ebb, it is comforting to remember that it is through art that one country can nearly always speak reliably to another, if the other can hear at all. Art, though, is never the voice of a country; it is an even more precious thing, the voice of the individual, doing its best to speak, not comfort of any sort, indeed, but truth. And the art that speaks it most unmistakably, most directly, most variously, most fully, is fiction. ("Place in Fiction" 782)

Reading fictions, the voices of individuals as Welty says, from both the American South and South Africa offers new inquiries into the perceived familiar as well as the lesser-known stories of Apartheid. The results dispel notions of regionalism, national boundaries, and time-bound literary styles such as modernism. Sandra Bermann expresses the potential impact of "transnational, interdisciplinary" study as contributing "to a new sort of global consciousness, one that would bring a keener sensitivity to the languages, cultures, and peoples of our polyglot planet and begin to draw us all into a broader, more responsive conversation" (432). Welty's fiction when read intertextually with the fictions by other women writers, black and white, from South Africa and the US South demonstrates that her writing is germane across time and space and that literature not only matters, but is essential. Transnational reading pushes us into the less familiar, less stable ground and makes us alert to how we are similar rather than how we are different. In this essay, I demonstrate how one might read Welty alongside South African writers Nadine Gordimer and Sindiwe Magona to illustrate the power of Welty's work to transcend time and space.

The catalyst for teaching Eudora Welty with Nobel Laureate of Literature Nadine Gordimer is Toni Morrison's 1977 statement: "They are fearless. Nadine Gordimer and Eudora Welty write about black people in a way that few white men have ever been able to write. It's not patronizing, not romanticizing—it's the way they should be written about" (47).[1] Morrison explained, "Perhaps it's because they [including Lillian Hellman] are all women who have lived in segregated areas of this country or in an area where there is apartheid" (47). Adding fiction by South African Sindiwe Magona, American Alice Walker, and other women writers, Renée Schatteman and I have team-taught graduate and undergraduate courses, delivered conference presentations, and published essays and syllabi.[2] Theoretical approaches of feminism, new historicism, Marxism, and postcolonialism proved the most beneficial for our students in experiencing how the literature transcended difference.

Reading Welty in a transnational comparative study is guided by several premises. First, Welty is an observant, participatory world citizen, not a cloistered, regional writer. Second, literature illuminates the individual and his or her subjective experience within the records of history. And third, comparative study of literature reveals that people share the difficult efforts to achieve human rights and that understanding the unfamiliar leads to new comprehension of one's everyday perceptions of personal experiences. The illustrative pairings I discuss here are "A Worn Path" by Welty with "Is There Nowhere Else Where We Can Meet?" by Gordimer and "Where Is the Voice Coming From?" by Welty with "Two Little Girls and a City" by Magona.

Both "A Worn Path" (Welty) and "Is There Nowhere Else Where We Can Meet?" (Gordimer) are stories of single women, faced with multiple obstacles on a cold morning as they traverse richly described landscapes. Welty's Phoenix Jackson emerges from the Natchez Trace, walks along a familiar path to town (Natchez) to buy medicine for her grandson who has swallowed lye. The unnamed woman in Gordimer's story is returning from town with a parcel, walking across a barren strip of land, toward the road leading home. Both women are confronted by men of another race—Phoenix by the white hunter who belittles her for her race, age, and poverty and threatens her with his gun,

Gordimer's white woman by a black man clothed in torn rags who frightens her, touches her shoulder making her lose her balance and drop her purse and parcel. Unharmed but afraid, she runs away. Both stories are replete with figurative language, similes (many suggesting animals and animal-like behavior), colors, smells, sounds—especially for describing place. Tracing these stylistic elements creates a rich tableau in which to see the world from the characters' perspectives.

Our students sought textual answers to essential questions about race, empowerment, and gender in "A Worn Path" and "Is There Nowhere Else Where We Can Meet?" They identified the gaps, silences, and negations in both stories. All of these critical thinking strategies open dense descriptions in these texts of minimal plot. Welty's story is accepted as an illustration of perseverance and success, while Gordimer's raises multiple questions that leave the ambiguities unresolved. Elizabeth Long's argument that fictions are "an especially fruitful mode of access to the subjective dimension of collective life in part because they explore the meeting places of self and society, of inner desires and external constraints" can be fruitfully demonstrated in "A Worn Path" and "Is there Nowhere Else Where We Can Meet?" and the two cultures read side by side add a powerful comparative dimension (3). Furthermore, reading unfamiliar fiction, such as Gordimer's story set in South Africa, alongside more familiar stories such as Welty's demonstrates the use of the Other as mirror to reflect the Self.

Readings of "Where Is the Voice Coming From?" by Welty and "Two Little Girls and a City" by Magona profit by guidance offered by Judith Langer and Homi Bhabha. Langer, as Schatteman explains, argues that fiction offers "room for *alternative interpretations, critical readings, changing perspectives, complex characters,* and *unresolved questions*" (130, my emphasis). Bhabha posits that literature, by detailing people's daily lives, illuminates the *translational moments* that happen in the spaces between historically recognized transformative events (38, Mitchell pars. 50–56). Both "Where Is the Voice Coming From?" and "Two Little Girls and a City" illustrate the power of imaginative renderings of harsh realities. Readers defamiliarize the history of Medgar Evers's assassination, and because Welty's and Magona's stories seem more different than alike, readers search beyond the surface plot for comparisons.

Welty's story is of an unnamed white man reporting to his wife how he has just shot a black man in the back, killing him; Magona's story is an impersonal narrative of two little South African girls in Cape Town. Both children, one a privileged white city girl and the other a poor black native from a village, are brutally raped, killed, and physically mangled. Reading the stories comparatively reveals remarkable similarities. Both are studies of the haves and the have-nots as determined by the characters' racial, economic, and social classes. The protagonists—Welty's victimizer and Magona's young victims—are out of their home environments. Both narratives tell of multiple tragedies, but the media (newspapers and television) tell only portions of the events. Distinctions also become clear in comparison. Despite social differences, Magona's victims' strong family bonds are in sharp contrast to the lonely brokenness of Welty's assassin. The intimacy of Welty's first-person narration highlights the absence of knowledge about Magona's unnamed predators. Welty focuses on the interiority of the murderer, but Magona objectively narrates tales of two curious, exuberant girls from opposite cultures. The contrast in the lives of Magona's two little girls invites readers of "Where Is the Voice Coming From?" to look between the lines and to listen carefully to realize multiple motivations for Welty's narrator. Readers are guided back to "Where Is the Voice Coming From?" to recognize the details of the black and white worlds of Thermopylae, Mississippi.

Byron De La Beckwith's murder of Medgar Evers became a transformational moment in civil rights history, but Welty's story that is a prescient fictional investigation into the 1963 white supremacist culture is replete with the opportunities for knowledge suggested by Langer.[3] Magona's story is of ordinary people, black and white, in the translational moments of apartheid South Africa. Both stories illustrate that danger is everywhere, regardless of precautions or good will. Readers readily feel empathy for Magona's fictional South African girls, and this pathos may open the reading of Roland Summers's assassin to some degree of understanding as well. The reading of a place and time that is unfamiliar helps us look beyond our anger and hatred of the assassin and our white supremacist history to at least identify the fictional murderer's situation. He is making his voice heard, trying to gain a foothold in a world where his social, racial, and economic status is being challenged by those who were heretofore at the bottom levels of society. Roland Summers's and other African Americans' gains of equality push Welty's protagonist further down.

For these and other comparative readings of stories from different cultures, a suggestion from "Revolution of Poetic Language" by Julia Kristeva is helpful. Kristeva speaks of "the *passage from one system to another*" (111), a transposition that allows readers to create meaning from considering the "intertextual potential (the *significance*)" of a text for linguistic or psychological analysis (Allen par. 4). Reading of Mrs. Bamjee's actions protesting South African apartheid (Gordimer, "A Chip of Glass Ruby") in conjunction with Dr. Strickland's complacency and inaction in 1960s Mississippi (Welty, "The Demonstrators") avoids the simplistic binaries that can emerge in comparative studies and leads to intertextual, layered, multivalent understandings. Similar transpositions may occur with concurrent readings of Gordimer's dystopian fairy tale "Once Upon a Time" and Welty's solipsistic complaint "Why I Live at the P.O.," both stories of dysfunctional families.[4]

For our comparative studies, Schatteman and I assigned focused annotation of passages that answered essential questions: How are the characters empowered to act? What role does race have in the plots, characterizations, and narrations (style)? What is gained by the transformation of the history into these genres?[5] We required close reading, starting with titles and opening sentences. Students analyzed micro-markers identified in opening sentences: (1) movement as in positing a "sensate body," (2) time-space orientation, (3) attention to the medium by use of symbolic or figurative language, and (4) conflict or threat to the character's well-being (Lohafer 67). Comparative studies also open other resources for consideration, so we viewed photographs, read interviews, studied historical contexts, researched newspaper reports, and watched films to enrich the understanding of how moments and lives not in the historical record are empowered with voice and presence in fiction as well as how the historical moments fictionalized open spaces for empathy. Students kept reading logs and wrote comparative essays.[6] One student reader in our undergraduate course commented, "Comparing/contrasting works from these two countries helped illuminate core similarities—what any kind of demeaning stereotype does to people, what the economics of racism wrecks—not just the lives and loves of the subjugated darker-skinned people but the lives/loves of those who subjugate" (McHaney, "Safundi" 3).

Students in our courses responded enthusiastically about the benefits of transnational comparative studies: "I quickly recognized the manipulative effects of relying heavily on one voice for authority. I also considered the unheard voice"; "I've become even more of a cultural relativist, aware of the gaps in my knowledge and sensitivity"; and "Cultures can differ but people as a whole ultimately struggle for the most basic human rights" (McHaney, "Safundi" 2, 3). Reading Welty's stories in conversation with work by writers as apparently different at Gordimer and Magona proves Welty's assertion that fiction offers a universal medium for communication.

Notes

1. I began teaching Eudora Welty, Alice Walker, Nadine Gordimer, and Sindiwe Magona in collaboration with Renée Schatteman, a colleague specializing in African literature, in a 2002 National Endowment for the Humanities Summer Institute.

2. See McHaney and Schatteman, "Women's Literature from South Africa and the American South: A Comparativist Pedagogy"; and Schatteman, "Teaching Africa through a Comparative Pedagogy: South Africa and the United States"; O'Brien and Schatteman's *Voices from the Continent: A Curriculum Guide to Selected Southern African Literature, Vol.* 3. Online resources that may be useful include South African History Online beginning with biographies of Gordimer and Magona at http://www.sahistory.org.za/, Northwestern University's "Apartheid to Democracy," online exhibits http://sites.library.northwestern.edu/southafrica/the-exhibit/, and a review of Gordimer's political positions integrated in her fiction at https://www.nobelprize.org/nobel_prizes/literature/laureates/1991/gordimer-article.html. We sometimes assigned Anne Moody's memoir *Coming of Age in Mississippi* and Lauretta Ngcobo's novel *And They Didn't Die*. We created class readers, found online texts, and placed books on library reserve. Several of the selections are variously anthologized and/or are brief enough to be read in class.

3. Medgar Evers, field secretary for the NAACP, returned home late in the evening of June 11, 1963, from a gathering where he had watched President John F. Kennedy deliver a civil rights address following the integration of the University of Alabama; https://www.youtube.com/watch?v=KVdZBtlSirI. He was shot in his driveway and died at 12:40 a.m., June 12, 1963. Evers's May 20, 1963, television speech is part of this NBC newscast of his death: Medgar Evers—www.NBCUniversalArchives.com.

4. Other comparative readings that have proven fruitful include "The Demonstrators" by Welty with "Six Feet of Country" by Gordimer and "Advancing Luna—and Ida B. Wells" by Alice Walker; and *Losing Battles* by Welty with *Mother to Mother* by Magona. Welty stories are profitably read in comparison with other stories by Walker as well: "Livvie" with "Roselily" and "Powerhouse" with "Nineteen Fifty-Five."

5. Other essential questions include the following: What is the relevant history that is being fictionalized or retold? What roles do rights have in the plots, characterizations, and narrations (style)? What role does resistance have in the plots, characterizations, and narrations (style)? Do characters' actions lead to personal or public (civic) changes? What results from reading the literature through a theoretical perspective?

6. See the website prepared for this volume for teaching resources and O'Brien and Schatteman.

Works Cited

Allen, Graham. "Intertextuality." *The Literary Encyclopedia*. January 24, 2005. The Literary Dictionary Company. Accessed January 2, 2006. Web.

Bermann, Sandra. "Working in the *And* Zone: Comparative Literature and Translation." *Comparative Literature* 61.4 (2009): 432–46. Accessed May 1, 2016. Web.

Bhabha, Homi K. *The Location of Culture*. London: Routledge, 1994. Print.

Gordimer, Nadine. "A Chip of Glass Ruby." *Life Times*, 117–28. Print.

———. "Is There Nowhere Else Where We Can Meet?" *Selected Stories*. New York: Penguin, 1975. 17–20. Print.

———. "Once Upon a Time." *Life Times*, 441–47. Print.
———. *Life Times: Stories, 1952–2007*. New York: Farrar, Straus and Giroux, 2010. Print.
———. "Six Feet of Country." *Life Times*, 19–31. Print.
Kristeva, Julia. "Revolution in Poetic Language." *The Kristeva Reader*. Ed. Toril Moi. New York: Columbia UP, 1986. 89–136. Print.
Langer, Judith. *Envisioning Literature*. New York: Teachers College Press, 1995. Print.
Lohafer, Susan. "The DNA of Genre: Micro- and Macro-markers of Genre in 'Best' American Short Stories and Essays." *Less Is More: Short Fiction Theory and Analysis*. Ed. Jakob Lothe, Hans H. Skei, and Per Winther. Oslo: Novus P, 2008. 63–74. Print.
Long, Elizabeth. *The American Dream and the Popular Novel*. Boston: Routledge, 1985. Print.
Magona, Sindiwe. *Mother to Mother*. Boston: Beacon P, 1998. Print.
———. "Two Little Girls and a City." *Living, Loving, and Lying Awake at Night*. New York: Interlink Books, 1994. Print.
McHaney, Pearl Amelia. "History and Intertextuality: A Transnational Reading of Eudora Welty's *Losing Battles* and Sindiwe Magona's *Mother to Mother*." *Southern Literary Journal* 40.2 (Spring 2008): 166–81. Print.
———. "Safundi Fall 2004 Evaluations Compiled." October 6, 2006. 1–6. Typescript.
McHaney, Pearl Amelia, and Renée Schatteman. "Women's Literature from South Africa and the American South: A Comparativist Pedagogy." *Safundi: Journal of South Africa & American Comparative Studies* 16 (2004). May 8, 2007. Accessed May 1, 2016. Web.
Mitchell, W. J. T. "Translator Translated: Interview with Cultural Theorist Homi Bhabha." *Artforum* 33.7 (March 1995): 80–84. Accessed March 25, 2016. Web.
Morrison, Toni. "Talk with Mel Watkins." 1977. *Conversations with Toni Morrison*. Ed. Danille Taylor-Guthrie. Jackson: UP of Mississippi, 1994. 43–47. Print.
O'Brien, Sharon Talis, and Renée Schatteman. *Voices from the Continent: A Curriculum Guide to Selected Southern African Literature, Vol. 3*. Trenton, NJ: African World Press, 2005. Print.
Schatteman, Renée. "Teaching Africa through a Comparative Pedagogy: South Africa and the United States." *Teaching Africa: A Guide for the 21st-Century Classroom*. Ed. Brandon D. Lundy and Solomon Negash. Bloomington: U of Indiana P, 2013. 128–39. Print.
Walker, Alice. "Advancing Luna—and Ida B. Wells." *You Can't Keep a Good Woman Down*. San Diego: Harvest, 1981. 85–104. Print.
———. "Nineteen Fifty-Five." *You Can't Keep a Good Woman Down*. San Diego: Harvest, 1981. 3–20. Print.
———. "Roselily." *In Love and Trouble: Stories of Black Women*. 1973. Orlando: Harvest, 2001. 3–9. Print.
Welty, Eudora. "Place in Fiction." *Stories, Essays, and Memoir*. Ed. Richard Ford and Michael Kreyling. New York: Library of America, 1998. 781–96. Print.
———. *Stories, Essays, and Memoir*. Ed. Richard Ford and Michael Kreyling. New York: Library of America, 1998.

VI

Teaching Welty in Our Writing Classrooms

Reading and writing can each teach us something,
eventually, about the other....
—*The Eye of the Story* (28)

I really don't know anything about teaching,
but my firm inclination is to tell them to read more.
—*Conversations* (62)

The only advice I give young writers is something that
is alarmingly new to some of them; that is to read.
—*Conversations* (312)

Finding the Freshman Voice

Using One Writer's Beginnings *in the Classroom*

—**Virginia Ottley Craighill,** Sewanee–University of the South

Increasingly, freshmen taking the introductory English class required at my university have a difficult time reading out loud. They know how to read, but when asked to read poetry or scenes from Shakespeare plays, the common core of all freshman English classes here, they do not seem to understand the emotional content of the lines, do not know how to use inflection, and often have difficulty reading syntactically through the line breaks. It's as if they cannot hear the text. As stated in the 2014–15 University of the South catalogue, English 101, a writing-intensive course, "is designed to develop the student's imaginative understanding of literature along with the ability to write and speak with greater clarity" (147). In order to achieve these goals, the students need to understand the concept of voice, the writer's voice and their own.

In her writer's autobiography *One Writer's Beginnings,* Eudora Welty describes how her own love of books as physical objects, of reading, of being read to by her parents, and of learning to listen for narrative grew out of her childhood in Jackson, Mississippi, and out of her intimate connection with her parents' passion for books and stories. I use the three chapters, "Listening," "Learning to See," and "Finding a Voice," to focus the first-year English class on these aspects: close reading, imagery, the construction of literary voice, and finally, learning to recognize, construct, and refine their own voices. Although Welty's memoir works well for a literature and composition course, *OWB* could also be used as a model in a creative nonfiction course or in an upper-level expository writing class.

In fact, I began teaching Welty's *One Writer's Beginnings* in a writing pedagogy course for new writing tutors and had them compose a literacy narrative à la Welty. Writing tutors are students chosen by the faculty after their freshman year for their skills in writing and peer editing. As one would expect, the student tutors, like Welty, have had childhoods filled with books, had parents or caretakers who read aloud to them and who encouraged their *bibliophilia*; it's evident in their sophisticated vocabulary and sentence structures. They relate to Welty's autobiography, despite its relative historical distance, and love to analyze her syntax and examine her word choices.

But having the tutors work with *One Writer's Beginnings* is not much of a pedagogical challenge. They love it because they can easily relate to her childhood. So I decided to take Welty to the English 101 students, most of whom, I suspected, spent more time on Facebook than they did in real books, and who are the Children of the Text. For these students, reading a book about a world with no technology but record players would feel like science fiction, so we started off with a short opinion editorial entitled "In Praise of (Offline) Slow Reading" by David Mikics (*New York Times*, January 3, 2014) and Welty's first chapter of *OWB*.

Mikics and Welty complement each other; Mikics's op-ed provides a contemporary spin on the pleasure and the necessity of reading books and describes the consequences of an increasingly digital world. He states, "The digital world offers us many advantages, but if we yield to that world too completely we may lose the privacy we need to develop a self. Activities that require time and careful attention, like serious reading, are at risk; we read less and skim more as the Internet occupies more of our lives." Mikics points to the "link between selfhood and reading slowly" and to studies that "suggest that reading books, a private experience, is an important aspect of coming to know who we are." Welty's autobiography illustrates Mikics's article concretely; as she says, "I learned from the age of two or three that any room in our house, at any time of day, was there to read in, or to be read to" (*Stories* 841). I wanted to see if Welty's childhood experience of reading resonated with my freshmen, so I had students write a comparative essay on the authors' ideas about reading and a literacy narrative about the influence of books on their own childhoods: Did their parents read to them? What books had a strong influence on them? What were their reading habits like presently? When, what, and where do they read?

This assignment had two purposes: to provide a contemporary version of Welty's narrative about books and the self, and to help me gauge where the individual students were as writers at the beginning of the semester. Not surprisingly, there was a strong correlation between students who were read to and who read a lot as children and the existence of a sophisticated writing style and a well-established writer's voice, as an excerpt from student Nora Walsh-Battle's essay proves:

> My upbringing was, much like Welty's, a hyper literate one. Almost all of my early memories feature books: my parents reading to me, reading themselves, going to the library on a weekly or bi-weekly basis, just running my hands over the spines lining our house's numerous bookcases.

Students like the writing tutors and freshmen like Walsh-Battle connected with Welty's narrative sensibilities and associated their love of reading with her stories, and they also exhibited the ability to write sophisticated prose and had clearly developed individual styles. Students whose backgrounds did not include much reading generally had unvaried sentences and a limited vocabulary. By having them read and analyze Welty's complex style, I hoped to expand their sense of what writing could be.

At the end of their essays on Mikics and Welty, I asked the students to choose a stylistically intriguing passage from "Listening" and to analyze the syntax and word choice, explaining how Welty creates her effect. Student Virginia Klemens responded, "Welty's word choice and syntax additionally adds flavor to her writing. One example of her careful word choice and phrasing is, 'It isn't my mother's voice, or the voice of any person I can identify, certainly not my own. It is human, but inward, and it is inwardly that I listen to it. It is to me the voice of the story or the poem itself'" (851). Klemens continues, "This passage captivated me because of the repetition of 'voice,' 'inward,' and 'it is.' The compound sentences create a pleasant rhythm and give the passage a poetic feeling. I also enjoy the shorter sentences that put together create a powerful message." Klemens touched on a key passage in Welty's first chapter: the concept of listening for the "voice of the story or the poem itself," as well as the voice Welty hears when she writes. Ultimately, the close reading of Welty's book and the concept of listening for the voice of the text prepared the students for the poetry unit, which I taught between the three chapters of *OWB*.

In preparation for their poetry unit, I began with the same quotation from "Listening" that Klemens identified above, which opens, "Ever since I was first read to, then started reading to myself, there has never been a line read that I didn't *hear*. As my eyes followed the sentence, a voice was saying it silently to me" (851). Following Welty's description, I asked the students to read passages from "Listening" out loud so they could hear what she is doing with language and sound. We paid close attention to the passage where Welty describes her "physical awareness of the *word*" moon and the sensory connection she makes between the object in the sky, the word, and its sound. When the passage was read aloud, the students could hear Welty's repeated use of assonance, the double *oo* sound of "moon" and "June" and the long *o* of "Ohio," as well as feel the physical sensation of making those sounds (847–48).

This prepared them to read poems aloud, after glossing unfamiliar words, and to describe, in writing, the poem's speaker and the emotional content of the poetic voice. In the next class, they performed a dramatic reading of a poem in that voice. With Welty's help, we worked toward an understanding of poetic voice and tone, and examined how the writer creates tone through word order and word choice, paying particular attention to the "physical awareness of the *word*" and "the connection it has with what it stands for" (847).

After this section of the poetry unit, I had them read "Learning to See" before we launched into imagery and figurative language. I connected Welty's description of the photograph of her grandmother Eudora Carden (889–90), who was pregnant when the picture was taken, to the need to closely observe the concrete imagery of a poem in order to see the symbolic significance. I wanted them to grasp that Welty's concept of "seeing" goes beyond visual observation to insight gained from understanding the tension between the image and what it hides, or reveals, a theme we dealt with in *King Lear* and *A Midsummer Night's Dream*, as well as in the poetry, and a theme that occurs in much of Welty's fiction. Reading *OWB* first in a course that deals with those more complex works would help students better understand Welty's narrative designs.

To conclude that section, I called their attention to Welty's description of the music box at her grandfather Welty's house and had them write a descriptive paragraph about a significant object from their childhood using only sensory imagery (910). From these paragraphs, I asked them to construct a poem using at least ten of the poetic devices they had studied.

For the final chapter, "Finding a Voice," we focused on style; I reminded them of the basic vocabulary of sentence structures, something they have generally forgotten if they ever knew, and gave them examples of literary and syntactical structures they would find in Welty's writing. I again asked them to find an intriguing passage, to post their passages, and to answer these questions: *Which literary devices does Welty use? Why are they appropriate for the narrative?* By looking at the construction of meaning through syntax, literary devices, and word choice in their chosen passage, they learned to identify Welty's use of these tools and discovered how voice can be consciously crafted. All the students posted their passages on the classroom website and presented their analysis in class. Two students chose this passage:

> The frame through which I viewed the world changed too, with time. Greater than scene, I came to see, is situation. Greater than situation is implication. Great-

er than all of these is a single, entire human being, who will never be confined in any frame. (933)

They noted the use of anaphora and remarked on the clever repetition of the word frame that literally frames the passage. In breaking down cumulative and periodic sentence structures and examining rhetorical tropes like anaphora and parallelism, students can begin to imitate these structures and devices in their own writing and move closer to developing their own distinct voices as writers.

When we moved to the Shakespeare unit, students were required to read out loud and, ultimately, to perform scenes for their final exam, as well as to write literary analyses of the plays. In those final scene performances, the students experienced the pleasure of the spoken word. While critical analysis of the text is a goal of the class, I continued to stress the ability to "speak with greater clarity" to illustrate a clear comprehension of the characters' voices and how Shakespeare conveys meaning through dialogue. Through Welty's instruction in *One Writer's Beginnings*, students were better able to hear the voices of poetic personas and literary characters not just in Shakespeare but in any literary work, to see through language to the concept of human nature, and to find their own distinctive mode of expression. These are, I acknowledge, high aims for freshmen in the digital age, but as Welty observes, "Children, like animals, use all their senses to discover the world. Then artists come along and discover it the same way, all over again. Here and there, it's the same world. Or now and then we'll hear from an artist who's never lost it" (847). The world of Welty, the poets, and Shakespeare, no matter how different it may seem on the surface, is the same world we are all born into, and through the voice of books, as Welty explains, we can come to understand our common humanity.

Works Cited

Mikics, David. "In Praise of (Offline) Slow Reading." *New York Times*. New York Times, January 3, 2014. Web. http://nyti.ms/1cqmNL7.

Welty, Eudora. *Stories, Essays, and Memoir*. Ed. Richard Ford and Michael Kreyling. New York: Library of America, 1998.

"He Going to Last"

Why Phoenix Jackson's Grandson Still Matters

—Dawn Gilchrist, Swain County High School

My Advanced Placement seniors are generally a good representation of our southern Appalachian high school, where over 50 percent of our students qualify for free and reduced lunch, and about 30 percent are members of the Eastern Band of the Cherokee. Our students, who share my southern Appalachian background (I entered Head Start in 1968, benefiting from LBJ's War on Poverty), are in a category that policymakers label "the underserved." They are also aware, much more than I was at their age, of how they are seen by the greater world. They recognize the stereotyping of and condescension toward people, both Cherokee and white, who are from this region. This understanding and empathy stem from the same source, from a growing recognition of the wrongheadedness of labels, that allows them to appreciate the careful renderings of Eudora Welty's characters in "A Worn Path"; from the rural white hunter and nurse, to Phoenix and her waiting grandson, my AP class appreciates the layered complexities of the characters and the respect that lies behind Welty's renderings of southern race and class.

Education has always been the best leg up out of poverty, and public school may still be the last best hope of social mobility. In my school, Swain County High School, every effort is made to level the playing field for our population in hopes that more of them will achieve their potential. One way that is done is to pay Swain students' AP test fees. Hence, all my students have to do to gain college credit is come to class, study, and pass the test—but therein lies the rub. The requirements for passing the three-hour AP Literature and Composition test include a multiple choice-based analysis of several passages of literature, requiring that students show an understanding of content, style, and form; further, in the free response section of the test, students must write three persuasive analytical essays that are scored on content, style, and mechanics. Those who do best on this test will always come from backgrounds in which the parents are readers, and the discussion of literature takes place around a dinner table. My students, for the most part, do not have this invaluable resource, and yet they must demonstrate the same perception and knowledge as students who have home libraries and deeply literate families. What they do have, however, is their unique perspective, one which they can access and employ almost as soon as they begin their first discussion of Eudora Welty's story. My challenge is to improve their analytical skills and to help them understand the mechanics of the story in order to help them pass the AP exam. At the same time, good literature helps readers to see through the eyes of another person, to understand other perspectives. I want my students to be able to do both, to read analytically, but also to see the relevance of this story to their lives.

"A Worn Path" is an eminently teachable work of short fiction for almost any high school class. But its allegorical structure lends itself exceptionally well to a tiered assignment that gives students in an Advanced Placement class discussion and writing material as they dig beneath the story's simple surface, thus practicing textual analysis somewhat painlessly. One assignment of this variety that I have used successfully requires the following:

1. Small student teams create informal writing and discussion questions, using questions taken from or inspired by the standard "Five Elements of Fiction" list: setting, conflict, characterization, plot, or theme (focus can also be on symbol/title if they prefer).
2. Two lists of ten or so analytical questions must be linked to their element: one list of five for discussion only, and one list of five for written responses.
3. The first list feeds the second.
4. Google Docs is the platform, allowing real-time collaboration with teammates.
5. Resulting lists of questions are projected onto a whiteboard for classmates' responses, oral and written, in that order.
6. Written responses may be used again later as students develop their unit essay on the short fiction genre.

When I first assign this activity, I tell students to use the Five Elements of Fiction as an approach, and to read the story as an allegory, specifically as a parable. This is often followed by groans as the students envision works such as

Pilgrim's Progress. Because of this, their engagement with the story, like their eventual grasp of its several meanings in the student-led assignment, always seems to begin a few pages in.

Students quickly begin to see how Phoenix seizes power in the story by exploiting the weaknesses of those who stereotype. Phoenix understands, for example, that the narrow views and sentimentalizing of the mainstream can be used to the advantage of those who are categorized and underestimated, if, for no other reason, because those who see other people in peripheral vision see them incompletely. In a long and thorough discussion of the story as viewed through different lenses and layers of meaning, students do a close reading of allegory, and in doing so, they also make discoveries about themselves.

While it might seem that students in rural poverty, coming from families that are often provincial and uneducated, would struggle with the sophistication of AP analysis, and struggle even more with a complex writer like Eudora Welty, using this particular story has the opposite effect. Because my students are so aware of the academy's interest in uplifting them as the downtrodden (sometimes even relying on that interest), as they create questions that require a delving into the story's meanings in conversation and writing, they make connections to their lives. One student grasped a more profound level of Phoenix's "stolen" nickel: she saw the equivalent as her own and her fellow students' emphasis on being Appalachian in their college essays, or, in her case, a further emphasis on being an enrolled member of the Eastern Band of the Cherokee (Brown). They see that the hand lifting Phoenix from the ditch is also the hand holding tightly to preconceived ideas of who she is, hence, of who they are; nonetheless, a hand up is still a hand up, and, as Phoenix tells the white nurse who offers her money, "Five pennies is a nickel" (*Stories* 179).

Again, because the students lead the class themselves, their discoveries and insights are slower in coming, but also more memorable for them than if I hand them a completed analysis in the form of lecture or notes. For instance, last fall, one group who asked discussion questions regarding symbolism did not see beyond the reference to slavery in the line beginning, "big dead trees, like black men with one arm" (173), until ten minutes into the conversation, but grasped that there was much more there when another student pointed out in the discussion portion of the assignment that this was also part of Phoenix's journey, and, because the story is a parable, the journey of the African American people, and, ultimately, of humans in general (Lane). Another discussion question from a group of students, this one regarding character, "What would Phoenix Jackson view as a good life?" (Barr), allowed a space for students to begin discussing the main character's similarities to themselves, which is, in a teacher's view, when real engagement begins.

It is in having students lead the class in an informal assignment, rather than in response to a strictly structured essay prompt, that they are given permission to move outside of pure analysis and explore the story's layers in relation to their own lives. They relate the story to their own experience, their own short history, but they also engage in the cerebral and analytical approach to literature that is the only means through which a student can achieve a high score on the AP Literature and Composition test. In watching the discussions that have taken place over the last few years, and in reading the unstudied responses that students write, I again realize why Eudora Welty's story goes far in helping my students understand that literature is more than craft, more than analysis, and even more than art. "A Worn Path" helps my readers understand why literature and its accompanying lexicon and analysis are worth their time because it helps them determine their own place in the world.

In recognizing the humanity they share with Phoenix, Swain County High School's AP seniors further understand how all aspects of the literary craft come together to create a work of endurance, and that such works endure not because they are artful—not because allegory, symbol, and theme are all cleverly organized to create a whole—but because that artful whole contrives successfully to deepen human insight into and awareness of our own actions and motivations. Ultimately, this is what the Advanced Placement Literature and Composition Test requires students to articulate. Using this ability to think deeply and critically is the means by which Educational Testing Services will take my students' measure. In using Eudora Welty's parable, and learning through analytical methods that it is a parable with authentic human love at its center, students see that the reason for an old woman's journey to procure "the soothing medicine" (178) for her chronically injured grandson is (as Welty herself responded to readers in a *New York Times Book Review* article) "the only certain thing at all" (Welty, "Selection" 1).

In 1968, between two bookends of Welty's accomplishments, an American president, though not of my ilk, chose to allocate a portion of governmental monies toward serving the poor, the traditionally underserved, among whom were my people, and that effort had an impact on my life. Eudora Welty, though not of her characters' ilk, nonetheless presents them in a way so finely rendered that they rise clearly in my AP students' imaginations, simultaneously embracing but also transcending category, nomenclature, race, and class. It is because of this that the story "A Worn Path" will continue to matter to my readers, and why my students will continue to care about Phoenix and her grandson. As Phoenix tells us on the last page, "He going to last" (178).

Works Cited

Barr, Caleb. "Eudora Welty Discussion and Writing Questions." Swain County High School. Bryson City, NC. October 2016. Presentation.

Brown, Brooklyn. "Eudora Welty Discussion and Writing Questions." Swain County High School. Bryson City, NC. October 2016. Presentation.

Lane, Gabbrielle. "Eudora Welty Discussion and Writing Questions." Swain County High School. Bryson City, NC. October 2016. Presentation.

Welty, Eudora. "Selection." *New York Times Book Review* March 5, 1978: 1. Web. October 10, 2014.

———. *Stories, Essays, and Memoir*. Ed. Richard Ford and Michael Kreyling. New York: Library of America, 1998.

How I Teach "Livvie" in Welty's Home County

—**Alec Valentine,** Hinds Community College

Many teachers have told me they avoid Welty because they don't understand her. Having had the opportunity to take a creative writing class with Welty long ago, I've always admired Welty's work, and have found that her fiction works well in my community college classes. This essay will discuss how I use several class periods to teach "Livvie" so that students become engaged in the story, learn to practice close reading, and develop their writing skills.

The Mississippi community college where I teach is one mile from the Natchez Trace, but many of my students don't feel connected to Livvie when they first read Welty's story. Even though many of them (black or white) surely have ancestors who "share-cropped" on farms like Solomon's and had no real chance for education or advancement, most students today know next to nothing about farming, by anybody. Everybody would rather forget that sharecropping ever took place and just not talk about it. Race and poverty are still painful to discuss. Mississippi's public schools reflect the legacy of sharecropping and all the forms of discrimination against nonwhite and poor people. In these schools, students often do not receive the education they need to succeed in our state's community colleges, which are much better integrated than most students' prior schooling.

I teach "Livvie" in the Freshman Comp II course at my college, a course that studies genres of literature and requires a concluding essay about each one. Welty is appealing for the short-story genre, but her work can be difficult even for good readers. My less skilled readers are very literal and look for action, solid facts, and clear concretes. If Welty at first glance seems to lack these, they may bog down. To give them something to hang onto, I focus first on characters and their challenges, as a way of drawing students into the story and its world. Many students regardless of race find that they can identify with Livvie's struggles. Then, through discussion and writing assignments, we discover literary dynamics within the story and learn to write about them.

During the first class, we begin by reading the first paragraph aloud, noticing the details of place, character, and situation. Then it's time to stop and ask for a journal entry. The students write *as Livvie* to say what she must think about this arranged marriage. Before writing, we take note of Livvie's personality traits that appear so far (passive, compliant), as well as her poverty. In writing this journal, students can gain an empathy with her. Afterward there is time for sharing a few journals.

The story is full of images, so I define that term for students at this point. As we continue, I ask one student to read through the second paragraph, stopping every couple of sentences, and ask others to volunteer each word they think is an image. We can actually see the several threes, so I lead on to ask what the threes might suggest? (Baby makes three, a romantic threesome, etc.) All the jelly, vinegar, pickled peaches and preserves, I point out, are things that in earlier times had to be sealed up tightly to be preserved. Who is sealed up tightly in this story? For the mousetraps in every corner, who is trapped? With the bottle trees a little further down, who must bottle up her feelings? Welty fills the story with images in order to *suggest indirectly*, not state directly, points about Livvie's predicament. The images also gain symbolic value as they portray Livvie's condition. Soon, students are doing a good job of finding images on their own and recognizing their metaphorical intent, and they are reading more deeply than literally. Before class is over we notice the "even balance" (*Stories* 277) of images in the third paragraph (is marriage an even balance?), the blood-red roses (like Livvie's monthly cycle), and the peach and pomegranate (female and male archetypes) in paragraph four. The assignment for the first night is to read the rest of the story, underline with pencil every image they find, and note whether it has any symbolic connotation.

I also ask students to begin an additional task of writing a paragraph with a topic sentence such as, "Welty's images in 'Livvie' suggest important points about Livvie herself"—or about another character. I assign it the first day but not to be completed until the following night. We go over it in class the second day—most don't have much, but it gives an opportunity for questions about it. I point out that we are looking for a topic for the big paper that will conclude the unit, and that we are learning how to write about literature: one way is to make a point and support it with examples, carefully explained. Already students seem to be identifying with Livvie and her problems. This means some have crossed a racial divide and recognized her humanity, and all have moved from merely *reading* literature to "getting into" it.

Students can readily see that Livvie's marriage is one-sided. She meekly answers, "Yes, sir," as Solomon and her parents arrange her marriage (276). And students identify with the cause: her poverty vs. his wealth, her relative youth. These elements are full of discussion and writing topics. A comparison of Livvie and Solomon is one. If there is time, instructors can assign a journal or letter of advice the student would give to Livvie before she marries, (1) as her mother or father, (2) as her friend. Why does Livvie marry Solomon? A good class discussion about marriage in contemporary society can liven things up. In Welty's youth there was little argument—marriage was *the* pathway, the goal—yet Welty herself remained single. Can women today remain single, or can men? What if they want children? I wrap up these speculations by bringing things back to Livvie's problem in her own day, when women had almost no way of earning money. We recall that life and thought have been quite different in other times, and we can't expect others to have lived by our values and understanding. An assessment of Livvie's marriage, examining what she gains and what she loses by it (or some other angle), is a good topic for a student willing to stick close to the text.

Several other topics can be floated now or soon. Comparison essays are easy to conceptualize: not only comparing Livvie to Solomon, but Livvie to Baby Marie, Solomon to Cash, or Solomon and Cash as Livvie's two imperfect choices for a husband. Livvie's status as wife/servant, a role common and accepted in her day, is shown throughout the story: all those preserves she would have made herself, just as she scrubbed the kitchen (281) and prepared trays of food every day (278–79). That role and other mentions like the excitement of the cosmetics Miss Baby Marie brings indicate Livvie's readiness for a change. The theme of Livvie's transformation (a likely topic) is also shown in imagery: the many references to spring and Easter, to flowers blooming, her restless thoughts in the paragraphs just before Baby Marie arrives, and many of the mentions of dreams.

Any topic in the two paragraphs above is good for an in-class paragraph or journal, as a way both of focusing students' attention on them and of getting them started on their essay. But another day of discussion is necessary. On the third day, instructors have the opportunity to introduce a couple more ways of reading in-depth. One is mythology. Various scholars have seen myths of Psyche or of Persephone (Livvie), of Hades (Solomon), of Pan or Dionysus (Cash) wavering beneath the surface of Welty's prose. Students can look up these myths online and with a little more reading discover how Welty does not retell the myth but amplifies her story with these ancient power packs.

Another is colors: Welty employs the colors of spring and rebirth and other motifs, and my students have written good papers analyzing colors alone. And names should not be missed. Welty always weaves some meaning into names in her stories.

Virtually every sentence in "Livvie," though in third person, relates something as Livvie might see or think it. Reading aloud through any paragraph, the teacher can show that this is so. As a classroom activity, I sometimes lead us in a few minutes of rewriting: the arrival of Miss Baby Marie as Baby Marie herself might tell it, first in first person, then in third person; or the exciting part of Cash's day as he might think it. Students then find it easier to write a journal as if they were Cash or Baby Marie. The author chose to keep the narration in Livvie's perspective, but why? This kind of question is hard to push further in this unit but is a prelude to what will come later when we analyze the point of view used in other literary texts.

Each class period on "Livvie" gives students practice in careful study of a rich and complex text, something my students are more successful at when they become interested in the characters. The approach I have described can also be used with other Welty texts: "The Wide Net," "Death of a Traveling Salesman," "A Still Moment," "First Love," *The Robber Bridegroom*, and others. Welty's charming ambiguity and opacity may at first frustrate and disappoint students with modest reading skills. But Welty knew people like my students. Many of her stories ("Livvie," "The Burning," "The Winds") can be presented as examinations of how a young person reacts to her own background and to the changes and possibilities which present themselves. With in-class analysis, guided writing, and suggestions for topics like those above, my students have produced some amazingly insightful papers. Young people can shed some of their racial provincialism and realize that a character like Livvie is facing the same existential choices and awareness that inform their own lives. They can give themselves over to Welty and let the gossamer webs and gentle breeze of her wording embrace, encourage, and even fortify them.

Works Cited

Welty, Eudora. *Stories, Essays, and Memoir*. Ed. Richard Ford and Michael Kreyling. New York: Library of America, 1998.

"Something Beautiful, Something Frightening"

Using Welty's Stories to Teach Critical Thinking in Undergraduate Writing Courses

—**Laura Sloan Patterson,** Seton Hill University

The contemporary undergraduate writing course, whether situated within a first-year composition program or within a specific discipline, is often founded on the goal of improving students' critical thinking and writing. In 2011, the Council of Writing Program Administrators, the National Council of Teachers of English, and the National Writing Project co-wrote a "Framework for Success in Post-Secondary Writing."[1] It defines critical thinking as "the ability to analyze a situation or text and make thoughtful decisions based on that analysis" (1) and encourages teachers to help students "move past obvious or surface-level interpretations and use writing to make sense of and respond to" a variety of texts (7). Eudora Welty's intricately constructed short stories allow instructors to challenge students to move to higher levels of critical thinking. Welty's stories can be dislocating for students because of the cultural contexts they portray and the layered imagery and voice they employ, but this dislocation can be used productively in the classroom. In my own first- and second-year college English courses, I have used the "something beautiful, something frightening" technique described in this essay with "Petrified Man," "The Purple Hat," "No Place for You, My Love," "A Visit of Charity," and "A Worn Path," but it might be used with any of Welty's short stories. Similarly, I have taught these stories to students in an Introduction to Literary Studies course and a writing-intensive Writing about Literature course, but this technique could be adapted for any high school or college course in which writing and critical thinking play a key role.

The WPA/NCTE "Framework for Success in Post-Secondary Writing" offers a clear call to action for helping students delve into complex texts in meaningful ways, and Welty's own essays echo this call and give specific guidance for understanding her work. In "Writing and Analyzing a Story," Welty thinks through the impulses behind storytelling: "What is the pull on the line? For some outside signal has startled or moved the story-writing mind to complicity: some certain irresistible, alarming (pleasurable or disturbing), magnetic person, place, or thing" (*Stories* 774).[2] From here, Welty recommends a system of analysis that recognizes the story's response to the outside world rather than an approach that subjects a story to "the method of critical analysis which would pick the story up by its heels (as if it had swallowed a button) to examine the writing process as analysis in reverse, as though a story—or any system of feeling—could be more accessible to understanding for being hung upside down" (774–75). While contemporary literary criticism is not in the habit of allowing writers to dictate the modes of analysis for their works and there are certainly many ways of productively analyzing Welty's texts, it is interesting to think about how we might develop a system of basic criticism that jibes with the author's own ideas about how literature is created, especially as an entry point for junior scholars.

I begin my first- and second-year courses for English majors with a unit on Welty stories and close reading, framing literary close reading as one convention of critical thinking and writing within the English discipline. My goal in asking students to dive into Welty's sometimes dislocating texts is to offer them a wide array of possible meanings rather than a single obvious theme—something they can sink their teeth into. In this way, students can more easily transition from general responses to the text to more sophisticated interpretive strategies that can be incorporated into longer research essays, ultimately comparing their own readings to those of established literary critics, which are some of the central goals of the course.

Students at my institution often find Welty's texts dislocating on a number of levels because of their own identities. Most students come from Pennsylvania or surrounding states and do not identify with southern culture or history, despite our college's western Pennsylvania location and its proximity to Appalachia. As a moderately selective school, we often admit students who have had little experience with complex texts and who may conflate "reading closely," which they define as reading carefully for comprehension, with literary close reading. A discussion on the first day of class often elicits frank responses about their current reading practices and interpretive strategies, including how they define close reading and interpretation. It's crucial to get these ideas on the table early in order to talk about new strategies for reading Welty's texts.

Instead of a contextualization of Welty's position in the southern canon, or biographical information, as I might give in a southern literature or southern women writers course, I offer contextualization as needed. For example, when students were confused about the events surrounding death customs in "The Wanderers," we discussed southern rural wake traditions, such as having a local person perform the "laying out," or the preparation of the body for burial. In the course of this discussion, it was important to emphasize that students could find this background information on their own to contextualize their close readings in a research essay.

One specific scaffolding framework for helping students move away from generalized emotion-based responses ("I love this text" / "I hate this text") is what I call "something beautiful, something frightening." As mentioned, this technique is, in some ways, born of Welty's own ideas about why writers write—"'This story promises me fear and joy and so I write it' has been the writer's beginning" (775)—as well as her ideas about how to approach a story as a reader. "Something beautiful, something frightening" also plays on Welty's tendency to linger on aesthetically pleasing imagery as well as emotionally confusing scenes. I use this technique because students' most pressing initial problem is often not *how* to close read but *what* to close read. They want to know how to determine which passages are worthy of closer attention. To guide them in this project, I ask them to read each Welty story and find "something beautiful" as well as "something frightening."

Because these are simplified categories, we discuss the subjective nature of beauty, as well as the idea that we might look for beauty as writerly craft—a particularly descriptive or aesthetically pleasing turn of phrase, a use of repetition that slowly reveals a new motif, a pattern of images drawn from the natural world. I also note that students should record passages where Welty's narrative voice seems to find something that she is describing beautiful, even if that something is in decay, in decline, or otherwise "beautiful" in an unexpected or grotesque way. We expand our definition of "frightening" to include not only that which is scary to characters within the text, but also confusing, odd, or troubling passages. While we could use one of these words instead, "frightening" seems most apt because it is often a fear of misunderstanding a text, of not getting it, that shuts down the reading and interpretive process.

In the first-year course, after the discussion of how we are using the terms "beautiful" and "frightening," students are given several minutes on their own to find passages that fit these categories—first using "beautiful," then "frightening." They are also asked to begin a close reading of the passage, defining what is beautiful or frightening, why it fits that category, and how the image, object, scene, or passage functions in the text. Next, students pair and share their responses. Finally, we hear some responses from each category as a larger group and comment on them briefly. Then we repeat the exercise, this time looking for a passage that could qualify as *both* beautiful and frightening. To conclude the lesson, students are asked to post to an electronic discussion board, where they are given the following prompt: "Below, post your best close reading moment of today's discussion. Next, expand your thinking using this close reading. If you had to create a thesis to write a close reading essay about one or both of Welty's stories, what would it sound like?"

In this activity, the framework of something beautiful, something frightening works particularly well on two levels. First, it works because those are the places Welty's own writerly eye seemed to linger in her descriptive passages: the twins in the bottle Leota describes to Mrs. Fletcher (26); the alternating clearing, jungle, and canebrake that forms the backdrop of "No Place for You, My Love" (564); Virgie's back porch view of cut flowers plunged "stem-down and head-down in shady water buckets" (524); "the little glass vial with a plunger" (271) decorating the purple hat. As each of these glimpses may indicate, one student's "something beautiful" may be another's "something frightening," which offers an excellent opportunity for student-to-student interaction and explanation of interpretations. Second, it works because it is not intimidating to students. They are reading complex texts, but they are reading with a clear goal in mind and with familiar terms that have been discussed in class.

A second exercise can be used with slightly more advanced students, and I have had success using it with sophomores in their writing in the discipline (or writing-intensive) English course. It asks students to be more precise with their close readings through visually mapping them on a chart. Groups of students are given a page range within a story, and they must find a passage to close read within that page range. Columns of the chart lead them through thinking about which kinds of literary techniques are being used, how those techniques might be described, and what significance they might attribute to these findings. A final survey of the "significance" column asks them to think about emerging patterns they see in Welty's work. They are instructed to think about how these patterns might lead them toward thesis statements for a short close reading essay on one Welty story. The chart is included at the end of this essay as an appendix.

The charting process strikes many students as a type of reverse engineering because they may be more accustomed to intuiting a thesis about a text from a preliminary reading, then going back to find examples that fit that thesis. However, the ambiguities of Welty's work resist the hunt for thesis examples. As in hasty interpretations of the Bible, evidence for a wide variety of thesis statements can be found in Welty's work, so it makes sense to practice a writing process that allows a thesis or argument to emerge more organically from a collection of textual readings.

At this point in the class, students are asked to move into small groups to formulate their own discussion questions about the stories, based on the passages they found intriguing. A primary focus on close reading, on trying to understand a story piece by piece, often leads students to notice even more of Welty's ambiguities and complexities: What does the final line of "Petrified Man" really mean? What are the results of the unplanned excursion in "No Place for You, My Love?" How can Virgie live within her community and still maintain her individuality? How does "The Purple Hat" overturn gender conventions? Welty's milieu—one of intricate beauty, but also one of fear and potential emotional and communicative misunderstanding—provides the ideal environment for the gradual emergence of larger questions from focused readings of individual passages. When these questions emerge, students begin the process of finding their own avenues for larger exploration through writing and research, a central goal of the college writing course and of instruction in critical thinking.

This type of focus on individual moments of something frightening or something beautiful may position students for the detailed textual work needed in new historicist or material culture approaches to Welty's work. An activity for an upper-division English capstone course or advanced research methods course might include looking at Welty research within the MLA International Bibliography database and asking students to identify moments that are seen as beautiful or frightening for particular critics and how they are using those moments as the basis for a larger analysis or evaluation of Welty's work. This activity would help students understand how even their preliminary close readings are the beginnings of contributions to the Welty discourse community.

How we choose to teach Welty's work is as significant as the choice to teach her work at all. Focusing even an introductory-level course on Welty's status as a southern author may backfire, leading students unfamiliar with her work to view her as a regional author or local colorist, thus missing her status as an important modernist with a global influence. It's my belief that it is worth the extra care to encourage students to view Welty's work as both complex and approachable. While there are inherent risks involved in combining their earliest experiences with close reading and their earliest experiences with Welty, such as leaving them overwhelmed, there is also risk in teaching close reading using less complex texts. Students may walk away from exercises such as these believing that basic theme or image identification "counts" as true analysis. The beauty of using a simple method of close reading with Welty's stories is that the results are far from simple. Students emerge from these activities with a sense of confidence that allows them to approach complex texts and complex writing tasks in the future.

Appendix: Close Reading Chart for Classroom Use

Word/words/ phrase/ sentence from your passage	**Literary term** or feature being analyzed (Exs: syntax [including punctuation features], symbolism, word choice, motif, mood, tone repetition, point of view, allusion, etc.)	**Description** of the literary term (i.e. "This sentence shows *clipped, staccato* syntax" or "This phrase shows word choice that creates a *tense* mood")	**Significance** or possible meaning of this word, phrase, or sentence via your interpretation of its literary features.

Now, read through your answers in the "Significance" column. What patterns are emerging? How could you synthesize several of your individual close readings into an argument about the passage? In other words, if you were crafting a close reading paper about this passage, what would your thesis be, given the work you've done so far? Write it below:

Notes

1. For further reading, see the Council of Writing Program Administrators website, which houses the framework: http://wpacouncil.org/framework.

2. Recommended further reading: Welty's essay "Writing and Analyzing a Story," which can be found in *Stories, Essays, and Memoir*.

Works Cited

Council of Writing Program Administrators, National Council of Teachers of English, and the National Writing Project. "Framework for Success in Postsecondary Writing." *Council of Writing Program Administrators*. Council of Writing Program Administrators, January 2011. Web. April 29, 2016.

Welty, Eudora. *Stories, Essay, and Memoir*. Ed. Richard Ford and Michael Kreyling. New York: Library of America, 1998.

"A Worn Path" in the Creative Writing Classroom

Writing, Attention, and the Ecological Thought

—**Amy Weldon**, Luther College

What are we really teaching when we teach creative writing? I say it's *attention*, which is vital for writing teachers to foreground because it's vital for writers ourselves. Eudora Welty's short story "A Worn Path" (1941) models the way everyday practices of attention can tilt a writer into what Welty herself called "the act of the writer's imagination I set most high"—observing, then imagining herself into, the heart and mind of another person, and giving that person's consciousness the same full, serious, and joyous attention she gives her own. In his book of the same name, eco-philosopher Timothy Morton has dubbed this type of seeing "the ecological thought": an awareness of our human interconnectedness with all the other human and nonhuman elements of life on earth, which begins, literally, with *seeing* them. Close attention to the world beyond one's head (in philosopher Matthew Crawford's phrase) orients students toward an understanding of craft—"be specific," "imagine this more fully," and "use good verbs"—that is built morally and imaginatively on participation in that world, enriching students' lives even if they don't become writers. "A Worn Path" shows them how attention can build a world on the page, image by image.

Creative writing, as I teach it, starts with focusing students less on "getting ideas" (receiving an external bolt of "inspiration") than on *working with images*, learning to draw out the dramatic and sensory potential of pictures or actions they observe or remember. We know that Welty herself wrote stories this way, "[d]rawing on bits of conversations she had heard, gestures she had observed or photographed, [and] notes she had jotted down on the back of an envelope or on whatever scrap of paper came to hand" (Marrs 48). And in her essay "Is Phoenix Jackson's Grandson Really Dead?" (1974), Welty even uses the word "image" itself, describing how "one day I saw a solitary old woman like Phoenix" walking through "a winter country landscape" and "the sight of her made me write the story": "I brought her up close enough, by imagination," Welty writes, "to describe her face, make her present to the eyes, but the full-length figure moving across the winter fields was the indelible one and the image to keep, and the perspective extending into the vanishing distance the true one to hold in mind" (*Stories* 816–17).

The imaginative and moral processes enabling the kind of craft that builds a story like "A Worn Path" begin with a particular inward posture—a continuous renewal of one's perceptions of the world through attention, to which both Welty and an important strand in environmental philosophy point the way. Timothy Morton begins *The Ecological Thought* (2010) with a simple statement: "The ecological crisis we face is so obvious that it becomes easy—for some, strangely or frighteningly easy—to join the dots and see that everything is interconnected. This is *the ecological thought.* And the more we consider it, the more our world opens up" (1). Morton's book claims that sustaining human and nonhuman life on earth in a time of climate change starts with readjusting our vision of the network of relationships within which we are embedded—understanding that we're not living over and against some distant realm called "nature" but as actors in systems that are acting on us. "The ecological thought doesn't just occur 'in the mind,'" Morton writes. "It's a practice and a process of becoming fully aware of how human beings are connected with other beings—animal, vegetable, or mineral" (7). Such awareness can banish the moral and ecological fallacy that we and our present needs and desires are all there is, and all there has ever been, to existence. Honoring the human and nonhuman beings who share the earth with us begins, literally, by *seeing* them.

Therefore, teaching creative writing, for me, means teaching how to pay attention to (Crawford's phrase again) the world beyond your head. My students learn early on to carry a paper notebook of any kind around with them and write in it, creating messy, exciting, and private grab bags of observations, drafts, and exercises (they may choose to read aloud from them, but I will never collect or grade them). In the first two days of class, we list ten specific sensory things we've seen that week, then write them on the board as material for additional writing exercises, asking, "does something you see up there spark another memory?" Students don't have to strain for some extraordinary description: "the fuzzy cloth buttons on my coat" or "the way new snow squeaks when you step on it" are worthy of notice as ways this world is present to our senses. A student who finds herself unable to list anything has just experienced for herself the results of habituated inattention—in fact, many students will freely exclaim, "I haven't been noticing *anything*!" during this activity—and can therefore begin to understand and change those habits on her own. Notebook-keeping and other writerly habits help students consider the impact of the omnipresent screens that surround them (laptops, smartphones, television) on their attention and their writing lives and ponder the value of a private self in control of where its attention might be directed; this, in turn, can lead them to claim thoughtful identities as artists. (And they do; in one recent class, my students concluded independently that Instagram would not be a good substitute for notebook-keeping because of the showy, for-public-consumption nature of the medium itself.) When they think about how attention works, and what may sharpen or dull it, students become aware of their bodies and minds as writing partners in a way they may not have before, and they consider how to be active, not passive, consumers of information and guardians of their attention. They're also well equipped to understand why "sensory and specific" are good qualities for language, and why using such language helps them speak to readers in our common human language—that of the body and the senses.

Helping students learn to pay attention also means helping them read a range of well-crafted work as *writers* read. Together in class, we scrutinize how writerly choices on the page create imaginative effects and then, through exercises, experiment with ways to create such effects ourselves. "A Worn Path," despite its foreignness in place and time for my young midwestern students, exemplifies the craft processes they're learning elsewhere in the class: close, open-hearted observation of another person and her world can enable a writer to build that world on the page, which in turn will help readers cross over into that world, imaginatively, word by word. It also reinforces what my students are learning about the power of an observed or remembered image, rather than an "idea" or a "plot," as the starting point for a story. Just as Welty did with the sight of an old woman crossing a field, we can notice a detail in the world and ask questions about it: Who is this person? What's at stake for her? Where is she going, and why? The answers to these questions will become the story's plot.

Reading "A Worn Path" with students, I start by discussing the careful descriptions and then ask where, artistically and morally, they lead. Our first sight of Phoenix Jackson is of a woman in motion: "moving a little from side to side in her step, with the balanced heaviness and lightness of a pendulum in a grandfather clock" (171). Her fragile suspension in time is established along with her persistent individuality: "Her eyes were blue with age. Her skin had a pattern all its own of numberless branching wrinkles and as though a whole little tree stood in the middle of her forehead, but a golden color ran underneath, and the two knobs of her cheeks were illumined by a yellow burning under the dark" (171). Such detail could only be written by someone who had looked closely enough at a woman like Phoenix—even across the boundaries of age, class, and race—to see her, yet this act of seeing avoids appropriation, cliché, or generality. While the observing narrative eye walks closely alongside Phoenix and sees what she sees—including things that may not really be there—it never has complete access to her thoughts and motivations, striking a balance of fully pictured personhood and of privacy and establishing a ground of human sympathy that soon the reader finds herself sharing as well. For this is the ultimate effect of Welty's close, precise vision: we will understand, even love, what we learn to see, and writing about something knits observation and care for it closer together in the wide net of language.

"A Worn Path" also shows students that readers need to see the details of a character's world, not only the character herself, in order to picture both more fully, since, as Morton would say, both are part of the same ecological whole. Welty renders her Deep South winter landscape with a particularity that helps readers picture it. In the "deep and still" woods, she writes, "the sun made the pine needles almost too bright to look at, up where the wind rocked" (171). The quail "[walk] like pullets, seeming all dainty and unseen" along a "wagon track where the silver grass blew between the red ruts" (174). As students read such lines, they marvel, "I can *see* that." Aesthetic philosopher Elaine Scarry's *Dreaming by the Book* (2000) tells us that prose which asks us to imagine light sliding over solid things, or the motion of an object or animal, makes these things cognitively "easier" for readers to picture; Welty's use of this principle here in the image of the bright sliding light along the pine needles, which sharpens the picture of them in our minds, indicates the sort of psychological connection with readers that the attentive writer can achieve, not entirely consciously, through faithful awareness of the living world. Word by word, she can then rebuild that world in our brains.

To help students achieve such observational precision, I guide them through a range of physical exercises to build a bodily awareness that can translate into language. When we work on verbs, we get out of our chairs and act out differences between a stroll, a strut, or a shuffle. Like Welty herself did, we treat revision as a physical act, cutting stories apart and rearranging them, and we read our work aloud, to ourselves and others. During class, we go for walks in order to incorporate one observed detail (the bristly tip of a cedar branch, a leaf tumbling end over end in the wind, bees bumbling over late-summer sage blooms) into our story in progress, no matter what it is, in order to set our characters in a more precisely imagined world. These processes help build students' sense of writing as something that is part of one's body and sensory habits, and it reminds students that—like Phoenix—every character lives in a physical landscape that the writer must be able to "enflesh" in her mind in order for readers to envision it too. Students tell me that the walking and nature-observing exercises tune up their vision, make their writing less cerebral, and even provide concrete story shapes and origins. One student found a bird's nest in a tree by the library during one of our excursions, and the moment in which her story's character discovers a nest—modeled exactly on her own experience—breathed with the same imaginative life as Welty's images of Phoenix Jackson.

Getting out in the world and touching things helps tune up our sense of the physical precision of language, fitting it to the thing we're describing. And it can tune up our moral selves as well. Like the biblical "Doubting Thomas"—more accurately translated as "Touching Thomas"—we humans need to put our hands on something to believe in it, and love it. This is a place where people of every stripe in our falsely and disastrously politicized landscape of conservation can meet: in attentiveness to and love for this breathing world, which will sustain us if we let it. That type of humility and knowledge of self in relationship to others is a feature of Morton's ecological thought and of Welty's humble, acute artist's eye. Even in our landscape of interstate medians and parking lots, it is worth reclaiming. Because then our students—even aside from implications for their artistic lives—will be positioned to ask for something better from their future, something as life-sustaining as art itself.

Works Cited

Crawford, Matthew. *The World beyond Your Head: On Becoming an Individual in an Age of Distraction*. New York: Farrar, 2015.

Marrs, Suzanne. *Eudora Welty: A Biography*. New York: Harcourt, 2005.

Morton, Timothy. *The Ecological Thought*. Cambridge: Harvard UP, 2010.

Scarry, Elaine. *Dreaming by the Book*. New York: Farrar, 1999.

Welty, Eudora. *Stories, Essays, and Memoir*. Ed. Richard Ford and Michael Kreyling. New York: Library of America, 1998.

VII

Casting Wider Nets: New Interdisciplinary Contexts for Teaching Welty

> As we discover, we remember; remembering, we discover; and most intensely do we experience this when our separate journeys converge. Our living experience at those meeting points is one of the charged dramatic fields of fiction.
>
> I'm prepared now to use the wonderful word *confluence*....
>
> —*One Writer's Beginnings* (946–47)

Teaching Welty in Dialogue with Other Artists in a Social Justice Course

—**Adrienne Akins Warfield,** Mars Hill University

The relationship between Eudora Welty's literary texts and works of art in other genres—visual, musical, and cinematic—has been a fruitful arena of exploration for Welty scholars. Such scholarship has been enhanced through consideration of Welty's own connections to these genres in her experiences as an art history minor in the 1920s, an accomplished photographer during the 1930s and 1940s, and a lifetime aficionado of both movies and music. Welty's works are well suited for interdisciplinary classrooms, as I discovered in teaching a course titled Social Justice in Literature and Culture. This course focuses on artistic representations of social justice issues and includes Welty's works among other literature, films, and music. Welty's fiction, when taught in conversation with works of other artists of diverse backgrounds and genres, holds great potential for encouraging dialogue on the connection between social justice and art. It is crucial for teachers and scholars of Welty's works to emphasize this potential in the face of misconceptions of Welty as an apolitical, narrowly regional writer unengaged with social issues.

Such misconceptions may derive from Welty's own assertions about the role of art, particularly within her essay "Must the Novelist Crusade?" They must, however, be answered with the more complex picture of her work and views that Welty scholars have explored over the years.[1] As Suzanne Marrs argues, "For Eudora Welty, an act of understanding—political, social, or personal—was typically an act of the imagination. Through fiction, art, and music, she sought to comprehend her world. Not surprisingly, then, she examined Mississippi politics through these prisms" (5). Marrs notes that Welty connected works by E. M. Forster, Pablo Picasso, and Fats Waller to politics, concluding, "Welty praised works of imagination that reject racism and hypocrisy" (10). We can bring students' attention to the unique ways that art engages issues of justice by teaching Welty's fiction in conversation with imaginative works in multiple media.

In my course, the first work of Welty's we study is "A Worn Path." I teach it alongside Ernest Gaines's story "The Sky Is Gray" and the film *The Great Debaters* as three different artistic depictions of African American life in the Deep South during the Jim Crow era. We first watch *The Great Debaters*, a fictionalized adaptation of the story of Wiley College's 1930s debate team. By depicting African American college students and professors who must balance their efforts for justice and advancement with the need for survival in the segregated rural South, the film helps students better visualize the settings and empathize with the characters of "A Worn Path" and "The Sky Is Gray." The class period after we cover *The Great Debaters*, we discuss Welty and "A Worn Path" and then move to Gaines, "The Sky Is Gray," and connections between the two works and authors.

In our discussion of "A Worn Path," I draw students' attention to Welty's understated but crucial depictions of how racial oppression and class status contribute to insufficient medical care and limited educational opportunity within the story. For example, we discuss how Welty subtly highlights the history of racist violence in Phoenix Jackson's life when the hunter points his gun at her, asking if it scares her, and she replies, "No, sir, I seen plenty go off closer by, in my day, and for less than what I done" (*Stories* 176). Our conversation focuses on the section of the story after Phoenix has arrived at the doctor's office. We discuss the staff's treatment of Phoenix as a tiresome "charity case" and Phoenix's assertion that she is "an old woman without an education" who was "too old at the Surrender" to attend school (178); this assertion subtly critiques the social structure of Phoenix's Mississippi, a structure that labels her a "charity case" without addressing the history of structural injustice that has defined her life. In our conversation about the doctor's office scene, I draw upon the research of Melissa Deakins Stang, highlighting that at the time of the story's publication, it was very common for children who swallowed lye to sustain serious injuries to the esophagus, often resulting in severe, even life-threatening symptoms similar to those Phoenix describes. As Stang explains, children who swallowed lye developed "a scarred esophagus that might immediately, or later, swell and constrict so that a child could neither eat nor drink," which could eventually lead to death by starvation and dehydration (14). Students are usually unaware of this medical phenomenon, and bringing their attention to this historical context underscores the social justice issues that provide the backdrop to Welty's story.

After focusing on the medical aspects of racial and class injustice in "A Worn Path," it is easy for students to make connections to Gaines's "The Sky Is Gray," a story narrated by an eight-year-old African American boy named James who is in urgent need of dental care. Gaines has stated in multiple interviews that "A Worn Path" served as a "model" for him in writing "The Sky Is Gray" (Gaudet and Wooton 223). Students are quick to notice the similarities between the two stories, both of which depict long, cold winter journeys from the country into town to obtain medical treatment. We discuss the role that racial segregation and poverty play in the way that medical problems are dealt with. Echoing the preoccupied demeanor of the nurse and attendant in "A Worn Path," the dentist's nurse in "The Sky Is Gray" tells the black patients in the waiting room they must leave until the dentist resumes work in the evening, unmoved by James's mother Octavia's pleas for more urgent care because "My little boy's sick [. . .]. Right now his tooth almost killing him" (103). A fellow patient in the waiting room tells Octavia that she should not feel rejected, stating, "I been round them a long time—they take you when they want to. If you was white, that's something else; but we the wrong color" (103). In class conversations, we also look at the way that both Welty's and Gaines's stories complicate the notion of charity and its relation to justice. In "The Sky Is Gray," Gaines depicts James's mother Octavia as a proud woman who deliberately refuses multiple attempts at charity from an elderly white storekeeper named Helena who calls the dentist's office to expedite James's care. By underscoring the fact that it takes a white woman's phone call to get James the dental care he needs, Gaines shows how unjust social structures define the terms of health care in the segregated South. While Octavia tells Helena, "Your kindness will never be forgotten" in reference to that phone call (117), she pointedly rejects Helena's other attempts at charity born of pity, perhaps in recognition of how easily such charity can be substituted for true justice. By examining "A Worn Path" in conjunction with "The Sky Is Gray," students are able to see the ways in which Gaines and Welty—authors of different races, genders, and generations—explore questions of medical ethics, class, and race in relation to social justice.

The course dialogue continues during a later class period dedicated to the study of various artistic responses to the murder of Medgar Evers.[2] Welty's "Where Is the Voice Coming From?" is discussed along with other responses to the murder, including Margaret Walker's poems "Micah" and "Medgar Evers, 1925–1963: Arlington Cemetery"; Bob Dylan's song "Only a Pawn in Their Game"; and James Baldwin's "Notes for Blues," the introduction to the published version of his play *Blues for Mister Charlie*, a work which Baldwin dedicated "To the memory of MEDGAR EVERS, and his widow and children, and to the memory of the dead children of Birmingham." Evers's legacy is largely unknown to my students, some of whom come into the course with the impression that the civil rights movement began and ended with Martin Luther King Jr. Studying artistic treatments of Evers's life and death helps to expand students' understanding of the many individuals whose leadership and sacrifices advanced the cause of justice within the long civil rights movement.[3] I begin the class period by outlining biographical information on Evers, emphasizing that as a World War II veteran, Evers returned to his home state of Mississippi with an increased awareness of the lack of freedom for African Americans in the South and spent the rest of his life organizing protests against racial discrimination and violence. We also discuss the significance of Evers's murder occurring on June 11, 1963, the same night as President Kennedy's landmark speech calling for a civil rights bill. Our conversation about the artistic responses to Evers's death begins with Baldwin's introduction to *Blues for Mister Charlie*, in which he reflects on a trip he took with Evers to "the back-woods of Mississippi" to investigate another murder. Baldwin felt compelled to write a play based on Emmett Till's killing, but his efforts were dampened by fear that he "would never be able to draw a valid portrait of the murderer." This statement sparks connections to Welty's and Dylan's works, both of which focus on Evers's murderer and his motivations.

After discussing Baldwin's reflections on his time with Evers and root causes of racist violence and injustice, we move to talking about Margaret Walker and her connections to the Evers family as a fellow member of the Guynes Street community in Jackson. "Medgar Evers, 1925–1963: Arlington Cemetery," a depiction of Evers's burial at Arlington National Cemetery, provides an interesting point of comparison to Dylan's description of Evers being lowered "down as a king" into his grave in "Only a Pawn in Their Game." Students make connections between Walker's poem "Micah" and Evers's biography and are particularly interested in the poem's final line, "Micah was a man," and its implied contrast of Evers's humanity, compassion, and courage with the hateful cowardice of his murderer. Our discussion of this contrast supplies a smooth transition to Welty's depiction of the murderer's mindset in "Where Is the Voice Coming From?" Students are both intrigued and repulsed by Welty's depiction of the psychology of racial hatred and violence within the story.

At this point, we discuss the composition and publication history of "Where Is the Voice Coming From?" as well as the identity and story of Evers's actual murderer, Byron De La Beckwith. I draw attention to the fact that, while both Welty and Dylan depict Evers's killer as a poor white man whose feelings of class resentment toward the middle-class civil rights leader serve as a major motivation for the murder, the socioeconomic status of Beckwith himself was far more complicated, as he had connections to the upper crust of Mississippi social life as well as some financial advantages. We watch footage of Dylan's performance of "Only a Pawn in Their Game" at a Greenwood, Mississippi, voter registration rally less than a month after Evers's death. Incidentally, Greenwood was also the hometown of Beckwith, who had been arrested for Evers's murder a little over two weeks prior to Dylan's appearance at the rally. This footage helps students to visualize the setting and context of both Dylan's song and Welty's story. The reactions of the African American attendees of the rally as Dylan sings about his version of Evers's killer provide a point of entry for discussing the complicated issues in representation involved in Dylan's and Welty's works: both "Only a Pawn in Their Game" and "Where Is the Voice Coming From?" are works by middle-class whites about the white murderer of a middle-class black man, and both depict this murderer as being of unequivocally low socioeconomic class, in contrast to the reality of Beckwith's actual class identity.[4]

By discussing "Where Is the Voice Coming From?" and "Only a Pawn in Their Game" together and in conjunction with other works, students are able to recognize problematic aspects of representation without being unfairly critical of either Dylan or Welty. In fact, after learning more of Beckwith's history, some students believe that both Welty's and Dylan's representations of Evers's murderer are appropriate from an artistic standpoint because both works deprive the killer of the power and recognition that he desired by depicting him as a victim. Our classroom dialogue raises important questions about race, class, and the relationship between fictional representations of events and the true stories on which these fictions are based.

Interpreting Welty's works in relation to political themes has always been complicated for teachers and scholars, perhaps made more so by the publication of her essay "Must the Novelist Crusade?" In responding to Welty's essay, Noel Polk describes the instructor's dilemma in regard to the relationship between art and politics: "[F]or the life of me, as a teacher and professor in *this* world, in *this* day and time, I do not know how I can teach" works by Welty, Faulkner, and Wright "without at least *hoping* that my students will not just be deeply moved by what they read but will take their deep feelings, and mine, to the next step, see the relationship between these dramatized sociopolitical problems and their own lives, and take whatever steps they can understand, by virtue of these books, to be essential to changing the way they live" (59–60). Teaching Welty's work within the context of an interdisciplinary social justice course has strengthened my own understanding of Welty as a socially engaged writer, one whose works can move students to greater social awareness and social action. When teaching stories such as "A Worn Path" and "Where Is the Voice Coming From?" alongside literary and cultural texts that have played key roles in American civil rights and social justice movements, Welty's voice emerges as one among many diverse voices concerned with these causes; and her unique methods of engaging with the political through her fiction are perhaps better understood as one thread within a tapestry of writers, artists, musicians, and filmmakers dedicated, each in their own way, to the cause of justice.

Notes

1. See the 2001 collection, *Eudora Welty and Politics: Did the Writer Crusade?* (LSU Press), edited by Suzanne Marrs and Harriet Pollack, for many key essays on this topic.

2. This chapter was written based on my experience teaching the course before the publication of Frank X Walker's *Turn Me Loose: The Unghosting of Medgar Evers*. Walker's poems have greatly enhanced the Evers unit in the most recent iteration of the course.

3. In my preparation for teaching artistic responses to Medgar Evers's life and death, I am greatly indebted to Minrose Gwin's *Remembering Medgar Evers*.

4. For background information on Byron De La Beckwith, see Gwin (63–64, 131) as well as Adam Nossiter's *Of Long Memory: Mississippi and the Murder of Medgar Evers* (105–43).

Works Cited

Baldwin, James. *Blues for Mister Charlie, A Play.* New York: Dial Press, 1964.
Bob Dylan: Don't Look Back. Pennebaker Hegedus Films, Inc. and Ashes and Sand, Inc, 1967. Director D.A. Pennebaker. Producer Albert Grossman.
Dylan, Bob. "Only a Pawn in Their Game." *The Times They Are A-Changin'*. Columbia Records, 1964.
Gaines, Ernest. "The Sky Is Gray." 1963. *Bloodline: Five Stories.* 1968. New York: First Vintage Contemporaries Edition, 1997. 83–117.
Gaudet, Marcia, and Carl Wooton. "Talking with Ernest Gaines." 1988. In *Conversations with Ernest Gaines*. Ed. John Lowe. Jackson: UP of Mississippi, 1995. 221–40.
The Great Debaters. The Weinstein Company: Harpo Films Productions, 2007. Director Denzel Washington. Producers Todd Black, Kate Forte, Oprah Winfrey, and Joe Roth.
Gwin, Minrose. *Remembering Medgar Evers: Writing the Long Civil Rights Movement.* Athens: U of Georgia P, 2013.
Marrs, Suzanne. "Eudora Welty: The Liberal Imagination and Mississippi Politics." *Mississippi Quarterly* 62.3 (2009): 5–11.
Nossiter, Adam. *Of Long Memory: Mississippi and the Murder of Medgar Evers.* Reading, MA: Addison-Wesley, 1994.

Polk, Noel. "Engaging the Political: In Our Texts, in Our Classroom." *Eudora Welty and Politics: Did the Writer Crusade?* Ed. Suzanne Marrs and Harriet Pollack. Baton Rouge: Louisiana State UP, 2001. 47–67.

Stang, Melissa Deakins. "Parting the Curtain on Lye Poisoning in 'A Worn Path.'" *Eudora Welty Review* 1 (2009): 13–24.

Walker, Frank X. *Turn Me Loose: The Unghosting of Medgar Evers: Poems.* Athens: U of Georgia Press, 2013.

Walker, Margaret. "Micah." *Prophets for a New Day.* 1970. In *This Is My Century: New and Collected Poems.* Athens: U of Georgia P, 2013.

Walker, Margaret. "Medgar Evers, 1925–1963: Arlington Cemetery." *This Is My Century: New and Collected Poems.* Athens: U of Georgia P, 1989. 176.

Welty, Eudora. *Stories, Essays, and Memoir.* Ed. Richard Ford and Michael Kreyling. New York: Library of America, 1998.

Using "A Worn Path" to Explore Contemporary Health Disparities in a Service-Learning Course

—**Casey Kayser,** University of Arkansas

Service-learning pedagogy is a method of teaching and learning in which students complete service work that is integrally connected to the academic learning goals of the course and meets a genuine community need. Service learning was formally recognized as a pedagogical practice in the 1990s and has grown widely since, engendering diverse models and approaches across disciplines. Numerous studies have demonstrated the positive effects that service-learning courses have on students' social, personal, academic, and civic development (Eyler et al. 1–5). Service learning provides an especially important learning tool for students in pre-health professions as a strategy for creating community responsive, culturally competent health-care practitioners; cultivating citizenship and achieving social change; and changing relationships between communities and educational institutions (Seifer 274; Housman et al. 275–76; Seifer, Hermanns, and Lewis 7).

This article examines my experience of teaching Eudora Welty's short story "A Worn Path" (1941) in a unique context, a service-learning Medical Humanities Colloquium for junior and senior premedical students housed in the English department at a large state university. My course combines literary and critical texts that attend to the social rather than technical aspects of medicine and requires an experiential and service-learning component in which students shadow physicians at community clinics and complete medically relevant service hours at community agencies such as the veteran's health-care center, a hospice home, organizations that serve individuals with disabilities, and mobile outreaches that deliver food and personal care items to surrounding rural areas. It is designed to instill in future physicians a commitment to compassionate, community responsive, and culturally competent medical care.

Medical humanities is an interdisciplinary field that acknowledges how the humanities, the social sciences, and the arts inform medical education and practice. In the late 1980s and early 1990s, scholars began to recognize narrative as a core component of the medical encounter. Scholars believe that studying literature can help practitioners understand the illness experience and the patient's and family's points of view. Literature offers insight into the human condition and leads practitioners to think critically and compassionately about moral issues, and ultimately, practicing literary analysis may help a doctor better read and interpret a patient's story and its multiple layers of meaning (Pellegrino 19; Belli 107; Rousseau 161; Hawkins and McEntyre 5). Further, the incorporation of the humanities, literary studies, and reflective writing into medicine can cultivate narratively competent, more effective practitioners (Charon 1898; 1900–1901).

I teach Welty's "A Worn Path" in a unit called "Medicine and Culture," and I pair the story with critical readings and discussions about gender and medicine, the relationship between socioeconomic status and health outcomes and treatment, the links between socioeconomic factors and race/ethnicity, statistics on health disparities, and how minority groups' relationships with health institutions have been shaped by historical exploitation. Though issues surrounding health permeate the story, it is more often read allegorically, as a mythical journey reflecting themes of racial struggle and progress. Very few scholars have noted the medical themes, though Melissa Deakins Stang establishes the historical foundation for lye poisoning and its effects and treatment, arguing that "the plight of Phoenix Jackson's grandson was alarmingly real, especially in the rural South" at the time the story was published (14). Annette Trefzer also notes Jackson's poverty and lack of access to medical care in the period before Social Security (106–7). Our discussion of the story is centered around Phoenix Jackson's race, class, gender, age, and rural home, and how the physical, environmental, and human obstacles she faces on her journey to the physician's office are symbolic of the challenges her positionality poses for access to health care and treatment. While the story is set in the 1930s, I lead students to see that the issues it raises are relevant to contemporary disparities in health treatment and access that may be a result of racial, geographical, environmental, and socioeconomic factors. Through reflection, a key component of service learning, students make connections between course readings and topics and their real-world experiences. The students placed in rural community clinics and at the mobile outreaches better understand the challenges that rural living and poverty present for health access and treatment, and the story of Phoenix Jackson's journey to the physician's office becomes more tangible for them.

I teach this text in the weeks leading up to one of the major writing assignments, the Literary Analysis Essay, and it helps me guide STEM students not accustomed to reading and analyzing literature at the college level learn (or relearn) how to engage in close reading and analysis. Because of Welty's "generous use of detail" (Pollack 21), the story provides a particularly good opportunity for encouraging close reading. I ask students to work independently to make three claims about the story, choosing textual evidence to support each one. I guide them toward making claims about Phoenix's positionality, introducing a sample claim and evidence: "Phoenix is old" with "numberless branching wrinkles" (*Stories* 171). I hope that students might make assertions like "Phoenix is poor," drawing upon textual details that suggest these aspects of her positionality. A common claim students make is "Phoenix may be suffering from dementia," pointing to such evidence as the little boy with the marble cake whom she apparently sees and who then disappears (172), in addition to her forgetting why she has made the trip at all upon her arrival. This exercise allows students to practice making claims and supporting them with evidence, as will be required for the upcoming essay, and drives our discussion and analysis of the story.

We link Welty's story to contemporary health disparities, studying a condensed version of the most recent Centers for Disease Control's Health Disparities and Inequalities Report, with statistics that demonstrate that "poor health status, disease risk factors, and limited access to health care are often interrelated and have been reported among persons with social, economic, and environmental disadvantages" (Meyer 3). We discuss how social determinants as well as race and ethnicity, sex, sexual orientation, age, and disability all influence health outcomes and treatment.[1] The students who shadow in a rural community clinic see these interrelated determinants and encounter issues surrounding poverty, low health literacy and education levels, and many medical and social problems connected to these factors. Further, they see that the journey Phoenix makes from her rural home to seek medical treatment has contemporary applications, as one student notes in her reflection journal, writing about the rural clinic in which she is placed for shadowing:[2]

> [The major city hospital] is a good 40-minute drive for most.... This makes it hard for people who must go to the hospital on a weekly or monthly basis. Most

of the population is hovering around the poverty line, and they simply cannot afford to make the trek into the city, so this clinic is a huge boon to the community.

I expected that students shadowing in that clinic and those working the mobile outreaches to rural areas would easily make connections between what they observed in those spaces and Welty's story, but students also made connections between the story and service experiences I had not seen as especially relevant. One student honed in on the themes of sacrifice and determination, linking it to his work at the hospice home:

> After reading Eudora Welty's "A Worn Path," I developed an even better understanding of hardship and perseverance. The sheer determination that the grandmother had in defeating every obstacle is very similar to that of the families of the patients at [the home]. Many times, the spouse, children, or even friends are determined to make their loved one's last days as happy and normal as they can.

From yet another interesting perspective, one student analyzes Phoenix's experiences in conjunction with our discussions of narrative medicine:

> Understanding patient background and stories also helps to provide access to healthcare for patients who might not otherwise receive medical help. This idea becomes especially important when working to provide healthcare to individuals of low socioeconomic or educational status. Without understanding what these people endure on a daily basis, we cannot hope to create healthcare plans that will actually work for them. One example of this was shown in the short story "A Worn Path" by Eudora Welty, as the main character in this story is allowed medicine that she may not otherwise be able to get if the nurse doesn't understand where Phoenix is coming from.

The student notes that because the nurses know Phoenix is poor, they "make a special exception" for her as a charity case, though in a condescending way. This theme came up often in our discussions, as students saw physicians give out samples instead of prescriptions or offer particular treatment choices with their patients' socioeconomic considerations in mind, fortunately in more respectful ways than the providers treat Phoenix. On the other hand, this particular student also recognizes that perhaps the health-care practitioners in the story fail to address Phoenix's true needs because they do not give her medical treatment or the support she may need for navigating her trip back and her potential dementia. Phoenix's experiences reflect a reality in contemporary health care, in which the rural poor and minorities often receive inadequate care. The story also opens up potential for discussions about the importance of recognizing a patient's humanity, as Welty's storytelling humanizes Phoenix for the reader in a way not accessible to the hunter or nurses, and those encounters call attention to the lack of compassion with which they treat her.

Teaching Welty's "A Worn Path" in this context, to premedical students, is valuable because its themes about health-care access are so relevant to their future careers. The service and experiential components of my course lead students to deeper understandings of course concepts, as they pair their analysis of "A Worn Path" and other literary texts with their experiences outside of the classroom. Further, this component of the course works toward an important civic goal of creating more compassionate, community-responsive future physicians. One student's final reflection seems to suggest this outcome:

> Shadowing really made me think about how dense of a bubble I live in. College was not just an option; it was a *requirement* for me. For many in [the rural area], college is not even a consideration. Having three square meals a day is something I hardly notice, whereas so many are lucky to get a couple decent meals a week. Having a child just because I want something to call my own is so unfathomable to me, but some do it without a second thought. My encounters have left me counting my blessings, and then counting them again. If anything, [this experience] has strengthened my resolve in conquering medical school. So many people need help and I want to do my best to someday in some way, shape, or form give them the help they deserve.

Reading Welty's story with an eye to how factors such as race, gender, age, and rural living affect health-care access and treatment places it in a new perspective, and supplementing the study of the story with real-world learning and service experiences in a course like this one offers potential to influence the knowledge base and philosophies of future physicians in ways that could help reduce health disparities in the future.

Notes

1. The World Health Organization (WHO) defines the social determinants of health as the conditions in which persons are born, grow, live, work, and age, including the health-care system. "Social Determinants of Health." World Health Organization. Web. http://www.who.int/social_determinants/sdh_definition/en/.

2. I received permission from my students to use their written work.

Works Cited

Belli, Angela. "The Impact of Literature upon Health: Some Varieties of Cathartic Response." *Literature and Medicine* 5 (1986): 90–108.

Charon, Rita. "Narrative Medicine: A Model for Empathy, Reflection, Profession, and Trust." *Journal of the American Medical Association* 286.15 (2001): 1897–1902.

Eyler, Janet S., Dwight E. Giles Jr., Christine M. Stenson, and Charlene J. Gray. "At a Glance: What We Know about the Effects of Service-Learning on College Students, Faculty, Institutions and Communities, 1993–2000." 3rd ed. Corporation for National Service Learn and Serve America National Service Learning Clearinghouse, 2001. Web.

Hawkins, Anne Hunsaker, and Marilyn Chandler McEntyre. "Introduction: Teaching Literature and Medicine: A Retrospective and a Rationale." *Teaching Literature and Medicine.* Ed. Anne Hunsaker Hawkins and Marilyn Chandler McEntyre. New York: MLA, 2000.

Housman, Jeff, Karen S. Meaney, Michelle Wilcox, and Arnoldo Cavazos. "The Impact of Service-Learning on Health Education Students' Cultural Competence." *American Journal of Health Education* 43.5 (2012): 269–78.

Meyer, Pamela A., Paula W. Yoon, and Rachel B. Kaufmann. "Introduction: CDC Health Disparities and Inequalities Report—United States, 2013." *Morbidity and Mortality Weekly Report* 62.3 (November 22, 2013): 1–187. Centers for Disease Control and Prevention. Web.

Pellegrino, Edmund D. "To Look Feelingly: The Affinities of Medicine and Literature." *Literature and Medicine* 1 (1982): 19–23.

Pollack, Harriet. "Photographic Convention and Story Composition: Eudora Welty's Uses of Detail, Plot, Genre, and Expectation from 'A Worn Path' through 'The Bride of the Innisfallen.'" *South Central Review* 14.2 (1997): 15–34.

Rousseau, G. S. "Literature and Medicine: Towards a Simultaneity of Theory and Practice." *Literature and Medicine* 5 (1986): 152–81.

Seifer, Sarena. "Service-Learning: Community-Campus Partnerships for Health Professions Education." *Academic Medicine* 73.3 (March 1998): 273–77.

———, Kris Hermanns, and Judy Lewis, eds. *Creating Community Responsive Physicians: Concepts and Models for Service-Learning in Medical Education.* American Association for Higher Education. Series on Service-Learning in the Disciplines, 2000.

Stang, Melissa Deakins. "Parting the Curtain on Lye Poisoning in 'A Worn Path.'" *Eudora Welty Review* 1 (Spring 2009): 13–24.

Trefzer, Annette. "'A Penny to Spare': The Question of Charity and the Rise of Social Security." *Eudora Welty Review* 6 (Spring 2014): 97–111.

Welty, Eudora. *Stories, Essays, and Memoir.* Ed. Richard Ford and Michael Kreyling. New York: Library of America, 1998.

Folk and Fairy Tales, Opera, and YouTube

Teaching Welty's Fiction in a Folklore and American Literature Course

—**Kevin Eyster,** Madonna University

For Dan Barnes (1940–2016)

Eudora Welty's "Why I Live at the P.O." and *The Robber Bridegroom* provide opportunities for students to explore the relationship between folklore and literature. "P.O." lends itself to what folklorists refer to as "performance analysis" (Bauman 3), and *Robber Bridegroom* is effective as part of a unit on the folktale. These texts have worked well in a course I have taught since 2004, Folklore and American Literature. Throughout the course, students come to an understanding of how the disciplines enrich and play off each other, providing a fuller reading of the subject texts. Welty's works are integral to this learning process.

My course, in which folklore is primary and literature secondary, fulfills an undergraduate upper-level literature requirement for general education. Students read and write about works primarily of American literature in which folkloric phenomena have been simulated and transformed for literary purposes. Whereas folklore emphasizes verbal, material, and customary art as expressive forms, literature emphasizes literary types or genres as texts produced by creative writers. Folklorists study such key cultural expressions as tradition, custom, and belief, and folktales, folk music, and folk art, as well as such folk groups as children and the family, and ethnic and occupational lore. Literary scholars study characteristic themes, styles, and techniques of specific writers and how their texts come alive through readers' responses to them.

Teaching both literature and folklore creates a significant learning curve for students, and a fruitful way to establish the latter as a discipline is by reading *Living Folklore: An Introduction to the Study of People and Their Traditions* (Sims and Stephens, 2012).[1] Since students have had little if any exposure to folklore formally, one way to make the discipline and its essential concepts concrete is through discussion of family folklore, which often is the general subject of their collection projects, and by connecting folklore to literature.[2] Before we get to "P.O.," the literary text we read first is Alice Walker's "Everyday Use."

I begin with Walker's short story for several reasons: how the story is told as Mrs. Johnson's personal narrative, a folklore genre; the setting as rural Georgia, with emphasis on the family as a folk group and the theme of sibling rivalry; the practice of customs (foodways, folk art, and family names); ritual (prayer and singing); and the tradition of quilting. Mama's decision to keep the handmade quilts for Maggie and her future husband instead of giving them to Dee-Wangero, who wants to return to the North and put them to use as decorative art, is best understood by students after viewing *Alice Walker: Everyday Use, Uncommon Art*, which includes a film adaptation of the story and an interview with Walker by her biographer, Evelyn C. White. Walker's story parallels the chapters in *Living Folklore* that introduce essential disciplinary concepts. Once students grasp these folkloric concepts, they are better prepared to consider how a performance-centered approach can be applied to a work of literature. The short story by Welty that most effectively embodies performance is "Why I Live at the P.O.," which also serves as another example of the genre of personal narrative.

Frequently, Welty writes in such a way as to suggest a conversation among her characters. Sister in "P.O.," Katie Rainey in "Shower of Gold," and Edna Earle Ponder in *The Ponder Heart* as well as Granny Vaughn's descendants in *Losing Battles* are humorous representatives of people who traditionally have been associated with a love of rhetoric and oratory, of visiting and talking, of communication through the spoken word. It is in such a context that Welty wrote "P.O.": "[B]eginning with my story 'Why I Live at the P.O.,' I wrote reasonably often in the form of a monologue that takes possession of the speaker. How much more gets told besides!" (*Stories* 853). What does "get told" reveals Welty's gift for creating storytellers and stories.

As folklorists Martha Sims and Martine Stephens note, "Most often . . . , performances of folklore happen naturally within daily conversations and situations . . . , [because] [p]erfomance is an expressive activity that requires participation, heightens our enjoyment of an experience, and invites response" (131). As a short story that simulates personal narrative, defined as a "framed and performed artistic expression, with both recognizable structure of the *performance* and . . . a familiar structure in the *narrative* itself" (Sims and Stephens 172–73), "Why I Live at the P.O." becomes Sister telling a specific personal experience to an implied auditor in the fictional world of the story. Welty creates this auditor explicitly: "someone" addressed as "you" within the text is the listening audience, a "someone" who never speaks but is spoken to by Sister. This triad of a character-narrator, her story, and an unidentified auditor calls attention to a special use of language. In the act of reading the short story, the reader is conventionally overhearing Sister's story and essentially becomes the auditor by inference. When we read "Why I Live at the P.O.," we have a sense of the auditor as the "you" Sister addresses directly. We become, hypothetically, a part of Sister's audience by aligning ourselves with her auditor in the literary audience. By extension, then, Welty's character-narrator engages us as inferred auditors whom Sister does not want to misunderstand her story. This dynamic narrative process further suggests that Sister's dramatic presentation of her story to an implied auditor can be interpreted and evaluated as performance. It is as if Welty is persuading us to participate in the act of fiction making.

As implied auditors, readers enjoy Sister and her story because the irony inherent in her comedic narrative has a lifelike quality to it. Her defensive nature and lack of self-awareness are common human traits, as is her desire to use language to regain her place as the favored sibling. Familial conflict, though not necessarily an everyday occurrence, happens frequently enough to be a central topic of conversation. In our discussion of the story, students see how Sister's judgmental character—"You ought to see mama, she weighs two hundred pounds and has real tiny feet" (62)—reveals the self-serving decisions in a humorous way. Welty depicts these disputes tongue-in-cheek, having Sister and by implication her family ensnare themselves in the very language they use to justify their behavior. As a wonderfully engaging character-narrator, Sister is testimony to the fact that Welty indeed has been "listening for stories."

Further augmenting our understanding of Sister's story as a performance, students are encouraged to listen to Welty's audio recording of the story available from the Internet. During class we also view her reading "P.O." in 1987 at the Faulkner and Yoknapatwpha Conference, as well as listen to select scenes via YouTube of Stephen Eddins's opera based on the story.[3] What we *imagine* about Sister, her family, and the implied auditor from a written text comes alive while watching Welty read "P.O." to a knowledgeable and appreciative audience in Oxford. Welty's audience knows this story well, and much like viewing the film adaptation of "Everyday Use," students are able to *see* how the text of a simulated performance and its reception varies depending on the physical and social contexts including setting, region, and the group in which it is shared. Moving from one medium to another, excerpts from Stephen Eddins's one-act chamber opera based on "P.O.," including the libretto written by Eddins and Michael O'Brien, are available from the Internet, adding yet another performance dimension to the short story. The opera, complementing the quickened pace one receives listening to Welty's audio-recording, utilizes two versions of Sister, one as narrator and the other as a character in the story, as well as giving voice to the other family members. Eddins and O'Brien enhance this multivocal approach by including several musical styles from the 1940s—gospel, spiritual, ragtime, and big-band jazz—enabling students to broaden their sense of the time period.[4]

Having navigated the two disciplines and how they intersect, students are equipped to consider a specific genre and how it relates to folklore and literature. Devoting a significant portion of the course to the study of folktales, specifically fairy tales, is a favorite of many students, especially those seeking teacher certification.[5] Whether or not they have grown up listening to and reading classic fairy tales, students are drawn to the oral-aural dimension and how it relates to written versions. The transactional nature of this process hinges, as Jane Yolen notes, on the all-important contribution of readers and audiences: "Told and retold or read and reread, the story exists neither in the mouth nor on the page, neither in the ear nor the eye. It is created *between*. No two listeners hear exactly the same tale. Each brings something of himself [or herself] to the story, and the story is then re-created between the teller and the listener, between the writer and the reader" (4). What excites students here is the "created *between*," because their engagement requires them to be active and participatory, similar to the role they embody reading and listening to "P.O."

We begin with the Grimm Brothers version of "Briar Rose," "Sleeping Beauty," and "The Robber Bridegroom," reading Maria Tatar's translation and annotation of each tale. In these early versions of the fairy tale, we consider tale types and motifs, as well as structure, characterization, and theme.[6] Once we have established a baseline, we consider how specific writers adapt and transform this genre for literary purposes. We read and discuss Yolen's young-adult novel, *Briar Rose* (1992), which uses the classic tale to explore the consequences of the Holocaust, as well as Nobel laureate Nadine Gordimer's fractured fairy tale, "Once Upon a Time," which inverts the fairy tale structure and satirizes the genre to allegorize the effects of Apartheid in South Africa. Students then are more prepared for the richness and complexity of Welty's *The Robber Bridegroom* (1942).

Initially, students are challenged by the layering of characters and subplots, but it is Welty's language—her diction, use of simile and metaphor, dialogue, and vivid imagery—that draws them in. Prior readings enable them to gain footing in this marvelous, paradoxical, and troubling fictional world. In comparison with the Grimms' version, Rosamond, the raven's refrain, the bandits' cabin, the maiden's severed finger and ring, and Jamie Lockhart as the "robber bridegroom" are readily identified. The addition of Clement Musgrove, Salome, Mike Fink, Little Harp, and Goat, and the specific setting along the Mississippi River and the Old Natchez Trace, resituate the fairy tale and repurpose its meaning. Most interesting for students is Welty's use of the *doppelganger*, as the doubling of characters works in tandem with the doubling of themes. As a proverbial liar who is chaste and unchaste, Rosamond is not "the perfect fairy tale princess she claims to be" (Merricks 6). As a berry-stained bandit who also appears gentlemanly in his aiding of Clement, Jamie is "actually a rapist" (Merricks 7). Clement adores his daughter but willingly complies with Salome in her avarice and greed.

The underbelly of the fairy tale tradition is exposed as the novella builds to an inevitable conclusion. Instead of a fantastical or magical otherworld ending in "happily ever after," *Robber Bridegroom* moves toward a series of compromises, significant losses, and a degree of poetic justice. Students anticipate Salome's inevitable demise as the wicked stepmother and are able to foresee Jamie and Rosamond's union even in a paradoxical situation. They approve of Goat receiving Jamie's reward money to help his sisters and mother but disapprove of his buying "a black cook" (*Novels* 80). Drawn to Clement "as an innocent of the wilderness" (87) who "wrestled with his" conscience "without any aid from the world at all" (51), they see the excess in his agreeing with Salome to become "a planter of Rodney's Landing" (87). While they too marvel at Rosamond and Jamie's bright future together, they puzzle over their ownership of "a hundred slaves" and agree with Clement asking, "Is all of this true, Rosamond, or is it a lie?" (88).

As a "literary or art tale" (Yolen 4), *Robber Bridegroom* takes otherworld conflicts and transgressions into the Mississippi frontier and the American experience. Surface and depth, appearance and reality contribute to "a multilayered story" (Merricks 1), culminating on one hand in a "joyous reunion of lover and beloved, father and daughter" (Ramirez 82) but on the other hand in "white settlers' displacement of Native Americans" in which "hero and villain are both culpable" (Marrs 95). By the end of the unit, students have learned how folk and fairy tales are part of a continuum that is recursive and best understood when several examples are considered.

Including Welty's stories in this course contributes to students' opportunity "to look both ways and to see a thing from all sides" (*Novels* 88). "P.O." augments their understanding of an essential concept in folklore studies, performance. *Robber Bridegroom* demonstrates how Welty Americanizes the subject matter while creating a trope to the fairy tale tradition. Students continue to be enriched by this learning experience.

Notes

1. For another key study of folklore, see McNeill. For a seminal study of fieldwork and ethnography, see Jackson. For a comprehensive study of the relationship between folklore and literature, see Brown and Rosenberg.

2. The course culminates with each student delivering an oral presentation based on the collection project. For an essential resource on the study of family folklore, see Baker, Kotkin, and Zeitlin.

3. Since Welty's reading in 1987 is only available in VHS format, for another audio-recording option, see Caedmon's *Essential Welty* or *YouTube*, uploaded by Tim Gracyk, April 7, 2015. www.youtube.com/watch?v=bmnzdozWfxw.

4. Augmenting our understanding of rural Mississippi during this time period, students view the photographs Welty took while working for the WPA in the 1930s included in the collection titled *One Time, One Place*.

5. As part of this unit, students also read Jack tales. See Perdue and Norman.

6. For other key studies of the fairy tale, see Warner and Zipes.

Works Cited

Alice Walker: A Stitch in Time. Films for the Humanities and Sciences, 2006. DVD.

Alice Walker: "Everyday Use." Films for the Humanities and Sciences, 2006. DVD.

Baker, Holly C., Amy J. Kotkin, and Steven J. Zeitlin, eds. *A Celebration of American Family Folklore: Tales and Traditions from the Smithsonian Collection*. Somerville, MA: Yellow Moon, 1992.

Bauman, Richard. *Verbal Art as Performance*. Prospect Heights, IL: Waveland, 1984.

Brown, Mary Ellen, and Bruce A. Rosenberg, eds. *Encyclopedia of Folklore and Literature*. Santa Barbara: CA: ABC-CLIO, 1998.

Eddins, Stephen, comp. *Why I Live at the P.O.* Lib. Michael O'Brien. August 2001, www.operaamerica.org/applications/NAWD/newworks/details.aspx?id=349.

"Eudora Welty, Why I Live at the P. O.—Opera by Stephen Eddins. Pt. 1." *YouTube*, uploaded by RichardGumby's channel, December 31, 2009. www.youtube.com/watch?v=FQbwKSqDerQ.

"Eudora Welty, Why I Live at the P. O.—Opera by Stephen Eddins. Pt. 2." *YouTube,* uploaded by Richard Gumby's channel, January 20, 2010. www.youtube.com/watch?v=QQ3FDsPj_34.

Essential Welty. Caedmon/HarperCollins, 2006. CD.

Gordimer, Nadine. "Once Upon a Time." Rpt. in *Jump and Other Stories.* New York: Penguin, 1992. 23–32.

Jackson, Bruce. *Fieldwork.* Urbana: U of Illinois P, 1987.

Marrs, Suzanne. *Eudora Welty: A Biography.* Orlando, FL: Harcourt, 2005.

McNeill, Lynne S. *Folklore Rules: A Fun, Quick, and Useful Introduction to the Field of Academic Folklore Studies.* Logan: Utah State UP, 2013.

Merricks, Correna Catlett. "'What I Would Have Given Him He Liked Better to Steal': Sexual Violence in Eudora Welty's *The Robber Bridegroom.*" *Southern Studies* 12.3-4 (2005): 1–16.

Norman, Gurney. *Ancient Creek: A Folktale.* 1975. Lexington, KY: Old Cove, 2012.

Perdue, Charles L., Jr., ed. *Outwitting the Devil: Jack Tales from Wise County, Virginia.* Santa Fe, NM: Ancient City, 1987.

Ramirez, Anne. "Gratitude, Greed, and Grace in *The Robber Bridegroom*: Eudora Welty's Intricate American Parable." *Eudora Welty Review* 1 (2009): 75–83.

Sims, Martha C., and Martine Stephens. *Living Folklore: An Introduction to the Study of People and Their Traditions.* 2nd ed. Logan: Utah State UP, 2012.

Tatar, Maria, ed. and trans. *The Annotated Brothers Grimm.* New York: Norton, 2004.

———, ed. and trans. *The Annotated Classic Fairy Tales.* New York: Norton, 2002.

Walker, Alice. "Everyday Use." 1973. Rpt. in *Women Writers, Texts and Contexts: "Everyday Use."* Ed. Barbara T. Christian. New Brunswick, NJ: Rutgers UP, 1994. 23–35.

Warner, Marina. *Once Upon a Time: A Short History of Fairy Tale.* New York: Oxford UP, 2014.

Welty, Eudora. *Complete Novels.* Ed. Richard Ford and Michael Kreyling. New York: Library of America, 1998.

———. *One Time, One Place: Mississippi in the Depression, a Snapshot Album.* 1971. Jackson: UP of Mississippi, 1996.

———. *Stories, Essays, and Memoir.* Ed. Richard Ford and Michael Kreyling. New York: Library of America, 1998.

———. "Where I Live." *Delta Review* 6 (1969): 61–72.

"'Why I Live at the P. O.' Eudora Welty reads her classic story RARE AUDIO." *YouTube,* uploaded by Tim Gracyk, April 7, 2015. www.youtube.com/watch?v=bmnzdozWfxw.

William Faulkner and Eudora Welty. Educational Film Production. University of Mississippi, 1987. VHS.

Yolen, Jane. *Briar Rose.* 1992. New York: Tor, 2002.

———, ed. *Favorite Folktales from around the World.* New York: Pantheon, 1986.

Zipes, Jack. *The Irresistible Fairy Tale: The Cultural and Social History of a Genre.* Princeton, NJ: Princeton UP, 2012.

Teaching Welty to Future Teachers

The Wide Net, The Golden Apples, *and Inquiry-Based Learning*

—**Rebecca L. Harrison,** University of West Georgia

Eudora Welty is disappearing from secondary school curricula; that is a fact. While "A Worn Path" hangs on as the token Welty text in a number of high school textbooks, many teachers elect not to teach it, and those who do often express hesitation at assigning it again. Teacher candidates, in particular, struggle with elucidating the complexities in Welty's work to adolescents and often provide unsatisfying readings in the context of southern regionalism and local color fiction. Their textbook tool kits, provided in woefully outdated teacher editions, offer little to support teacher efforts with Welty and encourage pedestrian interpretations of her works.

Those of us who teach college-level English can help fix this problem; that is a fact as well. Though pre-service teachers drive a significant percentage of English enrollments at accredited teacher training universities, major courses of study often have limited relationships to the actual curricula this group will teach. Thus, we miss a prime opportunity to infuse Welty into secondary environs in meaningful ways. Of course, doing so entails learning something about how high school standards work, but it also means directly impacting the intellectual enterprise of a significant number of adolescents who will, soon enough, populate our own college classrooms. In sum, we have a chance to change an entire teaching culture of Welty's work in reaching out to this population; let us seize it.

While much has been made of the wide adoption of the common core, these standards allow for more flexibility, rigor, and cross-curricular connections in high school classrooms which pave a way for integrating more of

Welty's work. What we need to do, then, is relatively simple: integrate Welty texts that pair well with secondary curricula maps in courses that target pre-service English teachers, and model inquiry-based pedagogical strategies that these students can one day adapt for the secondary environs. Incorporating such pedagogical supports with Welty benefits traditional English majors as well, many of whom go on to graduate programs where they teach adolescents in first-year writing classes.

Welty is a good fit for secondary curricula precisely because she recognized that we do not live, read, write, or interpret in isolation. Her work is simultaneously accessible and difficult, familiar and uncomfortable, and sharply focused but integrally linked to its cultural and historical moment. Reading her work requires that students learn close reading skills and the tenets of theoretical plurality, develop intellectual flexibility, and come to appreciate ambiguity, multiple perspectives, and alternative ways of seeing and configuring our world. High school students desperately need to read materials that confuse and challenge them, I tell my pre-service teachers, and, if you can teach them Welty, you are sending them out into the world with the ability to deeply read just about anything.

Approaching Welty with Teachers in Training

The Wide Net and Other Stories (1943) is an ideal fit for working with English Education students. A text that these majors can one day teach themselves, it offers selections that appeal to both genders and that can be taught either as the extended unit text or as part of the thematically linked shorter text-block of secondary curriculum maps.[1] As Welty designed the collection with the history of the Natchez Trace in mind, it is rife with historical figures and markers, mythological references, and allusions to multiple genres and forms. *The Wide Net* allows for the kind of cross-curricula pairings required by the common core. Teachers can couple the stories with essays Welty wrote about the Natchez Trace, along with her correspondence concerning the collection. They can use her photography to elucidate theme, and they can bring in documents from US and world history (from Burr to Audubon to the Windsor Ruins to the World Wars) to show the relevancy and intertextual nature of her work. In short, they can capitalize on its contemplations of nature—physical and human/moral—and of the colonial and postcolonial landscapes of the United States and the South to help adolescents come to understand the dynamic nature of social, political, and economic systems; individual and institutional behavior; and historical and spatial relationships.

In my Research and Methods course (ENGL 3000) for English Education students, *The Wide Net* anchors the last third of the class in which I model a myriad of teaching strategies on "First Love," "The Wide Net," "A Still Moment," "Livvie," and "At the Landing." These selections allow me to address a diverse number of literary devices and critical approaches to Welty and their distillation to adolescents, while demonstrating ways to teach the short story in isolation and, alternatively, as a larger collection. Welty's difficulty combined with the opaque nature of the links between the stories in this collection prove a strength for the main unit activities described below, as they help students come to see her rich web cast across the Natchez Trace as a puzzle to unravel, as a new way of reading and discovering.

For the first activity, students are strategically divided into four, four-person Welty learning communities that last for the duration of *The Wide Net* unit. These teams sit together in small pods and collaborate on all in-class activities. This model builds fluency with Welty's work and underscores the importance of purposeful collaboration, of talking to learn. Having students confront their confusion as teams galvanized in the effort to unpack the collection fosters an appreciation for her work but also for the diverse perspectives (critical and pedagogical) within their unit. The Welty community model becomes one of our last pedagogy lessons—something they have lived for one-third of the course—where I make visible the heuristics of building effective groups: from alternative methods for their composition to group task, role, and accountability strategies to keep them on task.

In addition to the learning community model, I use daily reading journals instead of giving reading quizzes on *The Wide Net*. Quizzes do not facilitate rich discourse with Welty's work, nor do they model the routine writing called for by the common core. Instead, I assign a reading journal that models methods for writing targeted, open-ended questions on Welty and sets students up for higher-quality class participation. The journal prompts hit four different learning goals with each story, covering some formal element, like POV or setting, explicit/inferred meaning and ambiguity, theme, and a deeper theoretical bend. Students complete one entry per story, but, over the course of the journal, they answer at least one prompt of each type. The journals feed class discussion in rigorous ways as students are prepared for each lesson's through-thread, a necessity with Welty, but they also reveal patterns of reading/misreading that help me address barriers more quickly. Additionally, they serve as a pedagogy lesson throughout. For example, I center my instruction of "First Love" on the four prompts and talk about my choices: what learning goals each was tied to, what I expected from students, and how tying the prompts to my delivery encouraged them to engage more in class.

Their second group of journal prompts on "The Wide Net" cements this skill set. Here, I show my questions next to poorly structured prompts. The Welty groups are then assigned one of my four journal prompts, and they work as a team to determine what its sound qualities are in connection to the story itself and in juxtaposition to the ineffective examples provided. Each team eventually deconstructs their question's structure for the class, and I lay bare approaches to sound question generation in connection to Bloom's taxonomy and principles of content differentiation for a variety of learning levels. They are not surprised when their next journal assignment on "A Still Moment" requires that they write four questions of their own and explain their choices—what they think their questions will yield, questions we workshop in our groups at the start of the next class. In addition to this kind of work with the journals, I also incorporate extension activities, like the following, that they can use with their own high school students:

- Reflection: For "Livvie," students review their own journal entry after class discussion. In the final ten minutes of class, they respond to their own thinking, addressing what they now know, how their thinking has changed or grown, and what they want to investigate as a result of discussion.
- Reflection/Response: For "At the Landing," students swap journal entries and respond to a peer's entry before class discussion begins; after class discussion, they write another entry on this established critical dialogue.
- Interrupted Journal: Depending on class composition, I may assign the entry on "At the Landing" as an in-class activity to model the use and import of expectation failures. I tell them they have ten minutes to write, but then call time after only five minutes. Students then swap journals with a classmate and, after review and reflection, finish their colleague's entry.
- Critical Hot Spot: Each student is assigned one source applicable to *The Wide Net* (e.g., a historical or mythological reference, a source explaining a character name, a key letter by Welty, etc.). Students write a one-paragraph report accompanied by a paragraph on how that information deepens our understanding of the Welty text in question. These entries serve as conversation starters for class discussion, usually three per class period.

These activities model how to engage reflectively as both readers of and collaborators on Welty's work—self to self, self to peer, and self to class—a skill they will have to teach their own students, and one specifically called for by the common core.

I reserve one final class period for connection boards, an exercise in synthesis and connected learning that brings to the fore the complex, connective threads of Welty's Trace. Five easel-size post-it boards are placed around the room, each with the title of one story on it. The Welty groups are given a unique color marker, and their task is to list at least two to three threads that connect each story to the others in the collection. These connections could be recurring signs, vocabulary, themes, character qualities, etc. The only rule is that they may not repeat an element already written by another group. The groups get five minutes per board, followed by one final five-minute period to go back and revise or add any element, as moving through the activity inevitably sparks additional connections they get excited about. Finally, I use the boards—their own observations—to underscore thematic linkage (while valuing student-directed learning) as we conclude *The Wide Net*. Seeing their own connections in this way crystalizes for them what was, at the beginning of the unit, an impenetrable imaginative landscape: Welty's sweeping, yet interconnected, engagement with a geographical region and a national historical consciousness rooted in colonization, the consequences of which still resonated across her South.

Welty teaching demonstrations augment the required research paper instead of traditional oral presentations. In this assignment, students are placed into four teaching teams, which are a different composition than their daily groups, thus giving them more practice with diverse discourse communities on Welty. These teams team-teach a selection from *The Wide Net* that we did not cover as a class. Further, they must do so via an assigned critical school of literary theory covered earlier in the term, demonstrating their ability to distill (and reconstruct) the theoretical lens in concert with their goals for elucidating the Welty selection. Their Welty-proficient peers, who role-play the intended grade level, offer oral and written feedback on the lesson and its dissemination. Each team, finally, submits a brief justification that addresses the common core standards for including the assigned story in secondary curricula.

Though successful with English Education majors, *The Wide Net* case study is fully accessible to a wide variety of students. I deploy it, including all pedagogy components, in courses for traditional English majors, such as the upper-level southern literature survey, and in classes filled mostly with non-majors, like the sophomore-level American literature survey. The only modification for these populations is that they teach their assigned story to the class, as opposed to a theoretical secondary audience.

Building Fluency with *The Golden Apples*

In my discipline-specific pedagogy class (ENGL 3400), Welty's *The Golden Apples* (1949) anchors the last unit. This volume gives my ENGL 3000 students yet another Welty text to contend with, and, as the class outcomes center pedagogy, space to provide them with significant practice with backward planning, instructional support materials, and assessment practices that go along with conveying such a challenging text.[2] This class redeploys the engagement strategies used with *The Wide Net*, but it more squarely articulates frameworks and variations of the assignments to help lead adolescents to their own discoveries with the entirety of this collection. In particular, we focus on how to scaffold necessary supports when teaching *The Golden Apples*, a text that is both a tightly woven tapestry and one intrinsically linked to external cultural references. The collection also provides an opportunity to address methods for taking on courageous conversations in high school settings with stories like "Music from Spain." This element pushes them out of their comfort zones and serves as a lesson in making sound, content-specific cases to administrators for teaching works with more controversial thematic content, a necessity given the conservative school systems in which our majors teach.

The culminating project for this class, a robust Welty teaching portfolio, honors their professional goals as *content*-specific teachers of English, since it measures their proficiency with the intersectional space that teachers, of any level, always occupy: that of scholar and pedagogue (see appendix). Students prepare a tripartite teaching portfolio in which they

- Write a sound, argumentative research paper on their assigned selection from *The Golden Apples*.[3]
- Theorize and articulate a persuasive justification for why it should be taught in public school.
- Narrate and position their own pedagogical approach to Welty.
- Present a detailed unit plan and handouts, including instructional supports, assessments, and rubrics.

Though these projects are graded individually, they also feed a common class Welty tool kit. The final portfolios are compiled into a collaborative class document, providing students with two full sample unit plans for *each* story in *The Golden Apples*, which they can reference and modify throughout their early teaching careers.

Though my English Education majors first profess that Welty is too hard to read, much less teach to adolescents, they all have grown scrappy with her and with each other. My fall 2014 cohort, in fact, grew tired of finding polite ways of saying "dig deeper" as they confronted her complex world and presented me with their own solution: permission to adopt a class safe word that would signal the end of what they described as "lazy reads," a phrase that would insist upon risk taking and remind each other of their communal commitment to that endeavor as future teachers. To my surprise, the vote for such a code went unopposed, and "It's Welty" became a commonly heard retort, a phrase synonymous with an entire way of actively reading and teaching, of what they told me later summed up both their truth with and appreciation of this figure. To thrive with Welty in the classroom, you first have to be taught how to wrestle with and survive her.

I must confess that, as a newly minted PhD in literature, I never anticipated one day working with pre-service teachers on Eudora Welty. It was an undiscovered country for me, and one about which I made many uninformed assumptions. Yet, this work has evolved into some of the most rewarding of my teaching career. I now have a concrete understanding of the environments for which 40 percent of our majors are training, and, armed with that knowledge, I can teach them Welty's world in a nuanced way that is relevant to their future careers. In turn, my students hopefully go better equipped to introduce Welty to young readers, increasing both her visibility and the reading skills of students who come into our collegiate classes. While we need not all go out and observe in high schools or teach pedagogy courses, by simply sticking our collective toes in the secondary waters, we can help a group of fellow teachers do more with this important figure. Let us take a lesson from Welty's "serious daring" and be bold in these waters as well.

Notes

1. See https://www.georgiastandards.org/Georgia-Standards/Pages/ELA-9-12.aspx and https://www.georgiastandards.org/Georgia-Standards/Frameworks/ELA-American-Literature-Curriculum-Map.pdf for examples.

2. This five-and-a-half-week case study devotes three and a half weeks to elucidating the collection and two weeks to the teaching portfolios.

3. Students submit a preference list that I use to make the assignments so that the full collection is covered. "Sir Rabbit" and "Moon Lake" rank the highest; "Shower of Gold" and "The Whole World Knows" typically rank the lowest.

Works Cited

Welty, Eudora. *Stories, Essays, and Memoir*. Ed. Richard Ford and Michael Kreyling. New York: Library of America, 1998.

Appendix: English 3400: Pedagogy and Writing

The Golden Apples: A Pedagogy Project

Project Layout

Each student will choose one chapter in *The Golden Apples* to center his/her final project. No more than **two** (2) students may choose the same selection of the collection, with the exception of "June Recital" where I will allow three. Your section of the text should be proposed **and** cleared by me by the time of our conference. Your final project will be divided into three distinct sections that represent the liminal spaces that teachers—good ones at least—always occupy. Students taking this class for honors credit are expected to write a **nine- to ten**-page paper for section 1 with a minimum of five secondary sources. They are also expected to write an argument for the book's inclusion into the curriculum (approximately three pages).

Section 1, "The Scholar": Develop a strong, sophisticated, critical reading of your selection and substantiate your claims with appropriate primary and secondary evidence. For this section, you should incorporate critical support from a minimum of **three substantial secondary sources**.

Length: 6–7 pages—not including the works cited page.

Section 2, "The Student": Compose a concise overview **and justification of your approach to teaching** your unit of this text. Consider the following: What are your end goals with this unit? What textual thematic principles (or foci) center your approach? Why are they important? How does this meet the ELA standards in question? How can you distill this for your students and assigned grade level? What specific pedagogical practices will facilitate student achievement of your goals and why? How will you measure achievement? Etc.

Length: 3–4 pages.

Section 3, "The Teacher": Create *original*, detailed, consecutive lesson plans (three minimum) and all instructional support materials for teaching your self-selected unit of this text in the secondary environment. This section of the project should represent *your* teaching self—your pedagogy—and how you envision enacting your goals with the selection. The lesson plans should incorporate a variety of techniques, primary and secondary materials, and include a writing assignment and rubric. Clearly, each lesson should be tied to appropriate ELA and Common Core standards.

Length: TBD by individual project parameters.

Schedule

Workshop Drafts: Your participation in two collaborative Welty teaching roundtables on this project count as a homework and class participation grade; see the reading schedule for dates and what to bring. Also, *each* missing roundtable draft *will* result in a deduction of *5 points* from the final portfolio grade.

Final Draft

The final portfolio is due the last day of class. Your hardcopy should be accompanied by a flash drive that has your full project, including support and assessment materials, in one well-organized electronic file. I will collate these so that each student leaves this class with a full teaching toolbox for Welty's *The Golden Apples*.

Finding Hope

Listening to Welty's Words in "Lily Daw and the Three Ladies"

—**Sharon Deykin Baris,** Bar-Ilan University

Eudora Welty knew she was "not a musician, not a teacher," but she felt a core likeness between herself and her character, Miss Eckhart the piano teacher. What "animates and possesses" both artists, Welty says, is the love of their art and the "love of giving it, the desire to give it until there is no more left." The student, as she continues, "always may have been my subject" (*Stories* 945). Today's student is empowered to take up her offer, now more than in decades past, using available technology such as Google, to research meanings that in Welty's time attached to particular phrases or objects. This essay will provide an example of how to lead students toward researching the cultural and historical valences of specific details of "Lily Daw and the Three Ladies." Our classroom quest is to uncover new or forgotten possibilities within her careful choice of language—in the case of our study, with a focus upon two seemingly disparate terms used in setting the stage for Lily as we first see her. This young woman sits near an open hope chest, her hair streaming, and her clothing style is soon described as "looking like a Fiji" (11). Discovering these terms' implications in Welty's time is an essential part of what the author loved to offer—and is our pleasure to get today.

As the story begins, we see a crowd gathered in a post office when the mail or the news of the day is being handed over. The student can share an atmosphere of expectation, emphasized when a then-current expression is used, appropriately to set the tone: "Everybody ... wondered what was up now" (5). Hearing that phrase in its 1930s lingo-like intimations, the online searcher may think of pleasure, yet with hints of trouble ahead. The phrase will appear again near the end of the story, for us to rethink these possibilities. (Students may delight in finding that Looney Tunes made comic use of that term's expectant aura, when by 1940 a cartoon uses the gravelly sound of "What's up, Doc?" and everyone then knows that fun and mischief are afoot.) The upshot of re-viewing this story in its cultural historical perspective is double: first, to move a somewhat neglected work by Welty onto current reading lists for study; second, to show that this—and her other stories and novels—may be more approachable and more hopeful than many readers, including some of my students, have found them.

We should first remind ourselves of some headlines of the late 1930s: lasting effects of America's financial crises, mounting racial strife in the South, and worldwide terrors spreading. These conditions are, I suggest, somewhat like the wavy scar on Lily's neck—visible "if you knew it was there" (8). Signs of hope, too, can be perceived. Hope first takes tangible shape in the form of a hope chest at the heart of the story, as if at the very heart of Lily's desires. "What will you all give me?" or "What will they have for me?" she asks, as if to fulfill her dreams (10–11). Few students today know or even care to know much about the facts of a hope chest, but for many in Lily's time, the collection of goods in a safe-like container was desired, or needed, as a sign of safety and of hope. An in-class online search prompts conversation about "what is up," or within, this hope chest. For example, a company called Lane Hope Chest promoted its benefits widely, as shown in one full-page color advertisement appearing in *Life Magazine*, 1941. In the picture three ladies surround a hope chest, touching linens and pointing to other goods to be stored in preparation for wedding scenes planned or dreamed of. Another relevant illustration can be found in a black-and-white advertisement at just about the time Welty began writing. It displays towels and lotions, with the sense of perfume and music virtually in the air. Students can appreciate Welty's art in this moment. They see the author's brilliance in evoking these aspects of hope chests' touting in her fiction: two soap bars and the washcloth that Lily handles. Our discussion also weighs the contrast between hope chest blandishments and realities in times of so much trouble.

Welty much later observed that "every writer, like everybody else, thinks he's living through the crisis of the age." A career of writing, in such times, may be the "least we can do, and the most," in response to "whatever situation we live through" (813). Along with a mounting appreciation for Welty's skill in conveying those times, the students have developed not only a critique of consumer presumptions but also an understanding of how tasteless and fruitless is a hope chest way of thinking. All too easily can troubles be packaged then stored away in a crisis. Such thinking is at work in the ladies' decision to send

Lily away to the Ellisville institution. They are quickly certain that Lily should be safely put away from real or putative harassments in town. Aimee will sigh about "how far away it was" (12). But Mrs. Carson is firm—for now—in her belief that it is best that thoughts of Lily's itinerant musician suitor be "gone and out of our lives for good and all." Mrs. Watts agrees (10). They arrange for Lily's train ride away, but the term introduced just after their decision to do so complicates our sense of the outcome. Looking "like a Fiji" connotes another desired, or dreamed of, way of life. It is also a way of looking at Lily's options. Her lifestyle is expressive of her own slant on life. This is noticed by the ladies as they sit on donated furniture in her home and look at Lily. She is easily resting on the floor in a natural way, birdlike and with flowers in her mouth, wearing a scant petticoat for her dress (11). Mrs. Watts invokes what purports to be funny when she gasps aloud about "looking like a Fiji!"[1]

What does it mean to look like a Fiji in this story? A student Googling "Fiji" and "1935" will find scenes of some barely clothed women or others decked out in flowers, to be appreciated in photographs alongside material concerning the Fiji Islands or Melanesian Islands, as sites of interest at the time of Welty's story. The Fiji Islands were repeatedly discussed in print during these same years, when social presumptions and racial prejudice came under heightened scrutiny. Anthropology had become important in the 1920s and 1930s, as this discipline looked to distant cultures to learn more about ourselves and others. Such study sought relief on social and financial grounds. Implicit in the observation of distant societies lay the recognition of a range of customs and beliefs as a source of hope. For along with new facts about variant lifestyles came a clearer understanding that no single-minded conformism or locked-in worldview should reign—at home or in Ellisville. The "relativity of culture," as anthropologists such as Margaret Mead and Ruth Benedict used those words, would be a basis for optimism, as Benedict reported her findings in her *Patterns of Culture* (soon to be called a major landmark in the twentieth century). A review of her book appeared in the *New York Times Book Review*, 1935. The review's summation of her findings can be brought to class for perusal. Its relevance to our discussion of hope is expressed in just such terms, as it quotes a subtitle in Benedict's final chapter: a "doctrine of hope, not despair." Students will be interested in looking at other resources such as the *American Anthropological Journal*, in 1936, and browsing more popular discussions, including *Time Magazine*, May 11, 1936. Its cover portrait and analysis of well-known anthropologist Franz Boas (who had written the introduction to *Patterns of Culture*) discusses his work and that of others. What these anthropologists found, as Boas put it, raises questions of "normal or abnormal [as] seen in a new light" (Benedict xv).[2]

Another dynamic of island life matched up especially well against current realities of financial ruin. An alternative to disastrous loss was suggested by study of island cultures, particularly of their practice of gift cycles. Benedict's book spends many pages on this since, as she put it, "much was to be praised," precisely *not* in an "accumulation of goods" but in a system of exchange enacted in the practice of giving and getting gifts. Gift exchange is "never a market transaction" but a promise kept in the form of ongoing social and material interactions (Benedict 143). Students should, however, be reminded that our readings of Welty's story serve not as a critique of materialist consumer culture; nor are our discussions to be seen as promoting Fiji-like existence in a small town's neighborhoods. But what the students' online search may better encourage, in light of Welty's often-stated warning about the dangers of indifference, is something else to ponder. If both hopes are alike in obliquely suggesting distant and distancing attitudes in a time of crisis, then what else can be done, at home, indeed in that "new light" that Boas, Mead, and Benedict were praising as a source of hope?

The ladies and Lily are on the train and ready to depart, when a change of mind occurs. What has caused this transformation?[3] Aimee is the first to disembark, since she has a post office job she must keep. Doing so, she bumps into Lily's suitor. As if to size up the situation, she looks at his musician's case then circles around him to check the possibilities. The now-weighted terms of the story are in focus, as the traveling musician's xylophone box is mentally placed alongside thoughts of the hope chest. Aimee looks from one to the other as if to ask: "Which was more terrible?" (13). Classroom participants may by now have taken sides, thinking hope chest versus Fiji to be the options of the day. Another option emerges: to imagine both concepts back home. Aimee sees this possibility and rushes to convince the ladies to change their minds. They should return home, perhaps with their own thoughts of a job to do. Lily enters the crowd in town and immediately hears the lingo-like refrain: "What's up—tricks?" The musician says this, and the couple kiss smack in the middle of it all. Lily "hung her head" (15), but that gesture may be seen not, or not only, as a nod to local conformities. For if students by now have felt empowered to find meanings of Welty's unfamiliar words in broader contexts, they should feel impelled to listen attentively to the fuller backstory of the ordinary words of Lily's narrative, reread on Welty's pages.

This was told, in part, when the ladies had crowded into a shared lift toward Lily's home and spoken of how she was provided a safe haven, supplied with food and even constant kindling (7). Many men and women in Lily's community have liked and understood her, as the story has shown, including the engineer and the bandleader-storekeeper. Shoppers have enjoyed participating in their local kind of gift exchange, seen in the matter of switched hats. Taking a look at the xylophone box in the middle of town, these ladies may by now have retraced outlines of ongoing give and take, somewhat like the cycle of gifts the students have discussed. Attention to others' patterns of conduct in a new nonjudgmental light becomes "what is up" for reconsideration. Not deciding whether Lily's lifestyle is "normal or abnormal," to quote Boas (Benedict xv), nor accepting all too swiftly presumed options, the story takes a turn toward the possibility of change, and hope, at home.[4]

I stop but do not conclude in recognition of much "more left" to consider. With band music in the background, we can play out the results of our classroom rereadings for the better.[5] Lily will marry a not-perfect musician, and she may often join him in his travels. She may also continue her own pleasures in the slant-roofed dwelling, with flowers, and pink straps visible. She can enjoy what she gives and receives as forms of attending to, not indifference to, one another's positions. A straw hat is tossed above to keep other hats in mind. Listening to Welty's words, the student can hear how carefully crafted is her offer of hope.

Notes

1. See Sarah Ford's essay on the subversive uses of humor in Welty's pages. Ford cites a sense of the uses of humor in my essay on Welty's *The Ponder Heart*, in which Edna Earle exclaims, "Isn't it a scream?"

2. Rebecca Mark shows how Welty's use of anthropological implications in "The Demonstrators" warns us not to "miss some important clues" in the world and in the news (212).

3. Commenting on another early story, in which Powerhouse "gives all he's got," Harriet Pollack traces a change of mind in the audience and in the reader, in her penetrating reading of Welty's own art of giving.

4. In *Conversations*, Welty disdains some students' literal use of hinted references. She drily adds that such students do "not treat your work as fiction; in fact they don't seem to know the difference between fiction and anthropology" (331–32). Our online work and class discussions clearly do.

5. Michael Kreyling includes a display of the story's colorful items, in a moving rendition of what has been going on in "Lily Daw and the Three Ladies," in his important early study of Welty. He does not condone the complacencies of "self-appointed guardians of order and purity" that others have found in the story (15–16); but his recent *Understanding Welty* opens with an invitation to find new facets in rereading this story, and other fictions, thus to see Welty "all new, full of surprise, always a step ahead" (8).

Works Cited

Baris, Sharon Deykin. "Judgments of *The Ponder Heart*: Welty's Trials of the 1950s." *Eudora Welty and Politics: Did the Writer Crusade?* Ed. Harriet Pollack and Suzanne Marrs. Baton Rouge: Louisiana State UP, 2001. 179–201.

Benedict, Ruth. *Patterns of Culture*. New York: New American Library, 1934.

Ford, Sarah. "Laughing in the Dark: Race and Humor in *Delta Wedding*." *Eudora Welty, Whiteness, and Race*. Ed. Harriet Pollack. Athens: U of Georgia P, 2013. 131–47.

Kreyling, Michael. *Eudora Welty's Achievement of Order*. Baton Rouge: Louisiana State UP, 1980.

———. *Understanding Eudora Welty*. Columbia: U of South Carolina P, 1999.

Mark, Rebecca. "Ice Picks, Guinea Pigs, and Dead Birds: Dramatic Weltian Possibilities in 'The Demonstrators.'" *Eudora Welty, Whiteness, and Race*. Ed. Harriet Pollack. Athens: U of Georgia P, 2013. 199–223.

Pollack, Harriet. "Words between Strangers: On Welty, Her Style, and Her Audience." *Welty: A Life in Literature*. Ed. Albert J. Devlin. Jackson: UP of Mississippi, 1987. 54–81.

Welty, Eudora. *Conversations with Eudora Welty*. Ed. Peggy Whitman Prenshaw. Jackson: UP of Mississippi, 1984. 331–32.

———. *Stories, Essays, and Memoir*. Ed. Richard Ford and Michael Kreyling. New York: Library of America, 1998.

RESOURCES FOR TEACHERS AND STUDENTS

Publications by Welty, Biographical and Historical Contexts, Teaching Aids, and a Brief Guide to Scholarly Interpretations of Welty's Works

A. Publications by Welty for Classroom Use
Major Stories, Novels, and Nonfiction

Two volumes, published in 1998 for the Library of America series, contain almost all of Welty's published fiction and a significant body of nonfiction. Coedited by Richard Ford and Michael Kreyling, these volumes provide the original versions of texts when first published in book form, along with explanatory notes, detailed publication information, and a chronology of Welty's life.

Stories, Essays, and Memoir includes forty-one stories: the collections *Curtain of Green* (1941), *The Wide Net* (1943), *The Golden Apples* (1949), and *The Bride of the Innisfallen* (1955), along with "Where Is the Voice Coming From?" (1963) and "The Demonstrators" (1966). Essays include "A Pageant of Birds" (1943), "Some Notes on River Country" (1944), "Writing and Analyzing a Story" (1955, revised), "Place in Fiction" (1955), "A Sweet Devouring" (1957), "Must the Novelist Crusade?" (1965), "Is Phoenix Jackson's Grandson Really Dead?" (1974), and "The Little Store" (1975). The final work is Welty's memoir *One Writer's Beginnings* (1984).

The second Library of America volume, *Complete Novels*, contains five works: *The Robber Bridegroom* (1944), *Delta Wedding* (1946), *The Ponder Heart* (1954), *Losing Battles* (1970), and *The Optimist's Daughter* (1972).

The Library of America books are the standard editions for the works they include, hence, the editions that our contributors cite in this book. For instructors' personal use and for many classrooms, the Library of America editions are also a good value, since each hardbound volume includes more than any other published collection. However, when teaching a smaller sampling of her work, paperback editions of the individual works or of *Collected Stories* (1980) may be less expensive.

Welty's Photographic Collections and Illustrated Books

One Time, One Place: Mississippi in the Depression (1971; rev. ed. 1996) contains black-and-white photographs Welty took during the 1930s, many while she was traveling and writing for the Works Progress Administration. In 1989, *Photographs* was published, a much larger collection of Welty's images with an extensive introductory interview with Welty conducted by Hunter Cole and Seetha Srinivasan, editors at the University Press of Mississippi. In 2000, *Country Churchyards* was released. Welty donated her photographs to the Mississippi Department of Archives and History and to the care of her friend Charlotte Capers, then the director of the archives. More of Welty's work has been published as archival materials have been released to the public. One such publication is *Eudora Welty as Photographer* (2009), edited by Pearl Amelia McHaney.

Welty's photographs are a great asset to the classroom, not only establishing context but also contributing to discussions of focus, framing, subject, and other techniques applicable to writing as well as photography. Some of Welty's photographs may be viewed at the websites hosted by the Eudora Welty Foundation or the Eudora Welty Society. Students may particularly enjoy two books by Patti Carr Black. *Eudora* (1984) contains photos of Welty's family and friends, and *Early Escapades* (2005) presents work from Welty's childhood through the early 1930s: drawings, poetry, crossword puzzles for her high school yearbook, a collage book written when she was twelve, cartoons sent in letters, and other visual treasures. Students will be inspired by Welty's creativity and visual gifts, and instructors may well find assignments inspired by these works.

Other Publications by Welty

Welty's nonfiction extends beyond that published in *Stories, Essays, and Memoir*. Additional literary criticism, reviews, and essays on life in Jackson were collected in 1980 in *The Eye of the Story*. Some of the essays in *Eye* and some previously uncollected material are collected in two 2009 books edited by Pearl McHaney, *Occasions: Selected Writings* and a collection of book reviews called *A Writer's Eye*. Welty wrote sixty-seven book reviews during her lifetime, fifty-nine for the *New York Times Book Review* in the 1940s. Instructors might use one or more of Welty's book reviews as a model for an assignment for their students. Welty wrote a children's book, *The Shoe Bird*, in 1964, and a one-act play, "Bye-Bye Brevoort," that was performed in 1956 (published in *Occasions*). In 1991 she coedited an anthology, *The Norton Book of Friendship*, with Ron Sharp.

Welty's correspondence provides a wealth of biographical information, but also merits study in its own right. Welty was a prolific and gifted letter writer, although she was very reluctant to make her correspondence available for study during her lifetime, and family correspondence is off-limits until 2021. After Michael Kreyling's 1991 *Author and Agent: Eudora Welty and Diarmuid Russell*, only Suzanne Marrs was given access to most of Welty's correspondence before it became available at the Mississippi Department of Archives and History after Welty's death. Marrs has edited and annotated *What There Is to Say We Have Said: The Correspondence of Eudora Welty and William Maxwell* (2011), and Julia Eichelberger selected, edited, and annotated *Tell about Night Flowers: Eudora Welty's Gardening Letters, 1940–1949* (2013). The latest book of letters, coedited by Suzanne Marrs and Tom Nolan, is *Meanwhile There Are Letters: The Correspondence of Eudora Welty and Ross Macdonald* (2015). Additional volumes are sure to be published.

B. Biographical and Historical Contexts
Biographical Sources

Welty claimed in her memoir that hers was "a sheltered life," but that life was well documented and filled with interesting people and achievements that spanned almost an entire century. Biographical materials are usually very successful ways to connect readers with Welty's writing. Students will enjoy exploring the "Life and Works" page on the Eudora Welty Foundation website, where they will find a short biography by Marrs, a bibliography, photographs and other artwork by Welty, a timeline, and other photos documenting Welty's friends, family, and career.

For instructors and students, Marrs's *Eudora Welty: A Biography* (2005), the standard biography of Welty, is a treasure trove of information about Welty's life, her friendships, and contemporary events that impacted her writing, including World War II and the civil rights movement of the 1960s.[1] Carolyn Brown's *A Daring Life* (UP of Mississippi, 2012) is well researched, informed by Marrs's 2005 biography and materials that became available after Welty's death;

this 144-page book is primarily intended for young adult readers. Other helpful resources include Ruth Vande Kieft's and Louise Westling's books, both entitled *Eudora Welty*, and both providing a basic introduction to Welty's life and works. These books, though published in the late 1980s, are still quite useful.

Noel Polk's *Eudora Welty: A Bibliography of Her Work* (1994) traces the publication history of Welty's works, including her writing and photography. It also includes a very helpful section entitled "A Publishing Log for the Career of Eudora Welty." This log documents her first publication, "A Heading for August" in *St. Nicholas*, a magazine for children (1920), and ends in 1992.

Significant biographical information also appears in Marrs's *One Writer's Imagination* (2002), Fuller's *Eudora Welty and Surrealism* (2012), McHaney's *A Tyrannous Eye* (2014), Pollack's *Eudora Welty's Fiction and Photography: The Body of the Other Woman* (2016), and in Welty's interviews and correspondence. Two books of interviews, *Conversations with Eudora Welty* (1984) and *More Conversations with Eudora Welty* (1995), are indexed, making them even more valuable for research.

Archives and Museums

The Mississippi Department of Archives and History in Jackson, Mississippi, is open to visitors; for those unable to visit in person, MDAH furnishes much material about Welty online, including a helpful introductory biography with photos, and another exhibit with photos documenting Welty's writing process ("Sense of Place"). The Welty House (1119 Pinehurst Street in the Belhaven neighborhood) gives tours by appointment and provides interesting displays and significant information in its Visitors' Center next door. For the virtual visitor, online photo tours of the house and garden are available on the house website, as well as photos of Welty and her family in the home from 1925 to the 1990s.

Other Historical and Cultural Contexts

Since most of Welty's works are set in the early twentieth century, many instructors will wish to provide historical and cultural background for students who lack detailed knowledge of the period or region. Besides the biographical material discussed above, instructors preparing to teach Welty have many other sources to consult and to provide to students as supplemental reading or visual aids.

Mississippi: A Guide to the Magnolia State is a guidebook produced by the Works Progress Administration in 1938, available online in full text via the Internet Archive. Welty, who worked for the WPA in 1936, knew some of the people who worked on this book. She did not help write it, but she did contribute two photographs to it. It is an invaluable guide to the Mississippi Welty encountered as she traveled the state in the 1930s. Welty's Natchez Trace fiction emerged from her exploration of the Trace's history and folklore. Robert M. Coates's book *The Outlaw Years: The History of the Land Pirates of the Natchez Trace* (1930) was an important source of material; today, students may begin with the National Parks' Natchez Trace Parkway website, or Elliott's "Paving the Trace" on *Mississippi History Now*. Many students are eager to learn more about life for African Americans in Welty's home region. Some instructors assign nonfiction by Richard Wright, another writer from Jackson and a contemporary of Welty's but on the opposite side of the color line ("The Ethics of Living Jim Crow," *Black Boy, American Hunger*). Among the many fine books that illuminate the twentieth-century South and Mississippi in particular, we suggest Grace Elizabeth Hale's 1998 *Making Whiteness: The Culture of Segregation in the South, 1890–1940*, John Dittmer's *Local People: The Struggle for Civil Rights in Mississippi* (1994), Ted Ownby's 1999 *American Dreams in Mississippi: Consumers, Poverty, and Culture, 1830–1998*. Readers may also wish to explore the *New Encyclopedia of Southern Culture*, twenty-four volumes in all, for essays reflecting the interdisciplinary nature of southern studies in the twenty-first century.

In addition to Welty's own photographs, instructors and teachers may be interested in photo essays from the region in the 1930s and 1940s: *You Have Seen Their Faces* (Erskine Caldwell and Margaret Bourke-White, 1937), *12 Million Black Voices* (Richard Wright and Edwin Rosskam, 1941), and *Let Us Now Praise Famous Men: Three Tenant Families* (James Agee and Walker Evans, 1941). A more recent book, *Passionate Observer: Eudora Welty among Artists of the Thirties* (ed. René Paul Barilleaux, 2002), furnishes examples of creative work by Welty's contemporaries and, in some cases, friends, who were visual artists.

Welty's cultural contexts went far beyond her region, and students are interested to see her texts in conversation with popular culture of the nation and the world, especially visual culture. Some of Welty's works first appeared in the *Atlantic Monthly, Harper's Bazaar,* and *Vogue*. Instructors may wish to show students Welty's works in their original publications, sometimes flanked by advertisements for lipstick and automobiles and articles on fashion. (Original publication information is in Polk's bibliography and in *Stories, Essays, and Memoir*.) Welty's works also reflect the influence of the culture of cities, especially New York City, where she found more opportunities than she had at home in Jackson to go dancing, hear jazz music and symphonies, and see theater, dance, movies, and museums. Articles such as David McWhirter's

"Eudora Welty Goes to the Movies" (*Modern Fiction Studies* 55.1, 2009) chart some of the connections between Welty and film. Students may also be interested in Ruth Weston's discussion of Welty's links to American art in Weston's chapter in *The Eye of the Storyteller* (1989, ed. Dawn Trouard). Other recent journal articles linking Welty to national popular culture include Lorinda B. Cohoon's "'A Woman's Serious Foot': Feet and Shoes in *Delta Wedding*, 'Asphodel,' and 'The Winds'" (*Eudora Welty Review* 3.1); Sarah L. Peters's "'Moon Lake' and the Summer Camp Movement" (*Eudora Welty Review* 6.1); Laura Sloan Patterson's "Sexing the Domestic: *Delta Wedding* and the Sexology Movement" (*Southern Quarterly* 42.2); Donnie McMahand and Kevin Murphy's "'Remember Right': Disenfranchised Grief and the Commemoration of Queer Bodies in Welty's Fiction and Life" (*Eudora Welty Review* 6.1).

Within the sea of excellent online materials related to the South that are now available, instructors with a little time on their hands may wish to explore the Digital Archive of the Mississippi Department of Archives and History, a tremendous array of photographs, publications, personal papers, postcards, government records, oral histories, and more. One digital exhibit presents records of the 1927 flood; another documents the activities of the Mississippi State Sovereignty Commission; audio interviews record individuals' memories of their involvement with Freedom Summer. *Mississippi History Now* and the Eudora Welty Foundation website are also rich online sources of historical material.

C. Teaching Aids
Films and Audio Recordings

Many film versions of Welty's works have been created, as Suzanne Marrs notes in her essay in this volume, including "The Purple Hat," "Why I Live at the P.O.," "The Hitch-Hikers," "The Wide Net," and "A Worn Path." For a Masterpiece Theatre version of *The Ponder Heart*, PBS has created a teaching website. PBS also created a documentary based on *One Writer's Beginnings* as part of its American Experience series.

Recordings of Welty reading her own work (several short stories, *The Optimist's Daughter*, the Massey lectures that became *One Writer's Beginnings*) are available through audio booksellers. Some recordings are available online; the *New York Times on the Web* has a page on Welty that includes links to her reading three stories in 1953 at the 92nd Street Y: "Why I Live at the P.O.," "Powerhouse," and "A Worn Path." Other recordings of Welty reading or being interviewed can be found in DVD form, streamed via library databases, or accessed online. Two films by Ross Spears feature Welty interviews: *Prophets and Poets: Southern Literature, 1941–1962*, and *Tell about the South: Voices in Black and White—The History of Modern Southern Literature* (both 1998). Welty's understated sense of humor is sometimes evident in television interviews with Dick Cavett, Roger Mudd, and others, some of which are now available online. Welty was an expressive reader of her own work with a charmingly distinctive Mississippi accent. According to a letter from William Maxwell, she once spent an entire day reading him *The Ponder Heart*; he recalled laughing for hours as tears flowed, and then laughing dry-eyed, "not because it wasn't funny, but because the tear glands gave up" halfway through her performance (qtd. in *What There Is to Say We Have Said* 33).

Maps

Visual learners and instructors interested in place/space/geography may become engaged with Welty's texts via maps of her settings. The WPA Guide mentioned above contains several maps of Mississippi towns and regions; students may also enjoy exploring online maps of Welty's home neighborhood ("Belhaven Heights Historic District") and of Jackson shortly after it was burned in 1865 ("Rebuilding Chimneyville"). Welty drew her own map of the fictional Banner, Mississippi, for the opening pages of *Losing Battles*. Another artist drew a map for the endpapers of the first edition of *Delta Wedding*; this can also be viewed in the *Eudora Welty Newsletter* (21.1). For a 2006 *Mississippi Quarterly* essay on "Music from Spain," J. Matthew Huculak used Google Earth maps to plot the day-long walk of Eugene MacLain in San Francisco, the city where Welty was living while writing the story. The map, "Eugene MacLain's San Francisco in Music from Spain," is available online; it could be a model for other projects in which students attempt to map Welty's geographies. (Part of an issue of the *Eudora Welty Newsletter* 28.2 also focuses on the topic "Welty in San Francisco"). Students may also use digital mapping to follow a "Driving Tour" available on the Eudora Welty House website; the tour includes the Welty family's first Jackson home and other settings found in her works. Students may glimpse these sites remotely using Google's "Street View," and then may access historic Google Earth images of these sites in earlier periods.

Other Classroom Materials

Teachers who wish to disentangle the Fairchild family history in *Delta Wedding* may benefit from Malinda Snow's "*Delta Wedding*: A Fairchild

Genealogy" in the *Eudora Welty Newsletter* (27.2). The Eudora Welty Foundation has a number of classroom resources on their website. In addition to a Reader's Guide for *The Optimist's Daughter*, the site includes a "Where Is the Voice Coming From?" Multimedia Teaching Unit and a "Welty and the Craft of Writing" media resource kit. *Mississippi History Now* also includes a Eudora Welty lesson plan.

More teaching resources, including sample assignments, handouts, and syllabi by several contributors to this volume, are available at a website, *Teaching Eudora Welty*, prepared by the editors of this volume.

D. For Further Reading: Scholarly Interpretations of Welty's Work

The field of Welty studies is dynamic and growing, with far more material being produced than many busy instructors have time to master. For those seeking a scholarly introduction to her body of work, Michael Kreyling's 1999 *Understanding Eudora Welty* is a fine starting point; studies by Vande Kieft (1962), Westling (1989), and Marrs (2002) are also very useful. As discussed in our introduction, critical understandings of Welty's work have broadened and deepened over time, particularly since the 1980s with the growth of feminist interpretations. Collections edited by Louis J. Dollarhide and Ann Abadie (1979), Peggy Prenshaw (1979), Albert J. Devlin (1987), Craig Turner and Lee Emling Harding (1989), and Dawn Trouard (1989) reflect the growing interest in Welty from the late 1970s to the 1990s. Patricia Yaeger may be the most-cited feminist scholar on Welty, especially her 1984 essay on Welty (*PMLA* 99.5), followed by readings in her 1988 *Honey-Mad Women: Emancipating Strategies in Women's Writing*, *Dirt and Desire: Reconstructing Southern Women's Writing*, and elsewhere, including an Editor's Column in *PMLA* (124.1, 2009). Other feminist readings include Franziska Gygax's 1990 *Serious Daring from Within: Female Narrative Strategies in Eudora Welty's Novels*, Peter Schmidt's 1991 *The Heart of the Story: Eudora Welty's Short Fiction*, Rebecca Mark's 1994 *The Dragon's Blood: Feminist Intertextuality in Eudora Welty's The Golden Apples*, and Suzan Harrison's 1997 *Eudora Welty and Virginia Woolf: Gender, Genre, and Influence.*

Welty studies in the twenty-first century has benefited from new scholarly approaches, many of these practiced by scholars working in "the new southern studies," including Kreyling, Yaeger, Prenshaw, Noel Polk, Barbara Ladd, Susan Donaldson, Annette Trefzer, David McWhirter, Sarah Ford, and Keith Cartwright, among others. Consonant with these developments are two collections that are frequently cited and of interest to students because of their wide-ranging approaches to Welty, her region, and her historical moment: Marrs's and Pollack's *Eudora Welty: Did the Writer Crusade?* (2001) and Pollack's *Eudora Welty, Whiteness, and Race* (2013). Instructors interested in following developments within southern studies may also peruse new journals (*Southern Spaces* and *Native South*) and new handbooks (*Oxford Handbook of the Literature of the U.S. South*, 2015; *Keywords for Southern Studies*, 2016).

Essays and books on Welty may be located via scholarly databases; in addition, Diana Pingatore's 1996 *A Reader's Guide to the Short Stories of Eudora Welty* conveniently summarizes the composition and publication history of each Welty story, as well as the scholarship on that story through the mid-1990s. *Mississippi Quarterly* has published two summaries of decades of Welty scholarship (1987–1997 and 1988–2009) in special issues devoted to Welty's work. The *Eudora Welty Review*, formerly a newsletter and since 2009 a peer-reviewed annual publication, provides an annual bibliography of scholarly work on Welty. The Eudora Welty Society regularly sponsors panels on Welty's work at academic conferences. Many EWS members have contributed to and supported this book. Information on how to join the society can be found on its website.

Note

1. An earlier biography, *Eudora: A Writer's Life*, by Ann Waldron (1998), provides a somewhat distorted portrait of Welty's long life. Having been unable to obtain interviews with Welty or most of Welty's friends and family, Waldron speculates about Welty's relationships and family secrets but reveals an incomplete understanding of Welty's literary achievements.

ABOUT THE CONTRIBUTORS

Jacob Agner is a PhD candidate at the University of Mississippi. His dissertation will focus on the early fiction and film of "rural noir." He won the 2012 Ruth Vande Kieft Prize for the best essay on Eudora Welty by a beginning scholar, and he has also published an essay on Cormac McCarthy. His teaching interests include southern literature and the crime tradition in American fiction and film.

Sharon Deykin Baris, senior lecturer in the Department of English and American Literature, Bar Ilan University, has published articles on Hawthorne, James, George Eliot, Stevens, Welty, and others, in journals including *Southern Literary Journal, Prospects, MLS, Common Knowledge, Henry James Review, Wallace Stevens Journal*, and in two collections of essays on Welty. Her topics have included the theory of American detective fiction; the influence of the book of Daniel in America; and Stanley Cavell on Emerson.

Carolyn J. Brown has written three biographies of Mississippi women, including *A Daring Life: A Biography of Eudora Welty*, winner of the Mississippi Library Association's Award for Nonfiction. She has published essays and book reviews about Eudora Welty in *Notes on Mississippi Writers*, the *Eudora Welty Review, Persuasions: The Jane Austen Journal*, the *Journal of Mississippi History*, and *Study the South*.

Lee Anne Bryan is the former education and outreach specialist of the Eudora Welty House, where she developed educational materials for teaching Welty and led educational tours. She continues to partner with the Eudora Welty Foundation and serves as the executive director of Alumni and Parent Relations at Millsaps College.

About the Contributors

Keith Cartwright is professor of English at the University of North Florida and the author of *Reading Africa into American Literature* (2002) and *Sacral Grooves, Limbo Gateways* (2013). He has taught Welty to students at Universidad de las Americas Puebla (Mexico), College of the Bahamas, Roanoke College, and Selma University, as well as in Jacksonville classrooms.

Stuart Christie is head and professor of the Department of English Language and Literature at Hong Kong Baptist University. He is the author of *Worlding Forster: The Passage from Pastoral* (2005), *Plural Sovereignties and Contemporary Indigenous Literature* (2009), and the coeditor, along with Zhang Yuejun, of *Modern American Poetry and the Chinese Encounter* (2012). He has also published numerous journal articles in venues such as *Modern Fiction Studies*, *College Literature*, *PMLA*, *Foreign Literature Studies* (外國文學研究), and the *American Indian Quarterly*. He recently guest edited a special volume of *Literature Compass* entitled "Twenty-First-Century Chinoiserie" (2015).

Virginia Ottley Craighill is a teaching professor at the University of the South in Sewanee, Tennessee, and has been director of Writing-Across-the-Curriculum. She teaches courses on the works of Tennessee Williams, modern American poetry, American literary journalism, and American women's literature, as well as teaching in Sewanee's first-year program, Finding Your Place, and English 101. She earned her PhD in English with an emphasis in creative writing at the University of Georgia and writes poetry and creative nonfiction.

Mae Miller Claxton is associate professor of English at Western Carolina University, where she teaches classes in southern, Appalachian, and Native American literature. She is the editor of *Conversations with Dorothy Allison* (2012) and coeditor, with Rain Newcomb, of *Conversations with Ron Rash* (2016). She has published essays in the *Southern Literary Journal*, *Mississippi Quarterly*, *South Atlantic Review*, *Southern Quarterly*, and the *Eudora Welty Review*, among others. She served as president of the Eudora Welty Society from 2010 to 2012.

David A. Davis is associate professor of English and associate director of southern studies at Mercer University. He studies southern literature and culture and teaches courses in American literature and southern studies. He has published dozens of essays on southern literature, and he edited a reprint of Victor Daly's novel *Not Only War: A Story of Two Great Conflicts* and a reprint of John L. Spivak's novel *Hard Times on a Southern Chain Gang*. He coedited *Writing in the Kitchen: Essays on Southern Literature and Foodways* with Tara Powell.

Susan V. Donaldson is National Endowment for the Humanities Professor of English and American Studies at the College of William and Mary. Eudora Welty's fiction is a regular fixture in most of the classes she teaches, from literature surveys to graduate seminars. Donaldson is the author of *Competing Voices: The American Novel, 1865–1914*, which won a *Choice* "Outstanding Academic Book" award, and some sixty essays and book chapters. She is coeditor of *Haunted Bodies: Gender and Southern Texts* and editor and coeditor of several special issues of the *Faulkner Journal* and *Mississippi Quarterly.*

Julia Eichelberger is Marybelle Higgins Howe Professor of Southern Literature at the College of Charleston and a past president of Eudora Welty Society. She is the author of *Prophets of Recognition: Ideology and the Individual in Novels by Ellison, Morrison, Bellow, and Welty* and the editor of *Tell about Night Flowers: Eudora Welty's Gardening Letters, 1940–1949*. She received the Phoenix Award for Welty scholarship in 2016. She has published essays in *Mississippi Quarterly, Southern Literary Journal*, and the *Eudora Welty Review*, among others, and in *Eudora Welty, Whiteness, and Race*, edited by Harriet Pollack.

Kevin Eyster is professor of English and chair of the Department of Language, Literature, Communication, and Writing at Madonna University in Livonia, Michigan. His appointment as an NEH Distinguished Teaching Professor in the Humanities led to the development of a course in folklore and American literature. He has published essays on a number of American writers, including Eudora Welty, William Faulkner, Nella Larsen, August Wilson, Colson Whitehead, and Gurney Norman.

Dolores Flores-Silva, associate professor at Roanoke College, is the coauthor of *The Cross and the Sword in the Works of Rosario Ferré and Mayra Montero* (2009). She teaches Welty as a bridge to crossings further south in her Latin American literature and Chicano Studies courses. She is currently working on a manuscript, "Cornbread, Quimbombo y Barbacoa: Mexico and the Gulf Shores of Our Souths," that addresses Welty's Natchez Trace fiction.

Sarah Gilbreath Ford is professor of American literature at Baylor University where she teaches early American literature, southern literature, and African American literature. She is author of *Tracing Southern Storytelling in Black* *and White* as well as numerous articles on Eudora Welty in journals such as *Mississippi Quarterly* and *Studies in the Novel*. She served as president of the Eudora Welty Society from 2014 to 2016.

Stephen M. Fuller is associate professor of English at Middle Georgia State University. He has taught Welty's fiction at MGSU and at the University of Southern Mississippi. His book *Eudora Welty and Surrealism* (2013) won the Eudora Welty Prize in 2013.

Dawn Gilchrist has taught at Swain County High School for nineteen years. She earned a BA from Western Carolina University, an MA from Columbia University, and an MFA from Warren Wilson College. She has published short stories, poems, and columns in various venues. In 2011 Gilchrist received the first Norman Mailer Writing Award for High School Teachers.

Rebecca L. Harrison, associate professor of English at the University of West Georgia, teaches courses on southern women writers, American literature, and discipline-specific theory and pedagogy courses for English education majors. A women's literature specialist, Harrison has published on writers such as Eudora Welty and Beatrice Witte Ravenel; her most recent book, *Inhabiting La Patria* (2013), is a critical collection on Julia Alvarez. Harrison, the 2015 Robert Reynolds Awardee for Excellence in Teaching, has forthcoming essays on Welty and Joan of Arc, STEAM English pedagogies, and two forthcoming books on inquiry-based learning.

Casey Kayser is a clinical assistant professor of English at the University of Arkansas, where she teaches courses in literature and medical humanities. Her work has been published in *Midwestern Folklore*, and she has essays forthcoming in *Mississippi Quarterly*, *Pedagogy*, and the *Journal of Medical Humanities*. She is the coeditor of *Carson McCullers in the Twenty-First Century* and is currently working on a book on gender, race, and regional identity in the works of southern women playwrights.

Michael Kreyling is Gertrude Conaway Vanderbilt Professor Emeritus at Vanderbilt. He is the author of *Eudora Welty's Achievement of Order* (1980), *Author and Agent: Eudora Welty and Diarmuid Russell* (1991), and many other publications. He is coeditor, with the novelist Richard Ford, of the 1998 Library of America editions of Welty's works.

About the Contributors

Ebony Lumumba is currently an assistant professor of English at Tougaloo College where she teaches courses in global and American literature. She specializes in postcolonial literatures of the global south and narratives of Africana mothering and foodways in her research and instruction. In 2013, Ebony was awarded the Eudora Welty Research Fellowship. Much of her scholarship cues in on Welty's incorporation of black life and culture within her fiction, nonfiction, and photography.

Suzanne Marrs is professor emerita of English at Millsaps College and the author of *Eudora Welty, A Biography* (2005), *One Writer's Imagination: The Fiction of Eudora Welty* (2002), and numerous articles about Welty's fiction. She is the editor of *What There Is to Say We Have Said: The Correspondence of Eudora Welty and William Maxwell* (2011), the coeditor, with Harriet Pollack, of *Eudora Welty and Politics: Did the Writer Crusade?* (2001), and the coeditor, with Tom Nolan, of *Meanwhile There Are Letters: The Correspondence of Eudora Welty and Ross Macdonald* (2015). Her book *The Welty Collection* (1988) is a bibliography of the Welty manuscripts, correspondence, and photographs at the Mississippi Department of Archives and History.

Pearl Amelia McHaney is the Kenneth M. England Professor of Southern Literature at Georgia State University in Atlanta where she also directs the Center for Collaborative and International Arts (CENCIA). In 2014, her book-length study *A Tyrannous Eye: Eudora Welty's Nonfiction and Photography* was published, and she received the Phoenix Award for outstanding achievement in Welty Studies from the Eudora Welty Society. She is the editor of *Eudora Welty as Photographer*, winner of the Eudora Welty Prize; *Occasions: Selected Writings by Eudora Welty*; *Eudora Welty: Contemporary Reviews*; *A Writer's Eye: Collected Reviews* by Eudora Welty; and the *Eudora Welty Review*, an annual peer-reviewed journal.

David McWhirter is professor of English at Texas A&M University, where he teaches classes in modernist literature and culture, early cinema, and US southern studies. He is the author of *Desire and Love in Henry James* (1989) and editor of *Henry James's New York Edition: The Construction of Authorship* (1995) and *Henry James in Context* (2010). McWhirter's essays on Henry James, Eudora Welty, Virginia Woolf, and other writers and topics have appeared in *Modern Fiction Studies*, *Mississippi Quarterly*, *ELH*, *ELN*, the *Henry James Review*, and numerous edited collections. He served as 2012–2013 president of the Eudora Welty Society and currently serves on the Executive Council of the Society for the Study of Southern Literature.

About the Contributors

Laura Sloan Patterson is professor of English at Seton Hill University in Greensburg, Pennsylvania, where she teaches first-year writing, gender studies, southern literature, and American literature. She has taught Eudora Welty's works in all of these contexts and published essays about sexuality, domesticity, and death rituals in Welty's stories. She is the author of *Stirring the Pot: Domesticity and the Kitchen in the Fiction of Southern Women*.

Harriet Pollack, professor emerita at Bucknell University, is the author of *Eudora Welty's Fiction and Photography: The Body of the Other Woman* (2016), the editor of *Eudora Welty, Whiteness, and Race* (2013), and of *Having Our Way: Women Rewriting Tradition in America* (1995), and coeditor with Suzanne Marrs of *Eudora Welty and Politics: Did the Writer Crusade?* (2001) and with Christopher Metress of *Emmett Till in Literary Memory and Imagination* (2009). Pollack received the Phoenix Award for Welty scholarship in 2008.

Gary Richards is associate professor of English and chair of the Department of English, Linguistics, and Communication at the University of Mary Washington, where he specializes in southern literature, US fiction and drama, and sexuality studies. He is the author of *Lovers and Beloveds: Sexual Otherness in Southern Fiction, 1936–1961* (2005) as well as essays on Truman Capote, Howard Cruse, William Goyen, Jim Grimsley, Allan Gurganus, Beth Henley, William Faulkner, Alfred Uhry, and Tennessee Williams. His current projects include a survey of literary representations of gay New Orleans and a study of representations of the US South in the contemporary Broadway musical.

Christin Marie Taylor is assistant professor of English at Shenandoah University, where she teaches African American and American literature. Her research interests include southern studies, working-class representation, and environmental literature. She has published in the *Southern Quarterly* and has taught Eudora Welty's short fiction in a variety of literature and critical thinking courses.

Annette Trefzer is associate professor of English at the University of Mississippi. She is the author of *Disturbing Indians: The Archaeology of Southern Fiction* (2007) and the coeditor with Ann J. Abadie of four volumes of critical essays on William Faulkner including *Global Faulkner* (2009), *Faulkner's Sexualities* (2010), *Faulkner and Formalism: Returns of the Text* (2012), and *Faulkner and Mystery* (2014). She teaches classes on Eudora Welty at the graduate and undergraduate level on a regular basis, and she is currently at work on a book on Welty's photography.

About the Contributors

Alec Valentine taught English at the community college level for thirty-one years. He began teaching in junior high schools in the first days of racial integration in Mississippi. His focus has always been on underprepared students, their use of language, and their awareness of literature. In college he was privileged to take a course in short-story writing from Eudora Welty.

Adrienne Akins Warfield is associate professor of English at Mars Hill University, where she teaches courses including Social Justice in Literature and Culture, Diversity in American Literature, Modern and Contemporary Literature, and others. She has published essays in *Southern Literary Journal*, *Mississippi Quarterly*, *Studies in American Indian Literatures*, *Southern Quarterly*, *Renascence*, *Journal of the Short Story in English*, *Eudora Welty Review*, *Critique: Studies in Contemporary Fiction*, and other venues.

Keri Watson is assistant professor of art history at the University of Central Florida. Her research and teaching interests include the history of photography, modern American art, and representations of disability. She has contributed essays to publications including *Disability and Art History*; *Eudora Welty, Whiteness, and Race;* and *Mosaic: A Journal for the Interdisciplinary Study of Literature*.

Amy Weldon is associate professor of English at Luther College in Decorah, Iowa. She is the author of *The Hands-On Life: How to Wake Yourself Up and Save the World* (forthcoming), and her essays, short fiction, and scholarly articles have appeared in multiple print and online journals and edited collections.

INDEX

Aeneid, 28
African Americans: agency, xvii, 75, 149, 160, 161, 162; characters in Welty's fiction, 35, 45, 71, 74–75, 79, 81, 82, 86, 89, 124, 127, 172, 196; communities, 78, 79, 80, 81, 82, 87; folklore, 88, 89, 152; history, 59, 150, 174, 196, 198, 203; identity, xvii, 69; minstrelsy, 88; performers, 87; representations of, 84, 86, 162, 199; toasts, 87; women, 81–82; writers, 72, 87. *See also* race
African literature, 162
African survivals, 94
Afro-creole cultural traditions, 91–93
Agee, James, 48, 52, 53
Agrarians and Fugitives, 134
Alexie, Sherman, 96
Algonquin Hotel, 11
allegory, 5, 105, 173–74, 175, 203
Allison, Dorothy, 110
ambiguity. *See* indeterminacy
American South. *See* South; US South
American studies, xv, 41, 42, 158
Anderson, Eric Gary, 56
Andrews Sisters, 27
Anglophone literature, 148
anthropology, xviii, 226, 228
Anzaldúa, Gloria, 64, 66, 67
Appalachia, xiv, 172, 174, 182; literature of, 59
Armstrong, Louis, 27

Arnold, Ellen, 56
art, 158, 175, 192, 195, 199, 224. *See also* visual art
artists, 27, 190, 195, 197, 200; in Welty's works, 124, 171, 224
Aswell, Mary Louise, correspondence with, 22. *See also* Welty, Eudora: correspondence
Atlantic Monthly, 235
Atlantic slave trade, 58, 92
audience: contemporary audiences for Welty's works, xvii, 13, 15; for oral narratives/storytelling, 60, 210–11; for Welty as speaker, 158, 210, 236; in Welty's works, 26, 27–28, 45, 84, 86–89, 120, 228. *See also* readers
Audubon, John James, 7, 216
Austen, Jane, 8, 9, 16; novels by, 8

Baldwin, James, 197, 198
Baym, Nina, 43, 124
Beckert, Sven, 90
Belcher, Wendy, 94
Benedict, Ruth, 226–27
Berman, Sandra, 158
Bhabha, Homi, 160
black Atlantic, xviii, 91, 94
Black Lives Matter, 78, 115
blues, 27, 28
Boas, Franz, 226

249

body/bodies, xviii, 99, 92, 120, 125, 190, 192; black, 75, 125; commodification of, 53; female, 25, 65, 66, 119, 123, 125, 126; queer, 109, 110, 112, 128; textual, 123, 124. *See also* disability; homosociality; literary theory; queerness; sexual trauma

borders/*la frontera*, 56, 62–66, 95

bottle trees, 152–54, 178

Bowen, Elizabeth, 8, 10, 15, 16, 131; novels by, 8–9, 11

Brooks, Cleanth, 122–23

Brown, Carolyn, xvii, 14, 233–34

Burr, Aaron, 7

Cabrera, Lydia, 64, 67, 91

canon (literary), xvii, 78, 79, 80, 82, 147; southern, 183

Carby, Hazel, 43

carnival, 50, 54, 64, 65, 66

Cartwright, Keith, xviii, 56, 94, 237, 238

Castellanos, Rosario, 64, 67

Cather, Willa, 134, 138

Chaney, Lon, 102

Chekhov, Anton, 8, 9, 16; works by, 8

Cherokee (Eastern Band), 55–56, 172, 174

Chicano literature, 62, 63. *See also* Latin America

Chickasaw, 56, 59

Choctaw, 56, 57, 58, 59

Chopin, Kate, 42, 138

cinema. *See* film

Cisneros, Sandra, 66

civil rights, 73; civil rights movement (American), 5, 54, 72, 147, 161, 163, 198, 200, 233, 235; post–civil rights, 54. *See also* protest

Cixous, Hélène, 124, 125, 143–45

class, xvi, 19, 25, 26, 34, 41, 42, 44, 49, 53, 54, 73, 81, 84, 103, 111, 128, 134, 138, 160–61, 172, 175, 179, 191, 196–99, 203. *See also* privilege (white)

close reading. *See* literary theory

Cold War, 158

Collins, Merle, 94

colonialism and postcolonialism, 58, 63, 65, 138, 148, 179, 216, 219

comedy/comic, xiv, 25, 39, 42, 43, 44, 45, 46, 104, 107, 114, 117, 122, 209, 210, 228; comic mugging, 27; comic parody, 28; comic play, 25; comic quest, 29. *See also* humor

community, 76, 127, 149, 202, 203, 204, 205, 217; in works, 4, 39, 42, 44, 49, 51, 79, 80, 128, 227

Conrad, Joseph, xviii, 134, 135, 138

consumerism, 49, 62, 66, 134, 136, 138, 190, 225, 227

Corn Mother, 64–65

cosmopolitanism, xiii, xviii, 22, 141, 142, 145

Council of Writing Program Administrators (WPA), 181, 182, 186, 187

critical race studies. *See* literary theory

cultural studies, 133. *See also* literary theory

culture, 112; African American, 79, 87, 94; Anglo-American, xvii, 42, 133–34, 136, 138, 145; death, 49, 53; global, xvii, 142, 158, 160–62, 226–27; indigenous, 55–57, 59–60, 65; Latin American, 62; material consumer, 49, 102, 138, 185, 227; modernist, 136–37, 138; patriarchal, 124–25; plantation, 73–74; queer, 113; southern, 182; visual, 43; white, 86, 161

Dash, Julie, 43

Davis, David A., xvii, 134

death, as theme, 4, 48, 52, 54, 183; cultural, economic, and religious issues of, 48, 50, 51, 53; funeral industry, 48, 51; mortality and immortality, 4, 49, 50, 51, 52, 53

De La Beckwith, Byron, 161, 198–99, 200

diaspora, 91, 93, 94

DiBattista, Maria, 136

Dickey, James, 110

Dickinson, Emily, xiii, xvi
Dinesen, Isak, 16
disability, xvi, xviii, 33, 101, 102, 103, 104, 107, 126, 128, 203, 204; studies, xv, 107, 122, 126, 127, 128; disabled characters, 126–27
Donaldson, Susan, xvii, 73, 82–83, 238
doppelganger/doubling, 118, 212
Dos Passos, John, 143
Dow, Lorenzo, 7
drug use, 113–14
Dunbar, Paul Laurence, 72, 75
Dylan, Bob, 197, 198, 199

ecology, 188, 189, 191, 192. *See also* environment; landscape; nature
Edwards, Laura, 42
Eichelberger, Julia, xvii, 83, 150, 233
Eliot, T. S., 133, 134, 135, 136, 138
empathy, xiv, 5, 33, 91, 161, 162, 172, 178
England (Cambridge), 142, 158
Entzminger, Betina, 42
environment, 147, 203, 204. *See also* ecology; landscape; nature
Eudora Welty Collection, xv, 19; student research in, 19–20, 22. *See also* Mississippi Department of Archives and History
Eudora Welty Foundation, teaching aids to works, 6, 7, 8, 15, 232, 233, 236, 238
Eudora Welty House and Garden, xiv, 6, 8, 9, 13, 14, 15, 16, 234
Eudora Welty Review, 22
Eudora Welty Society, 232, 239
eugenics, 25, 30, 102
Europe, 141, 142. *See also* travel
Evers, Medgar, 7, 150, 160, 161, 163, 197, 198, 199, 200; house, 7

Fahy, Thomas, 102
fairy tales. *See* folklore
family: middle-class (white), 49, 53; as theme, 32–35, 39, 48, 50, 53, 54, 161, 162, 210, 211, 213; working-class, 49, 53
Fantasticks, The (musical), 120
Farish Street Baptist Church, 81
Farm Security Administration, 102
Faulkner, William, 56, 66, 85, 94, 102, 126, 133, 134, 138, 139, 143, 144; *As I Lay Dying*, 48, 52, 53
Federal Writers' Project, 57
feminist criticism. *See* literary theory
femininity, 141, 143, 144, 145. *See also* gender; lady (southern white); southern womanhood
Ferré, Rosario, 64, 66, 67
Fiji Islands culture, 226–27
film, 136, 137, 195; versions of Welty's works, 6, 236–37
Fitzgerald, F. Scott, 143
folklore, xv, 18, 60, 137, 208, 209, 211, 213; African (black Atlantic world), 88, 90–92, 94; Choctaw, 91; folktales, 58, 64, 93, 96, 117, 208, 213; initiation tales, 92; medicine, 90–91, 92, 93, 95, 96; ritual, 94
Ford, Richard, xviii
Ford, Sarah Gilbreath, xvii, 37, 83, 228, 238
formalism. *See* literary theory
Forster, E. M., 5, 9, 15, 112, 133, 150, 195; *A Passage to India*, racial prejudice in, 5, 9
Fort Rosalie, 65
free indirect discourse, xv, 33, 37, 145
Fugitives, 134
Fuller, Stephen, xviii, 21–22, 139, 233, 234

Gaines, Ernest, 48, 53, 196, 197
gardens and gardening, 20, 23, 51, 71, 72, 73, 74, 75, 124
Garland-Thomson, Rosemarie, 102, 128
gender, 73, 75, 125, 147; and disability, xvi, 103–4; and health care, 203, 206; identity, xvi, 107, 111–13; performance of, 112, 113; roles in society, 41, 111,

125, 134, 137, 142; and sexuality, 123; in Welty's works, 34, 42, 49, 73, 75, 81, 95, 145, 160, 185, 197, 203; and writing, 144
Gilbert, Sandra M., 124
global consciousness, xv, 158. *See also* South: global
global modernism, 113, 137, 144, 158
globalization, 157
Glymph, Thavolia, 42
Gone with the Wind, 42, 86
Gordimer, Nadine, xviii, 158, 159–60, 161–62, 163, 211
Great Debaters, The (film), 196
Great Depression, 7, 8, 101
grotesque, 39, 127, 183. *See also* disability
Gubar, Susan, 124
Guinn, Matthew, 48, 53
Gullah Geechee, 93
Gwin, Minrose, 200

Hale, Grace Elizabeth, 73, 235
Hall, Alice, 126–27
Hansen, Miriam, 136
Harlem Renaissance, 86, 87, 88; connection to modernism, 87, 88; writers of, 86
Harper's Bazaar, 235
Harris, Joel Chandler, 85
Harrison, Suzan, 8, 11, 37, 41, 43, 139, 238
health care, 197, 202, 203, 204, 205, 206
Hellman, Lillian, 159
Hemingway, Ernest, 36, 111, 112, 133, 139, 143
hero, 28, 34, 81, 104, 212
heroine, xviii, 25
historically black colleges, xiv, xvii, 78
history: African American, 78, 86, 196; American, 7; cultural, 49, 63, 90; disabilities, 128; family history, 236; Latino, 63, 66; as literary context, 62, 156–57, 159–63, 198–99; minorities, 78; Native American, 55–60; queer, 114; southern, xvii, 39; women's, 25, 73; world, 216. *See also* Mississippi; Natchez Trace

Hobson, Geary, 60
Hollenbaugh, Carol, 123
Holm, Tom, 57
home, as theme in works, 5, 52
homosexuality, 110, 111, 112. *See also* homosociality; queerness
homosociality, 110, 111, 112, 114. *See also* homosexuality; queerness
Hong Kong, 147; Umbrella Movement (2014), 148, 150, 151–52, 153–57
hope chests, 128, 224, 225, 227
Howe, LeAnne, 55, 56, 58, 59
Hughes, Langston, 87
humor, xix, 17, 44, 237. *See also* comedy/comic
Hurston, Zora Neale, 42, 91, 103, 111
Huyssen, Andreas, 136

indeterminacy, 3, 20, 21, 75, 177, 185
Indians. *See* Native Americans
indigenous studies, 56
initiation tales, 91–92, 95
interdisciplinary studies, xviii–ix, 158, 193, 195, 199, 203
internationalism, xviii, 109, 131, 134, 141, 142, 143, 145. *See also* global modernism
internet, 136, 168, 210, 211, 226, 235
intertextuality, 32, 34, 158, 161, 162, 216
Irigaray, Luce, 124–26

Jackson, Andrew, 90, 96
Jackson, Mississippi, xiii, 5, 14, 16, 19, 20, 21, 57, 81, 90, 94, 112, 141, 167, 198
Jackson Clarion-Ledger, 7
Jacobs, Harriet, 42
jazz, 27, 86, 211, 235
jigsaw method, 73–74, 76
Jim Crow, 27, 42, 46, 72, 74, 127, 196
journeys, as theme in works, 4, 20, 59, 90–91, 93, 95–96, 174–75, 193, 197, 203–4
Joyce, James, xviii, 133, 135, 138, 139, 144

Kenan, Randall, 48, 52
King, Martin Luther, Jr., 72, 75, 198
King, Thomas, 60
Knopf, Alfred and Helen, 11
Kreyling, Michael, xviii, 18, 21, 22, 37, 38, 56–57, 145, 228, 233, 231, 233, 238
Kristeva, Julia, 161. *See also* intertextuality

Ladd, Barbara, 238
lady (southern white), xiii, xvi, xviii, 26, 33, 42–46, 74, 86, 125, 135, 142. *See also* southern womanhood
La Llorona, 64
landscape: geographical, 59, 159, 189, 191–92, 219; global, 155, 159; modernist, 135–37; social, 64, 74. *See also* ecology; environment; nature
Langer, Judith, 160, 161
language, 171, 190–92; disability, 126; feminist, 123–25, 137, 145; literary, 25, 116, 118; Native American use of, 57–59; other than English, 62, 64, 150, 158; race and language, 84; Welty's use of, xv, 10, 11, 21, 122, 169, 212; in Welty's works, 28, 33, 85, 92, 119, 210, 224
Latin America, xv, xvii, 62; history of, 62, 63; literature of, 62, 66; writers, 64, 66, 67
letters. *See* Welty, Eudora: correspondence
Library of America (editions of Welty's works), xix, 231–32
Limón, José, 64, 67
literary criticism. *See* literary theory
literary theory, xv–xvi, xviii, 122, 128, 129, 145, 182, 219; close reading/formalism/New Criticism, 122, 123, 128, 141–45, 182; critical race studies, 115, 128; ecocritical, 145; feminist, 41, 122–26, 128, 145, 159; intersectional, 128–29; Marxism, 159; materialist and cultural studies, 128, 133, 145, 185; new historicism, 159, 185; postcolonialism, 159; poststructuralism, 143;

psychoanalysis, 124, 125, 128; textuality, 129. *See also* disability: studies; sexuality
logging, 135
love, romantic, 18, 25, 26, 65, 113
Lyell, Frank, correspondence with, 21–22. *See also* Welty, Eudora: correspondence

Macdonald, Ross, 8, 9, 10, 11, 16, 18, 22; correspondence with, 18; novels by, 9, 10, 11. *See also* Welty, Eudora: correspondence
magical realism. *See* realism
Magona, Sindiwe, 158, 159, 160, 161, 162, 163
Mardi Gras, 49, 50, 54. *See also* carnival
Mark, Rebecca, 41, 83, 104, 139, 228, 238
Marmion, 4, 33
marriage (heterosexual), 25, 34, 101, 111, 112, 113, 123, 128, 143, 178, 179
Marrs, Suzanne, xvi–xvii, 15, 16, 18, 21, 22, 79, 83, 107, 133, 142, 195–96, 233, 234, 236, 238, 239; courses taught, 7–11
Marshall, Paule, 91
Maxwell, Emily, 18
Maxwell, William, xviii; correspondence with, 9, 18; novel by, 9. *See also* Welty, Eudora: correspondence
McCullers, Carson, 17, 20
McHaney, Pearl, xviii, 21, 107, 139, 163, 232, 233, 234
McKay, Claude, 72, 87
McRuer, Robert, 127, 128
McWhirter, David, xviii, 37, 83, 89, 235, 238
Mead, Margaret, 226
media, xvi, 62, 117, 134, 136, 161, 162, 163, 168, 190, 196, 206, 210, 211
medical care, access to, 196, 197, 203, 205
medical humanities, xviii, 203
medicine journey, xviii, 90, 92–93, 96
Medusa, 120, 125, 128, 136, 144
memory in fiction, 26, 28, 48, 49, 50, 51, 52, 53, 74

Mexico, 63–64, 67, 92, 94, 142
Mikics, David, 168, 169
Millar, Kenneth. *See* Macdonald, Ross
Mississippi, xiii, xiv, 4, 5, 14, 32, 42, 44, 64, 66, 81, 84, 85, 87, 90, 101, 133, 142, 161, 177, 198, 199; 1930s, 27, 43, 85, 135, 196; folk culture, 65, 91, 94; history of, 63, 64, 213; Mississippians, 13, 117; Native American history in, 56, 57, 59, 60, 65; politics of, 195; sharecropping/tenant farming in, 15, 177; State Fair, 101, 104; in works, 7, 44, 64, 87, 212
Mississippi: A Guide to the Magnolia State, 57, 234–35
Mississippi Department of Archives and History (MDAH), 16, 19, 57, 83, 232, 233, 234, 236
Mississippi River, 58, 212
modernism, xvi, xvii, 51, 86, 103, 112, 133, 134, 136, 137, 138, 185; American modernism, xviii, 88, 109, 111, 137, 138, 139, 158; Anglo-American, 134, 145, 149; global/international, xviii, 112, 137, 144, 145, 185; mass culture, 136–37, 138; modernist artists, 133, 142; modernist studies, xv, 133, 134, 137, 138; modernist writers, 36, 88, 133, 134–35, 136, 138, 144; postmodernism, 7, 84, 144, 145; southern modernism, 134; urban modernism, 135; Welty fiction as, xvi, xvii, xviii, 24, 29, 34, 41, 48, 61, 133, 134, 135, 144
Moi, Toril, 124
Moody, Anne, 163
Morrison, Toni, xviii, 78, 79, 82, 85, 83, 159
Morton, Timothy, 188, 189, 191, 192
Mozart, Wolfgang Amadeus, 17
Mudd, Roger, 15. *See also* Welty, Eudora: friendships
Munro, Alice, xviii
Murrell, John, 7

music, 26, 28, 136, 137, 195, 208, 210, 211; lyrics, 27; musicians, 6, 27, 28, 84, 128, 200, 224, 226, 227, 228; song, 27. *See also* art; artists
mystery, as theme in works, 21, 29, 65
myth, xv, 4–5, 32, 34, 64, 90, 96, 116, 118–19, 120, 138, 147, 148, 149, 150, 151, 152, 154, 155, 157, 179, 203, 216, 218; cultural myths, 42, 86, 88

narrators, 26, 27, 33, 44, 86, 127, 128, 210, 211; unreliable, 45, 86, 128, 161
Natchez, Mississippi, 45, 58, 63, 64, 95, 159. *See also* Natchez Trace
Natchez Indians, 56, 59, 65
Natchez Trace, 177; history of, 57, 58, 64, 216, 235; in Welty's works, 15, 45, 57, 58, 59, 60, 62, 63, 117, 159, 212, 217, 219. *See also* Natchez, Mississippi
National Council of Teachers of English (NCTE), 181, 182
National Intimate Partner and Sexual Violence Survey (NISVS), 116–20
National Writing Project, 181
Native Americans, 57, 58, 60, 104, 118, 119, 212
Native American studies, 55, 57; community vs. individual, 57, 58; historical and cultural contexts, 55, 56, 58, 59, 60; language (story), 58, 59, 60; resources for, 55; writers, 56, 59, 91
Native South, 56, 59–60
nature, 20, 21, 29, 72, 73, 76, 183, 189, 191, 192, 216. *See also* ecology; environment; landscape
New Criticism. *See* literary theory
New Negro Renaissance, xvii
New Orleans, 50, 54, 63, 94. *See also* Mardi Gras
new southern studies, xv
New Women, 41, 43
New York City, 110, 112, 117, 119, 141, 142, 235; Welty's travel to, 11, 86

New Yorker, xiii, 18
New York Times Book Review, 175, 226, 232
Ngcobo, Lauretta, 163

O'Connor, Flannery, 56
Ohio, 36, 142, 170
oral narrative, 58, 87, 173, 210, 211
Ownby, Ted, 235

parables, 174, 175
parody, 25, 28, 44, 107
Patchett, Ann, xviii, 8
Patterson, Laura Sloan, xviii, 22, 236
Paz, Octavio, 66
"peoplehood," in Native American studies, 57–58
performance, 26–27, 28, 102, 88, 103, 104, 112, 113, 171, 208, 209, 210, 211, 213; performers, 27, 28, 84, 86, 87, 102, 103, 104
Persephone, 32, 34, 149, 179
photographs/photography, xv, 151–53; 1930s, 42–43, 149, 213, 232; African American subjects, 79, 81; in archives, xv, 83, 232, 236; in correspondence, 18, 22; displayed at Eudora Welty house, 9; at Eudora Welty Foundation website, 232–33; fair photographs, 101, 102–4, 107; family photographs, 13, 15, 170, 232; Farm Security Administration, 102; gender in, 79, 81; as inspiration for writing, 189; photo essay books, 235; photographer, Welty as, 43, 81, 149, 195; photographs in *Mississippi: A Guide to the Magnolia State* (WPA guide), 57, 235; photography exhibit, 14; in teaching Welty's works, 6, 13, 15, 24, 29, 79–80, 82, 107, 157, 216, 232; travel/global photographs, 141–42, 226; in Welty's works, 113
Picasso, Pablo, 195
Pierpont, Claudia Roth, xiii
place, in fiction, 39, 55, 59

plantation, 64, 66, 73, 74, 94; capitalism, 90; myth, 74, 86, 88; post-plantation, 91, 115
Poe, Edgar Allan, 112
poetry, 169, 170, 171
politics, xiii, 8, 20, 43, 45, 84, 85, 114, 154, 155, 195, 196, 199, 200, 215–16
Polk, Noel, 39, 199, 234, 235, 238
Pollack, Harriet, xvii, 41, 43, 67, 72, 79, 82, 83, 89, 107, 200, 204, 228, 234, 239; courses taught, 30
postmodernism, 7, 84, 144, 145
poverty, 5, 7, 15, 53, 102, 127, 159, 160, 172, 174, 175, 177, 178, 179, 197, 203, 204, 205
Prenshaw, Peggy, 30, 41, 238
Price, Reynolds, 8–9, 10, 112; novels by, 9, 11
privilege (white), xiii, xvi, xvii, 75, 104. *See also* class; lady (southern white); social position; southern womanhood; whiteness
protest, 71, 75, 78, 148, 150, 151, 152, 154, 155, 156, 157, 161, 198. *See also* Hong Kong: Umbrella Movement; race
psychoanalysis. *See* literary theory

queerness, xviii, 109, 110, 111, 112, 113, 114, 128; queer studies, 112, 127, 128; queer subculture, 113; representations of, 112. *See also* homosexuality; homosociality
quest, 28, 29, 91, 92, 93. *See also* journeys

race, xvii, 39, 46, 72, 74, 76, 81, 84, 103, 172, 175, 178, 179, 180, 197, 198, 203, 204, 206; in blues, 27; critical race studies, xv; knowledge of, 85; performance of, 28, 84, 86, 87, 88; prejudice, 5, 9, 107, 177, 226; race relations in 1930s, 6, 27, 196; racial encounters, 45; racial identity, xvii, 84, 88, 107; racial injustice, 79, 196, 197, 198; racial purity, 26; representations of, 25, 29, 84, 85, 87, 88, 199;

representations of in Welty's works, 25, 28, 29, 42, 71, 73, 75, 81, 104, 111, 160, 177, 196, 199; roles, 41; segregated society, 43, 160, 196, 197, 203; and stereotypes, 85, 86, 88, 104, 172, 174, 226; teaching about, 71, 75, 84, 203, 204; and trauma, 91, 196, 198, 225

racism, xvi, 32, 35, 80, 101, 104, 135, 162, 196

Randall, Alice, 42

rape. *See* sexual violence

readers: expectations of, xvii, 24–25, 29, 72, 104, 144; inspiring empathy in, 21, 29, 33, 95, 161, 173, 191, 206; of other writers, 16; student readers, 13, 42, 71, 91, 96, 122–23, 162, 175, 177, 221, 233; Welty as reader, 8, 16, 183; of Welty's letters and works (literary audience), 4, 5, 15, 16, 18, 21, 32, 210–11. *See also* audience

reading Welty's works: aloud, 167, 169; for character, xvii, 33, 45, 191; for context and history, xiv, xvi, 55, 59, 90; difficulty, xiv, 21; reading beyond South, 145, 147, 160–61

realism, 53, 148, 152; historical realism, 53; magical realism, 53, 64, 65. *See also* surrealism

region: regional contexts, 110; regionalism, xv, 131, 147, 158, 185, 215; regionalist writers, xiii, xvi, xviii, 66, 133, 138, 143–44, 159, 185, 195; regionalized modernity, 134; regionalized sexuality, 110, 112; regional settings, 131, 147, 219. *See also* South; southerners

ring shout, 93

Robinson, John, 112; correspondence with, 18, 22. *See also* Welty, Eudora: correspondence

rural settings, 203, 204, 205, 206

Rushdie, Salman, 142

Russell, Diarmuid, 56, 133; correspondence with, 18, 22. *See also* Welty, Eudora: correspondence

San Francisco, 110, 141, 142

saraka, 94–95

Scarry, Elaine, 191

Schatteman, Renée, 159, 160, 162

Schmidt, Peter, 41, 43, 139, 238

Sedgwick, Eve Kosofsky, 110

segregation/apartheid, 46, 71, 73, 74, 75, 101, 102, 137, 158, 159, 161, 197, 211. *See also* Jim Crow; race

service learning, 202, 203, 206

sexism, 101

sexuality, 109, 110, 113, 114, 119, 123, 125, 128, 134, 204; of characters, 113, 123, 128; female, 111, 125, 126, 128, 136, 137, 145; heterosexuality, 127, 128; male, 112; theories of, 122. *See also* gender

sexual maturity, 26

sexual violence, 115–18, 120; rape, 116, 117, 118, 120, 123, 125, 160, 212

Shakespeare, William, 167, 171

Silko, Leslie Marmon, 91, 95, 96

slavery, 58, 92

Smith, Lillian, 48, 53

social change, 5, 49, 72–73, 135, 202

social commentary, 114

social construct, 84, 101, 104, 107, 116, 124, 126–28. *See also* class

social justice, xviii, 195–96, 200

social media, xvi, 117, 196

social position, 81–82, 103, 126, 172

social protest, 75

socioeconomics. *See* class; poverty

song. *See* music

South: 1930s, 6, 110, 125, 196; contemporary, 53, 54; cultural myths of, 42; economic development of, 53, 54, 135; funeral customs of, 51, 53, 183; global, xv; migration from, 48, 54; modernity, 51, 53–54, 133–38; other "Souths," xviii, 62–64, 67, 94; post southern, 141–42, 145; rural/small town experiences, 53, 110, 196, 203; social change in, 49. *See also* race; region

South Africa, xv, 160, 161, 163, 211; writers, xviii, 112, 134, 158, 159, 160, 185. *See also* Gordimer, Nadine; modernism
southerners, 143; 1930s, 110; white expatriates, 54; white middle-class, 54; working-class, 54
southern gothic, 84
southern literature. *See* southern studies
southern studies, xiv, xv, xvii, 3, 39, 48, 50, 52, 56, 60, 91, 133, 135, 141, 183, 237; new, xv; queer, 112
Southern Tenant Farmers Union, 7
southern womanhood, xvii, 22, 42, 46, 73, 75, 142, 143; black and white womanhood, 42, 43; mythology of, 42, 43, 73; stereotypes of, 42, 86. *See also* lady (southern white)
Spencer, Elizabeth, 109
Stang, Melissa Deakins, 96, 196, 203
Steinbeck, John, 102, 111
storyboard assignment, 149, 150, 155–56
students, reactions to Welty's works, 19, 20, 24, 59–60, 63, 72–73, 154–56, 162, 174–75, 177, 221
surrealism, 66, 117, 136, 139, 145
surveillance, 43, 73

Taylor, Christin Marie, 17, 22
Taylor, Melanie, 60
Taylor, Peter, 54
teaching: Advanced Placement, xviii, 172, 173, 174, 175; Africana courses, 91; African American courses, 91; American literature courses, 72, 78, 84, 91, 95, 96, 134, 208, 219, 221; anthology, 109; apartheid, 163; Bloom's Taxonomy, 218; Caribbean courses, 91, 96; citizenship, 202, 206; close reading/literary analysis, 162, 167, 169, 177, 182, 183, 184, 185, 186, 204, 208, 216; Common Core, 215, 219, 221; community college, xviii, 177; community responsive, 202, 203, 206; creative writing, xviii, 167, 177, 188, 189; critical analysis/thinking, xvi, xviii, 72, 115, 160, 171, 181, 182, 185, 186, 203, 204; elementary students, 13–14; first-year-experience courses, 41–46, 72; folklore, xviii, 208; gender studies, 109; global South, 142; groups, 217; high school students, 13–15; historically black college, 78; inquiry-based learning, xix, 102, 107, 215, 216; interdisciplinary contexts, xviii; international contexts, 147; international modernism, 142; introduction to literature courses, 134, 170, 181; journals, 217, 218; learning community, 217; liberal arts college, 48, 62; literacy narratives, 168; literary theory, 122, 142; medical humanities, xviii, 202; middle school students, 13–15; modern US fiction, 109, 111, 149; Native American studies, 59–60; reading skills, 180, 216, 221; research methods course, 185, 217; secondary school curricula, 215, 216, 217, 219, 221; service learning, xix; Shakespeare, 171; short story, 149; social justice, xviii; southern literature courses, 91, 96, 109, 183, 219; teacher education, xviii, 215–21; teaching aids to works, 6, 7, 8, 15; Teaching Learning Activity (TLA), 149, 155–57; teaching portfolio, 220, 221, 223; teaching techniques, 73, 76; undergraduate writing courses, xviii, 41, 42, 72, 109, 110, 112, 165, 167, 177, 181, 184, 185, 216; Visual Thinking Strategies (VTS), xvi, 103, 107; women's literature courses, 72, 109, 142, 183. *See also* reading Welty's works; students; writing and writing techniques; writing assignments
textuality/intertextuality, 32, 34, 123, 129, 139
Till, Emmett, 198

time, as theme in works, 4, 51, 52, 59
Tolkien, J. R. R., 91
Toomer, Jean, 134, 138
transnational interpretation, 137, 158, 159, 162. *See also* global consciousness; internationalism
trauma, xviii, 30, 115, 116, 117, 120; visual, 119
Trefzer, Annette, xviii, 22, 57, 203, 238
Tretheway, Natasha, 66
"tribalography," Native American studies, 58, 59, 60
Trouard, Dawn, 145, 236, 238
Truong, Monique, 112
Turner, Lorenzo Dow, 93
Twain, Mark, 85, 88, 109, 112

US South, xv, xvii, 39, 42, 133, 134, 147, 150, 158, 159. *See also* South
Utica, Mississippi, 14

Vande Kieft, Ruth, 234, 238
Vidal, Gore, 111
violence, 65–66, 72, 75, 123, 196. *See also* sexual violence
vision, 13, 93, 129, 137, 174, 189, 191, 192
visual art, 13, 15, 22, 83, 189, 195, 232, 233, 235; paintings, 119, 136, 149. *See also* photographs/photography; surrealism
Vogue, 235

Walker, Alice, 159, 162, 163, 209, 210
Walker, Frank X, 200
Walker, Margaret, 42, 197, 198
Waller, Fats, 6, 27, 85, 195
wanderer, as theme, 20, 27
Warren, Robert Penn, 122, 123
Waverly, 4
Welty, Edward, 15
Welty, Eudora
  audio recordings of, 236–37
  awards, Pulitzer Prize, 13, 15

biography, biographical materials, xvii, 13, 17, 232. *See also* Marrs, Suzanne
correspondence, xvii, 17–21, 18, 157, 216, 233; about art and artists, 19–20; about creative process, 23; about flowers and gardening, 18, 20, 23; comments on other writers, 17, 20; daily life in Jackson, 19, 20; political views in, 19, 20
film versions of works, 6
friendships, xiii, 8, 11, 15, 112; with writers, 10, 16. *See also* Aswell, Mary Louise; Bowen, Elizabeth; Lyell, Frank; Macdonald, Ross; Price, Reynolds
homes: Congress Street house, 14; Pinehurst Street house, 14, 15, 16
humor, xix, 17, 44, 237. *See also* comedy/comic
"lady," xiii, xvi, 133, 142
maps of works, 237
nonfiction, body of work, 232
politics, xiii, 5, 8
as reader, 8, 16
revision process, 14
travel, xiii, 141, 142; Ireland and Bowen's Court, 10
Works: **children's book:** *The Shoe Bird*, 233; **fiction:** "Asphodel," 139; "At the Landing," 65, 66, 67, 217, 218; *The Bride of the Innisfallen*, 8, 9, 11, 29, 141, 142, 231; "The Bride of the Innisfallen," 8; "The Burning," 8, 29, 180; "Circe," 8; *The Collected Stories*, 109, 232; *A Curtain of Green*, 7, 8, 9, 25, 28, 41, 42, 43, 44, 46, 60, 231; "A Curtain of Green," 21, 22, 71, 72, 73–76, 109, 122, 124–25; "Death of a Traveling Salesman," 4, 8, 180; *Delta Wedding*, 4, 8, 10, 32–36, 59, 115, 231, 237; "The Demonstrators," 8, 29, 83, 161, 163, 228, 231; "First Love," 7, 64, 180, 217, 218; "Flowers for Marjorie," 8, 117, 127; "From the Unknown,"

7; "Going to Naples," 8, 109, 141, 142–43, 144–45; *The Golden Apples*, 4, 7, 8, 9, 10, 11, 29, 36, 41, 118, 134–38, 215, 220, 221, 222, 223, 231; "The Hitch-Hikers," 6, 8; "June Recital," 4, 7, 22, 41, 135, 137, 222; "Keela, the Outcast Indian Maiden," 8, 29, 104, 107, 127; "The Key," 107; "Kin," 8; "Lily Daw and the Three Ladies," 20, 22, 24, 25, 30, 43, 44, 46, 104, 107, 111, 128, 224, 228; "Livvie," xiv, 22, 149, 150, 152, 154, 163, 177, 178, 179, 180, 217, 218; *Losing Battles*, 8, 59, 163, 209, 231; "A Memory," 24, 25, 26, 30, 29, 127–28; "Moon Lake," 22, 118–19, 137, 221; "Music from Spain," 110, 135, 139, 220; "No Place for You, My Love," 4, 7, 22, 181, 184, 185; *The Optimist's Daughter*, 8, 9, 11, 15, 48–54, 231; "Petrified Man," xiv, 6, 19, 20, 22, 25, 30, 43, 44–45, 46, 111, 117, 122, 125, 127, 133, 181, 184, 185; "A Piece of News," 25, 117, 122–23; *The Ponder Heart*, 6, 209, 228, 231, 237; "Powerhouse," xiv, xvii, 6, 8, 21, 22, 24, 25, 26, 27–28, 45, 84, 85–89, 127, 163, 228; "The Purple Hat," 6, 181, 184, 185; *The Robber Bridegroom*, 8, 55, 56, 58, 59, 63, 66, 117–20, 147, 149, 150, 180, 208, 211, 212, 213, 231; "Shower of Gold," 22, 118, 209, 221; "Sir Rabbit," 137, 138, 139, 221, "A Still Moment," 7, 180, 217, 218; "A Visit of Charity," 6, 181; "The Wanderers," 4, 7, 22, 135, 183, 184, 185; "Where Is the Voice Coming From?," 7, 8, 22, 29, 109, 159, 160, 161, 197, 198, 199, 200, 231; "The Whistle," 6, 7, 8, 14–15, 127; "The Whole World Knows," 136, 221; "'Why I Live at the P.O.," xiv, 6, 22, 43, 44, 45, 46, 107, 110, 111, 112–14, 133, 162, 208, 210, 211, 213; "The Wide Net," 22, 28–29, 58, 64, 109–10, 111, 112, 114, 139, 180, 217, 218;

The Wide Net and Other Stories, 8, 55, 56, 62, 63, 64, 215, 216, 217, 218, 219, 231; "The Winds," 21, 22, 64, 180; "A Worn Path," xiv, xviii, 4, 6, 8, 14, 15, 22, 29, 45, 59, 60, 80, 81–82, 90–91, 92, 93, 94, 95, 96, 133, 159, 160, 172, 173, 175, 181, 188, 189, 190, 191, 196, 197, 200, 202, 203, 204, 205, 206, 215; **miscellaneous collections**: *Early Escapades*, 232; *The Eye of the Story*, 9, 16, 83, 165, 232; *The Norton Book of Friendship*, 11, 233; *Occasions*, 16, 232, 233; *A Writer's Eye*, 233; **nonfiction**: "Cindy and the Joyful Noise," 82, 83; *The Collected Stories*, preface to, 21, 36, 63, 95; "Essays of E. B. White," 157; "Ida M'Toy," 83; "'Is Phoenix Jackson's Grandson Really Dead?,'" 4, 6, 189, 231; "The Little Store," 14, 231; "Looking at Short Stories," 123, 129; "Must the Novelist Crusade?," 3, 9, 29, 195, 199, 231; *One Writer's Beginnings*, xiii, xvi, 1, 14, 58, 142, 167, 168, 169, 170, 171, 193, 231; "A Pageant of Birds," 81, 231; "Place in Fiction," 4, 158, 231; "The Reading and Writing of Short Stories," 24; "Reality in Chekhov's Stories," 9, 16; "Some Notes on River Country," 57, 231; "A Sweet Devouring," 231; "Writing and Analyzing a Story," 7, 115, 120, 182, 186, 231; **photography**: "Bottle Trees," 153; "Choctaw girls," 57; *Country Churchyards*, 232; "Courthouse Steps," 43, 46; "Delegate," 43, 46; *Eudora*, 232; *Eudora Welty as Photographer*, 101, 232; "Headless Girl," 107; "Hello and Goodbye," 43, 46; "Hypnotist," "Hypnotized," 102–3, 105; "Mule Face Woman," 103–4, 106; *One Time One Place*, xv, 69, 80–81, 83, 101, 213, 232; *Photographs*, xv, 29, 83, 101, 102, 142, 232; "Sunday

morning," 151; "Twisto the Rubberman," 103–4, 106; "A woman of the 'thirties," 43, 46; **play:** "Bye-Bye Brevoort," 233
Westling, Louise, 234, 238
Weston, Ruth, 236
West Virginia, 142
whiteness, 74; female, 30, 35, 75; privilege, 104; white supremacist culture, 161. *See also* privilege (white); race; segregation
Williams, Tennessee, 110, 112, 143
Wisconsin, 142
Wolof tale, 91
Womack, Craig, 56
womanhood. *See* southern womanhood
women's narratives, 25, 29, 41, 94, 124, 144; female pastoral, 29; "girl stories," 30, 137; southern women writers, 41–43; white and black women writers, 46, 79, 159
Woolf, Virginia, xviii, 8, 112, 133, 134, 138, 139, 142, 144; *Mrs. Dalloway*, 135; *To the Lighthouse*, 8, 9
Works Progress Administration (WPA), 57, 101, 104, 142, 149, 152, 213, 232, 234–35, 237
World War I, 7, 135
World War II, 7, 8, 112, 135, 198, 233
Wright, Richard, 7, 82, 110, 134, 143, 235
writing and writing techniques: allusions, xv, 4, 5, 25, 28, 32, 33, 34, 119, 138, 149, 216; character, xvii, xix, 32, 33, 34, 35, 36, 42, 45, 107, 118, 123, 144, 145, 149, 162, 163, 173, 178, 180, 191, 192, 219; context, 33, 41; craft, 189, 190; description, 183; dialect, xv; diction/vocabulary, 168, 169, 170, 212, 219; figurative language, 160, 162, 167, 170, 211; focalization, 25, 33; form, 32, 33, 36; genre, 25; image, 51, 170, 178, 179, 181, 183, 184, 186, 188, 189, 190, 212; indeterminacy, 3, 20, 21, 75, 177, 185; intertextuality, 32, 34; irony, 79; lyricism, 20–21, 118; narrative gaps, 20; narrative strategies, 32; oral tradition, 87; parody, 25, 28, 44; performance, 21; plot, 25, 29, 32, 118, 122, 123, 144, 145, 149, 160, 162, 163, 173, 190; point of view, 6, 25, 32, 33, 34, 36, 37, 45, 85, 87, 88, 144, 180, 203, 217; politics in, 5, 9–10; postmodern, 7; process, 14, 15, 20, 182, 185, 189; reflection, 203, 204, 206, 218; setting, 145, 173, 196, 209, 211, 217; sound, 169–70; symbolism, 48, 49, 51, 52, 145, 150, 152, 170, 174, 175, 178, 203; syntax, 168, 169, 170, 171; "system of feeling," 115, 120; theme, 123, 126, 144, 145, 173, 175, 186, 212, 216, 217, 219; theoretical perspectives on, xv, xvi; tone, xiv; voice, 5, 167, 169, 170, 171, 181; word choice, 168
writing assignments, 19, 80, 162, 163, 167, 173, 180, 183, 189–90, 192, 217–18, 222–23

Yaddo, 17
Yaeger, Patricia, 26, 83, 123, 125, 139, 238
Yeats, W. B., 5, 133, 134, 136, 137, 138, 139
Yolen, Jean, 211
Yoruba initiation tale (Osain), 95

Zeus, 118–19